Fundamentalism and Tolerance

FUNDAMENTALISM AND TOLERANCE

An Agenda for Theology and Society

Edited by Andrew Linzey & Peter Wexler

Bellew Publishing
London
1991

First published in Great Britain in 1991 by
Bellew Publishing Company Limited
7 Southampton Place, London WC1A 2DR

ISBN 0 947792 75 9 (cased)
ISBN 0 947792 74 0 (limp)

Phototypeset by Intype, London
Printed and bound in Great Britain by
Billings & Sons Ltd

Contents

Introduction

We have been here before. Seventy years ago, in a sermon entitled 'Shall the Fundamentalists Win?', Harry Emerson Fosdick warned that the 'apparent intention' of the fundamentalists 'is to drive out of the evangelical churches men and women of liberal opinions' on such questions as 'historical' miracles, especially the virgin birth and the inspiration and inerrancy of scripture: 'Such are some of the stakes which are being driven to mark a deadline of doctrine around the Church.'[1]

It sometimes seems that Church history is set eternally to repeat itself; but must it be in ignorance of the tendency to do so? Just over fifty years ago the report *Doctrine in the Church of England*, attempting to resolve a controversy whose terms sound all too familiar, concluded:

> The theological and religious values of the doctrines of the Virgin Birth and of the Resurrection are set out clearly. It is, however, allowed that some members of the Commission, while accepting the reality of the Incarnation, regard the Virgin Birth as less consistent than a purely normal birth with the completeness of the Incarnation; and that a variety of answers is possible to that question.[2]

Yet in 1989 a Bishop could be attacked for holding one of the 'variety of answers' regarded as permissible by the Archbishops' Commission on Christian Doctrine in 1938.

Is there not something to be learnt from this *déjà vu* experience? Healthy controversy is necessary for the refreshment of understanding; by that criterion repetitive controversy cannot be healthy – as a small voice reminds us whenever we find ourselves falling into the quasi-automatic repetition of familiar lines of argument, or yielding to the temptation of well-tried formulae, whether of derogation or arrogation. What makes for this repetitiveness is the dominance of one of the four tendencies John Robinson detects to some degree in each of us: the cynicism of the foolish, the fundamentalism of the fearful, the scepticism of the wise, and the conservatism of the committed.[3] Our best (and perhaps our only) chance of reducing distortion is not by seeking to eradicate each of these defects in isolation; they can at best be neutralized, each by its antithesis, and only if their existence within us is admitted. Separated from its twin quality, each defect is too easily seen as inhabiting the opponent only.

Collected here are seventeen essays written against an increasingly stark background of doctrinal embattlement. As such they offer ways in, through and between the conflict between fundamentalism and tolerance, scepticism and conservatism, that characterizes our time. They provide an agenda of unfinished business for both schools of theology and the Churches themselves. Some essays report work in progress, some give accounts of previous debates, and some offer innovative, even original, contributions to move those debates one stage further. Half of the contributions address issues within theology as it wrestles with its own problems of authority, history, gospel and spirituality. The other half concern theology set outwards, engaging those topics – sexuality, science and society, to take three examples – that seem most to exercise the thought of our contemporaries, religious and secular.

Eight topics and seventeen papers later, it might seem that all around is strife and discord; not one issue in theology or society brings simple unity. Far from being a sign of the end, we suggest it is rather a sign that we are just beginning. The first paragraph of Paul Tillich's classic work *Systematic Theology* suggests the inevitability of formation and reformulation.

> A theological system is supposed to satisfy two basic needs: the statement of the truth of the Christian message and the interpretation of this truth for every new generation. Theology moves back and forth between two poles . . . Not many theological systems have been able to balance these two demands perfectly.[4]

These poles we have chosen to characterize in terms of 'fundamentalism' and 'tolerance' or 'conservatism' and 'scepticism'. That there is a balance to be struck rules out all sense of smug modernity on one hand, and complacent traditionalism on the other. In short: there is a dialectic to be forged – one that requires the capacity to listen even and especially sympathetically to voices one may think are seriously mistaken.

And shall the fundamentalists win? Fosdick answers his own question in the negative: 'I do not believe that the Fundamentalists are going to succeed. Nobody's intolerance can contribute anything to the solution of the situation which we have described.' But lest liberals themselves are unheedful of this message, he adds this warning which seems applicable to us all:

> Speaking, as I do, from the viewpoint of liberal opinions, let me say that if some young, fresh mind here this morning is holding new

ideas, has fought his way through, it may be by intellectual or spiritual struggle, to novel positions, and is tempted to be intolerant of old opinions, offensively to condescend to those who hold them and to be harsh in judgement on them, he may well remember that people who held those old opinions have given the world some of the noblest character and the most rememberable service that it ever has been blessed with, and that we of the younger generation will prove our case best, not by controversial intolerance, but by producing, with our own opinions, something of the depth and strength, nobility and beauty of character that in other times were associated with other thoughts.[5]

All these papers owe their origin to the weekly Open Seminar arranged by the Centre of the Study of Theology in the University of Essex. We are pleased that they have now found a place in the prestigious series of Canterbury Papers. We would like to express our gratitude to the contributors, to the Theology Centre and to the General Editors of the series for their help and encouragement. Our special thanks to Margaret Middleton and Lynn Bowman-Burns for their kind help in the preparation of the manuscript.

Andrew Linzey
Peter Wexler

Centre for the Study of Theology
in the University of Essex
May 1991

Part I
THINKING WITHIN THEOLOGY

1 THEOLOGY AND AUTHORITY

The Authority of Scripture in a Contemporary Theology

Maurice Wiles

That scripture has authority is a tautology. For to call a group of writings 'scripture' automatically implies that they have some kind of authority for the person who so calls them. The question is: what kind? A distinction is sometimes drawn between 'hard' and 'soft' forms of authority.[1] An example of the former would be a legal statute. It doesn't mean, of course, that a law is always obeyed. But whatever the statute says is the law *is* the law; it automatically effects what it affirms. But the 'authority' of an expert, in antiques for example, is a very different thing. We turn to the expert and usually take his word without further ado. But we know that sometimes authorities differ. Our expert may be wrong. The fact that he or she, speaking authoritatively, has declared something to be a genuine antique does not make it so.

The emergence of the canon, that is, of a precisely defined set of writings with clear limits that constitute them as 'scripture', was a gradual process, taking about three centuries. As time went on, the range of issues on which scripture was expected to speak with authority grew. The nature of the authority ascribed to it varied, but it tended towards the 'hard' end of the spectrum. God was the ultimate author, the ultimate author indeed of every detailed word. So, if one could be sure that one had understood it right, what one read in scripture was absolutely binding. It made no sense to say: this is what scripture says, but is it true?

But the qualification about understanding it right is no mere formality. Even with legal statutes, drawn up with careful attention to the need for comprehensiveness and clarity, there can still be disputes about their proper interpretation which have to be determined by some supreme court of appeal. And the Christian scriptures are very different in form from a legal statute. Most of them were written to fulfil quite other sorts of role. Many of them were written for specific occasions, and many have the elusiveness of poetry. So the need for interpretation was paramount. In effect, church leaders determined how scripture was to be understood, and so became hidden authorities, not infrequently manipulating the text to their own advantage. When Augustine discusses how one should determine the meaning of difficult texts, his first principle is that the true meaning must be one that agrees with the teaching of the Church; only secondarily does he suggest consideration of what meaning fits the overall context of the passage.[2] The use of allegorical interpretation served to make the meaning of the text extremely pliable in the hands of the church authorities.

One way in which the Reformation set out to challenge the power of the leaders of the Church was by emphasizing the need to get back to the literal meaning of scripture. Then, it was implied, scripture could function once again in a properly authoritative way. So the sixth article of the Church of England declares: 'Whatsoever is not read therein or cannot be proved thereby is not to be required of any man that it should be believed as an article of faith.' But, as I have already indicated, the very nature of the scriptural writings makes it extremely difficult for the Bible to fulfil that role, however much stress is placed on the literal sense. And that inherent difficulty has become more and more evident as time has gone on. The so-called 'critical study of the Bible', which developed so rapidly during the nineteenth and twentieth centuries, has brought that fact home with increasing force. In assessing its significance it is important to recall at the outset that the word 'critical' in that context does not mean 'finding fault with'; it means 'making judgements about', and you cannot read any book (the Bible included) without doing that. A few examples may serve to illustrate the types of problem that such an approach, with its careful attention to the biblical text, brings to the fore. I will indicate briefly three such types.

1 *Historical accuracy.* The books of Kings and of Chronicles sometimes describe the same historical events, but do so in ways which are in conflict with each other. So too do the Gospels of Matthew and Mark. They cannot both be literally true. We cannot therefore treat scripture as a fully reliable authority for the detail of what happened historically.

2 *Differing theological standpoints.* 2 Samuel 24:1 says that God incited David to number the people, for which he was then punished; 1 Chronicles 21:1 says it was Satan's doing. This factual discrepancy derives from the more advanced theological judgement of the author of Chronicles, in whose eyes the earlier ascription appeared immoral and therefore unacceptable. The books of Ruth and Ezra take fundamentally opposed views about the acceptability of mixed marriages. It is not only, therefore, on matters of fact, but

on matters of faith and morals as well, that scripture does not speak with a single voice.

3 *Rootedness in the socio-cultural understanding of the time.* The scriptural authors, as the last few examples have shown, wrote out of a general understanding of the world and of society that they shared with their contemporaries. Even when they challenged many aspects of that understanding with a sharpness of prophetic protest, there were other aspects, often unexpressed, that they accepted without question, but which we may now believe to warrant similar challenge. Two examples are the institution of slavery and the patriarchal ordering of society.

The problem, therefore, with which the contemporary Christian is faced is this: if that is the character of the scriptural writings, how can they function as an authority for us?

One reaction is to revert to fundamentalism. Christian belief and practice, it is sometimes argued, are in need of strong and unchallengeable authority; only in that way can we know what God is like and what is his will for us. We have every reason, therefore, to believe that God has given us an absolutely reliable authority of that kind. If critical method suggests otherwise, so much the worse for critical method. Its approach must be wrong, and cannot be appropriate in this case. Such an argument flies in the face of all the evidence. And even then, it cannot deliver what it promises to deliver. For however authoritative the text, the interpretative task remains. There is no real escape from human subjectivity.

But it is not only fundamentalists who have been concerned to find a way in which scripture can function authoritatively in the twentieth century. The same concern has been felt by many critical scholars too, and it has not infrequently helped to determine the form and style of the critical scholarship that they have developed. Three such styles of scholarship merit brief description.

1 *Biblical theology.* This name was given to a broad approach to the study of the Bible that was highly influential some thirty or forty years ago. It accepted without question the main findings of critical study. It recognized that in the light of those findings it would indeed be absurd to suggest that every detail of the scriptural records should have binding authority for us. But what such study did do, it was claimed, was to enable us to see more clearly the dominant themes of the Bible as a whole. Above all it revealed a coherent developing history of God's providential activity, leading up to the coming of Jesus and God's decisive saving activity in and through him. It was that overall picture, not the details either of history or of faith and morals, that was authoritative and binding for Christian belief. There is much to be said for such a view, but it is less than fully satisfactory as an answer to our problem. It is highly

questionable whether there is a single overall picture, emerging from detailed critical study, that is as clear or as consistent as such an account affirms. And even in so far as that objection might be met, is such an account of God's providential guidance of history one that can authoritatively command our acceptance?

2 Demythologizing. This approach from about the same time, linked primarily with the name of Bultmann, is usually seen as a much more radical alternative, less concerned with the authoritative character of the scriptural text. It certainly is much more radical in its questioning of the idea of direct divine action, especially through miracles such as the resurrection of Jesus. But the positive purpose of demythologizing was to bring out the existential meaning of scripture, as conveying a spiritual message of how life lived in true relation to God ('authentic existence') is possible. That, it was argued, was the necessary process for getting to the true meaning of the text. And the meaning revealed by such a manner of interpretation was indeed authoritative for the Christian believer.

3 Narrative exegesis. This approach, which is prominent today particularly in the United States, draws on literary critical studies, especially the study of realistic narrative, for its exegesis of the scriptural text. It does not deny the validity of historical criticism in its own sphere, but does not see that as crucial for the primary understanding of scripture, which in itself is a text rather than a series of past happenings. If we follow out the significance of the narrative to be found in the canon of scripture, an appropriate reading of it as a narrative text will provide us with what has been called 'an identity description of God'. It is that, it is argued, which is authoritative and determinative for Christian faith. There is much of value in such a narrative approach as a corrective to an excessive concern with detailed historical questions. But here too there are problems. Is there, in fact, a single narrative theme running through all the writings that make up the Christian canon? Or is that something which the Christian reader, reared in the tradition of earlier teaching, imposes on the text?

Each of these approaches has important insights to offer in our attempts to understand the Bible in a way appropriate for the life of the Church today. But none of them in my view is wholly successful if we look to them as ways of re-establishing the authority of scripture for our time. Is there any other way open to us that might fulfil that role more fruitfully?

There is one feature that all the three approaches I have been describing have in common. In each case their proponents are more or less consciously looking for a style of criticism in the light of which scripture would be enabled to maintain a virtually unchanged role in relation to the life of the Church and the content of Christian faith. The goal in each case is to provide a manner of interpretation, which may make it possible for the interpreter to say at the end of the day: this is what scripture really means, and this therefore is what is binding for Christian thought.

There is an oft-quoted saying of Leonard Hodgson, my predecessor but one in my present post: 'As one who has been a professional teacher of theology for forty-three years, I now publicly declare my hope that no pupil of mine will ever be guilty of using the saying. . . . "the Bible says . . .".'[3]

That has been widely accepted as legitimate criticism of a 'proof-text' use of the Bible. But perhaps it has wider implications that are not so generally accepted. Most of us (and I deliberately include myself in the description) still want to be able to say that our beliefs and action should be being determined by what we are enabled to grasp as 'the overall theological view implicit in the scriptures' or 'the existential significance of Paul's teaching' or 'the characterization of God given by the biblical narrative'. Is not at least that implicit in the tautology of having an authoritative scripture at all?

But it is that expectation that, I want to argue, needs to be changed. We ought not to be looking for a revised way of handling the biblical material which will enable it to continue to play unchanged within the Church the same role as in the past. What needs to be changed is precisely our expectation of the kind of role it should fulfil. And that change can be seen in strongly positive terms. As I tried to suggest at the start of this article, the way in which scriptural authority has functioned in the history of the Church has not always been an unmixed blessing. Some scholars have been so conscious of that fact that they have even spoken of the 'curse of the Canon'. That is an exaggeration, but there has certainly been a negative side to its functioning in the past. In so far as critical study has helped to rescue us from that, we ought not to be seeking to be 'entangled again in a yoke of bondage' (Galatians 5:1).

The interpreter of scripture in the life of the Church is rightly concerned with what it has to say of significance for the life of the Christian now, in the very different conditions of life and knowledge in the twentieth century. If we work with a comparatively 'hard' sense of scriptural authority, that practical concern is liable to lead us to distort what scripture has to say and to lose sight of some important aspects of what is really there. We shall be tempted to get round or to ignore those features of scriptural teaching which do not easily fit with our contemporary knowledge or understanding of the world. But if we do not ascribe that kind of role to scripture, we will be less liable to succumb to those temptations. Working with a 'softer' sense of authority, which leaves us free to say on occasion, as to the expert, that what it says is wrong, there will be less pressure on us to impose our desired meanings on the text. Indeed, I want to take that reflection a stage further. Despite what I said at the outset about authority as an inherent element in the very meaning of the word 'scripture' itself, there is a case for eschewing its use altogether. In practice the word 'authority' is almost always and inevitably heard and understood in the inappropriate sense of a 'hard' authority. A better way of describing its proper role for Christian thought and life might be to speak of it as an 'indispensable resource'.

What difference might this change in expectation make? I have already mentioned the existence in scripture of conflicting theological or moral attitudes, such as those characteristic of the authors of the books of Ezra and of Ruth. John Fenton has described the New Testament as 'a book of rows', claiming that there are only three books in the New Testament which were not significantly influenced by internal controversy.[4] If that is anything like fair, it has important implications for Christian belief and for the life of the Church. It would mean that we ought not to expect to come up with a single, uniform Christian doctrine and we ought not to regard all controversy as simply the result of sin and blindness (important factors though those no doubt frequently are). Stephen Sykes has described Christianity (like democracy) as an 'essentially contested concept'[5] – that is to say a concept which cannot be exhaustively defined, but whose meaning is always in search of more precise definition through the process of discussion and argument. Christian truth is not something that is authoritatively given in the past; it is something always to be discovered in the present with the help of the past. And there is no way of doing that which does not run the risk of error and conflict.

Theology in the past has often been more creative than it has been prepared to admit. It has often claimed to be doing no more than to repeat old truth, when in practice it has been affirming new truth appropriate to new circumstances. Its appeal to scripture has helped to convince it that it really is doing no more than reiterate the truth expressed in its foundation documents. But often the meanings it has claimed to be finding there have been read into the text rather than out of it. An appeal to scripture involving interpretation of that kind has been an effective disguise of the measure of change which has characterized Christian thought down the ages.

We need to bring into the open what is always in some measure going on. There is always an interplay between past and present. The best insights of our time help to determine the way in which we understand and accept scripture; and the wisdom of scripture can serve to challenge and correct the intellectual fads or myopia of our day. Neither has the automatic 'authority' to override the other. It is to avoid any such suggestion that I prefer to speak of scripture as an 'indispensable resource'.

How then may we summarize what scripture has to offer as an indispensable resource? It provides, first, the primary historical witness of the founding events of Christian faith. Then it embodies also profound theological reflection on those events from that same initial period of the Church's existence. Moreover it constitutes a varied body of literature of proved transformative power in relation to human life. None of this, of course, in the light of all that has been said, makes it directly determinative of our theological convictions or way of life. But it makes a crucial contribution to their formation. And this means that neither the factual inaccuracy of much of its historical witness nor the conditioned character of its theological reflection (sometimes involving assumptions that we do not and cannot share) is as problematic as it would be for those still desiring older and stronger styles of authority. For however great its historical precision or its theological force, it would not be binding on us just because it is scripture. Its role is to contribute to the process whereby we have to 'judge for ourselves what is right' (Luke 12:57). In that way it takes its place, a peculiarly important place, along with the varied other ways in which God addresses us as responsible beings, whom he is seeking to lead into the ways of his kingdom.

Authority and Freedom – Yesterday and Today

Gordon Roe

Two political theorists with more than a passing interest in theology devoted much of their life to the themes of authority and freedom. Lord Acton, author of *The History of Freedom and Other Essays*, collected notes on the subject but never completed the work. Harold Laski, on the other hand, did write *Authority in the Modern State*, which is still a classic of its kind. Both of them, Laski in his book and Acton in his manuscript notes now in the Cambridge University Library, recognized that there was one person in the nineteenth century who in his life brought both themes into sharp focus. There were plenty, mainly on the right, who carried the banner for authority in a century of revolutions and who therefore were resistant to the claims of individual freedom. There were even more – and Acton listed them frequently in his notes – for whom the achievement of freedom took precedence over the claims of authority. There were few who sought radically (and not compromisingly) to see *both* as essential to the right view of the individual and society. Among them Lamennais was by far the most interesting, lucid and colourful. Acton devoted a whole file of notes to him,[1] and Laski said of him: 'There is a sense indeed in which his career is little less than the mirror of his age.'[2]

Hugues-Félicité Robert de la Mennais (1782–1854), known to his friends as Féli and more widely in later years as Lamennais, lived through times of great and sometimes violent change, which must inevitably have influenced his search for an authority and certainty which would be not the adversary but the context of the freedom for which he strove.[3] Early attempts to send him to school were unsuccessful, because of his naturally rebellious nature. Subsequently, however, he was privately educated according to the liberal educational methods of Jean-Jacques Rousseau by his uncle, one of the new aristocracy whose library was well stocked with the works of eighteenth-century rationalism. Under this rather ambiguous influence and with the help of his elder brother Jean, who was destined for the priesthood, he came gradually to believe that liberty and reason without religion made for tyranny and slavery. It was not until he was twenty-two years old, in 1804, that he made his first confession and communion.

By that time Chateaubriand had published his Romantic apologia, *Le Génie du Christianisme,* and Napoleon had negotiated a concordat between Church and State which had within it the seeds of future conflict. The limits of the Church's freedom to order its own life and its authority in relation to that of the State were to provide material for much of Lamennais' most trenchant writing. In theory the restoration of the Church after years of suppression *should* have provided the conditions for which Lamennais and others were looking. In practice, however, the relationship was such an uneasy one and conditions on both sides changed so drastically in the next half century, that Lamennais' perception of what true authority was, and what freedom really was, never remained constant for long. In consequence he was regarded as a traitor to a series of causes: royalism, ultramontanism, liberal Catholicism (which meant different things in different countries) and socialism. In fact, if there is a key to his nature, it lay in his constant struggle to synthesize on the one hand the inner certainty that comes from true authority and, on the other, freedom from any form of tyranny.

The first stage of this struggle was represented by his book *Réflexions sur l'état de l'église* (1809), a call to the Church to arouse itself from lethargy and subservience to the Napoleonic State, a reminder of its apostolic vocation, much as *Tracts for the Times* were to the Church in England twenty years later. In these *Réflexions* and in *La Tradition de l'église sur l'institution des évêques* (1814), the authorship of which he shared with his brother Jean, he outlined a position to which he was to adhere throughout many apparent changes of view, namely that Church and State each had its own proper authority and that each should be able to exercise its own freedom. In an attack on the State's control of education he called for unrestricted liberty in the founding of new schools and colleges, the excellence of which would be guaranteed by what the 1980s would call market forces. The sharpness of his attack on Napoleon led him to believe that flight from the country would be wise. A seven-month stay in London in 1815 had two serious effects on him. It led to his ordination to the priesthood, a decision to subject himself to ecclesiastical authority in a way which was to have serious repercussions on the rest of his life. Of his ordination to the sub-diaconate, he said: 'This step has cost me a prodigious amount.'[4] Just before his ordination to the priesthood a friend wrote to his brother Jean: 'He walks with a determined step in the way of the Cross, through the darkness of pure faith, living by sheer obedience, without any taste for it nor any consolation.'[5] It seems that he was ordained not out of a sense of vocation to pastoral or priestly ministry (he was never appointed to such a post) but out of a personal need to subject his burning imagination to a strict discipline.

The second effect of his stay in England was his exposure for the first time to Protestantism, in his view religion without sufficient authority. It was one of the influences upon his great work *Essai sur l'indifférence en matière de religion* (1817–23).

The *Essai*, despite its ponderous title, is an impassioned plea for the freedom of the human spirit to be exercised under the authority of religion, in particular that of the Catholic Church. It is a violent attack upon protestants, deists and atheists who reject authority, that is to say the source of certainty about what is true, 'this ardent search for the truth, and this pure and living joy which we experience when we find it', and replace it with human reason, in one form or another.[6] It is easy to caricature it as a Romantic rejection of the value of human reason in favour of Chateaubriand's aestheticism disguised as the philosophy of *sensus communis*. But even a cursory reading of the book reveals that it is really about the peace and happiness both of the individual and of society, guaranteed by certainty about the truth provided by the authority of the Church. The dominical link between truth and freedom, 'the truth shall make you free', lies not far beneath the surface.

In politics, Lamennais had been regarded since the restoration of the monarchy as a monarchist. He believed that freedom was guaranteed by order, and that France under the moderate, if unexciting, Louis XVIII stood some chance of reviving as a society where the Church was free to play its part of regeneration. The apologetic he had outlined in the *Essai sur l'indifférence* was intended to rally the Church and to encourage it to play this active part in the nation's life:

> There are therefore two societies, the political or civil which relates to the temporal order, and the spiritual which relates to eternity.
> Therefore there are two authorities, and these two authorities are infallible, each in its own order. The political society witnesses to contingent truths and the facts on which they are based, its institutions, laws etc.; and its witness, an expression of the general reason, is certain. The spiritual society witnesses to the unchangeable truths on which it is based, its dogmas, precepts, etc.; and its witness, an expression of the general will, is also certain.[7]

With the accession of Charles X in 1824, things changed. Charles's very devotion to religion threatened the infallibility and autonomy of the two orders, the freedom of the spiritual society to check any hint of tyranny in the temporal society. Paradoxically a king who should have been most sympathetic to Lamennais' aims for the Church was seen as infringing its liberty. As a result, Lamennais moved more and more from his form of monarchism, towards ultra-montanism, the belief that in the end all religious authority on earth rested in the Pope, who would be a guarantee of the freedom of states and of individuals. His book *De la religion considérée dans ses rapports avec l'ordre politique et civil* (1824) began to make public the movement of his thought away from monarchy as a support for stability and order towards the Pope.

Between 1824 and 1829 Lamennais could see the political forces of reaction and repression, dressed very often in the robes of religion, face to face with forces of popular revolution. That very *sensus communis* which had been the basis of his apologetic for Christianity and Catholicism was threatening to divorce the desire for freedom from the acceptance of the authority of God. The importance for him of freedom was beginning to emerge clearly. Vidler puts it thus:

> Lamennais always loathed, dreaded, and denounced tyranny. The reason why he wanted the spiritual and moral authority of the papacy made effective was his belief that that was the only way of *preventing* civil governments from 'crushing all freedom, both in church and in state'. He never ceased to point the contrast between tyranny, which is based on the arbitrary use of force, and order, which springs from willing obedience to an authority morally entitled to obedience.[8]

The publication in 1829 of his book *Des progrès de la révolution et de la guerre contre l'église* marked publicly the point towards which he had been moving for some time, namely that the only authority which could be trusted to encourage that liberty was that of the Pope. He rejected, as he had long rejected, any idea of the sovereignty of the people because he still believed (and this was the heart of the argument of the *Essai*) that it relied upon individual reason. On the other hand, he at last rejected the authority of monarchs, because in practice it tended always to subject the Church to the State and led to tyranny and oppression.

The 1830 revolution in Europe proved him right. For the most part, God was seen as an oppressor, not, as Lamennais would have hoped, as a regenerator of society. Yet Lamennais believed there was still hope that the Church might represent the essential principle of authority in society, the authority of God, and at the same time take the lead in humanity's struggle for freedom. After the accession of Louis-Philippe at the end of July 1830, Lamennais believed that there were three parties in France: the jacobin revolutionaries, small in numbers but great in influence; the royalists, reactionary and making for disunity; and a third group 'incomparably the most numerous', disposed to unite for the maintenance of order, on a wide basis of liberty.[9]

The rallying point for this third party was the newspaper *L'Avenir*, which bore the significant motto *'Dieu et la liberté'*.

> Soon, a word, both powerful and peaceful . . . will give the signal which the world awaits, for its last regeneration. Imbued with a new spirit, led to science by faith and to liberty by order, peoples will open their eyes and will recognize each other as brothers, because they will have a common Father, and weary of their long ages of discord, they will rest at the feet of this Father who stretches out his hand only to protect and opens his mouth only to bless.[10]

High-flown and naive though they may be, these words represent in an extreme form Lamennais' belief that liberty and authority must go hand in hand, and that the authority that transcends all others is that of Christ's Vicar on earth. The picturesque story has often been told of Lamennais' journey to Rome with his companions, 'pilgrims of God and liberty' as they called themselves, to seek the Pope's approval for their campaign for the separation of Church and State, for freedom of conscience, freedom of religion, freedom of teaching, freedom of the press and freedom of association. They met with a cold reception: in a Europe in ferment, Gregory XVI could not dissociate himself from the forces of established order. The ideas were tactfully rejected in the encyclical *Mirari vos*, published on 15 August 1832, although Lamennais himself was not condemned. By that time, however, it is fairly certain that Lamennais had finally been forced to abandon his belief that the Pope would be the guarantee of true liberty. By his support for the Orthodox Tsar Nicholas against the Catholic insurgents of Poland, expressed in a letter to Polish Bishops on 9 June, Gregory XVI had revealed at worst his complicity in power politics and at best the fatal inability of this particular human system to express divine authority.[11]

An uneasy few months passed, in which Lamennais submitted and half-submitted to papal authority, proposing distinctions between religious and political opinions which he must have known would never be accepted. Then, at the end of April 1834, he published *Paroles d'un croyant*, a book quite unlike anything he had written before, a prose-poem which achieved its effect as much by its style as by its content, by its imagery, as by its argument. In forty-two chapters divided into verses in biblical fashion, scenes of human misery alternated with apocalyptic visions, poems of lyrical simplicity with litanies of helpless sufferers crying to the God of mercy, exhortations to patience and faith with outbursts of hatred and revolt.

It had an extraordinary effect both in France and in the rest of Europe. People queued at reading rooms to borrow it by the hour. It was read in drawing-rooms, cafés, studios and in public squares.

Groups of people clubbed together to buy a copy. Lamennais, the priest, was now unambiguously on the side of the people.[12]

The book is almost entirely visual and consists essentially of two visions, sometimes quite distinct and in contrast to each other, sometimes merging with three-dimensional effect. The first is of the condition of the world, the slavery of the people and the tyranny of rulers. The second is of the kingdom of God, the reign of Christ and the divine reality beyond the veil of earthly appearances.

'And I saw the evils which come on the earth, the weak oppressed, the honest man begging his bread, the wicked raised to honour and loaded with riches, the innocent condemned by corrupt judges, and his children wandering alone in the heat.'[13] In these and many other generalized pictures of human misery, which he believes all his readers will recognize, he portrays the poor and oppressed as the real people of faith. In contrast, his visions of tyranny are horrifying and specific. In Chapter 13, for example, he sees seven kings seated in the darkness around a throne made of human bones. Before the throne is a reversed crucifix, a pitcher of foaming blood and a skull. One of the tyrants pours blood into the skull and drinks, crying 'Cursed be Christ who has brought liberty to the earth'. Elsewhere he sees seven shadowy figures seated on rocks covered with slime, cursing Christ who has triumphed over their tyranny. In the famous Chapter 33, he paints more recognizable pictures of these tyrants, including William IV, Louis-Philippe, Tsar Nicholas and Pope Gregory XVI.

The other vision is a vision of the kingdom of God, expressed in biblical and apocalyptic terms which most of humanity can recognize and acknowledge: 'The unbeliever is alone in the universe. All creatures praise God: all that have feeling bless him; all that have thought adore him; the day-star and the stars of the night sing to him in their mysterious language.'[14] This is the authority claimed by the author of the *Essai sur l'indifférence* for the universality of belief in God. In this case the vision is rather less pictorial than the visions of slavery and tyranny. Although Christ is invoked throughout the book, he is less the flesh and blood Jesus of the Gospels than the symbol of redemption and the embodiment of those principles which need to prevail if man is to be free: 'The reign of God is the reign of justice in the mind and of charity in the heart. It is founded on faith and faith through Christ who has promulgated God's law, the law of love and the law of justice.'[15] In the last chapter, Lamennais is transported beyond the region of the shadows of this life to the clear light and sound of reality. Here he sees three oceans in one ocean, an ocean of power, an ocean of light and an ocean of life, penetrating each other without losing their identity, yet forming an indivisible, absolute, eternal unity. That unity is God, he who is.

This great ocean is the context of all creation, that which gives it meaning, and life, and harmony.

These two visions reveal the two passions of his life, liberty and authority, in a new way. He had never caught the same tone before, and he was never to catch it again. However unfair the assertions, over-simplified the issues or naively romantic the images, he had found a medium for his message. So striking was the book that it revealed, more clearly than his other work, two obvious difficulties in the way of one who tries to reconcile liberty and authority.

The first is the tension between acceptance and struggle. Parts of the *Paroles* praise the virtues of faith and trust. Chapter 16, for example, has a parable about two men, each with wife and children, struggling to survive. One is plagued with anxiety about the future, the other trusts in God: 'God never abandons his own. His love has secrets which we cannot know. Let us believe, hope, love and follow our way in peace.' This commendation of trust in a loving and omnipotent God, very much in the spirit of the *Imitation of Christ* which Lamennais had successfully and profitably translated in earlier years, if taken literally could paralyse all struggle. But such passages are side by side with unequivocal calls to arms: 'You will recover liberty, security, and peace only by fighting unremittingly against those who oppress you'; 'Do you believe that the idiot serf, seated at his Lord's table, has more taste for his delicate dishes than the soldier of liberty for his morsel of black bread?'; 'Young soldier, where are you going?' There follows a litany of combat against tyranny: 'Blessed be the arms that you bear, young soldier, seven times blessed.' Temperamentally we feel that Lamennais is on the side of struggle, but since the *Paroles* is more of a poem than an argument he does not have to reconcile the apparent contradiction. We see glimpses of a way through: God's order – in which man trusts and finds serenity – has been upset by man's sin. It is a mark of man's faith in that order that he is prepared to struggle to restore it.

The other difficulty is that, in places, Lamennais seems to be reconciling liberty and authority by an extreme form of idealism which hovers on the brink of denying the reality of present existence.

> What your eyes see and your hands touch are only shadows, and the sound that strikes your ear is but a crude echo of the intimate and mysterious voice which adores and prays and trembles at the heart of creation. For every creature trembles and every creature is suffering the pangs of childbirth and is struggling to be born to real life, to pass from darkness to light, from the region of appearances to that of reality.[16]

Here and elsewhere he speaks of the reality at the heart of all things as transcending time and space. He speaks as if the end of the struggle of liberty will be the removal of the veil of unreality and the realization of God's kingdom of justice, love and peace.

It was this unrealistic utopianism at the heart of Lamennais' belief which finally alienated him from Marxists and other social revolutionaries. And it was his tendency to take less than seriously the realities of the flesh and what Christians have always meant by the incarnation (a tendency which had always been there for those who had eyes to see) which marked off his later work from orthodox Christianity.

Neither of those objections, however, should obscure the nature of Lamennais' vision. It was in his day a uniquely powerful assertion of the significance of both liberty and authority.

In less than two months after the publication of the *Paroles*, Lamennais was condemned in the papal encyclical *Singulari nos*, not for his defective Christology but for the violence of his attacks on monarchs and popes. Although he was never formally excommunicated, from that time onwards he was effectively outside the Church.

This did not, however, mean that he abandoned his quest for an authority which would guarantee liberty. He became a popular hero, identifying himself with the struggles of the people to make a reality of the revolutionary slogan (which he rearranged as 'Equality, Liberty and Fraternity' because he believed that while equality was simply a fact of nature to be recognized, liberty and fraternity flowed from its recognition and were to be fought for). *Le Livre du peuple* (1837) paints a picture of the slavery of the people as man's failure to fulfil the divine will. The people's right to freedom (and all that goes with it) is balanced by the duty to co-operate with the Trinity of creative power, wisdom and love. Work, thought and love will bring about the perfecting of humanity and union with God, if not quite in this world, then in the next.

Throughout the rest of his life Lamennais portrays man's struggle for freedom in terms of obedience to that essentially religious demand. No longer is it expressed by the teaching of the Church, but by a system of philosophy already hinted at in his *Paroles* expressed in trinitarian terms, coloured with Christian imagery, having much in common with idealist philosophies, whether of Catholic origin like Schelling's, or Protestant like Hegel's. Obedience to authority is still a consistent theme. *Une voix de prison* (1843), for example, begins with Christ telling the author to speak to tyrants, to pour his threats into their ears, to afflict their soul with cold fear. 'They have said that I did not exist. They will soon learn whether I do or not.'[17] Christ is an icon of the supreme one who cares for the poor. He is not an example, but an imperative issuing from the nature of things.

There is, however, some development in the way that he describes this new religion. In his *Discussions critiques* of 1841 he speaks of a 'flux divin' which unites humanity with God in ways other than those of conventional religion. In saying this he appears to be denying any supernatural order, and therefore any supernatural authority for human obedience. Religion arises from purely natural laws and consists in the proper development of the divine element inherent in all people. He clarifies this in *De la société première et de ses lois, ou De la religion* (1848) by saying that dogmas and science converge. Belief in incarnation, he now says explicitly, is an outmoded fable. Religion is the law of life itself. This interpretation of the natural order in terms of traditional Christian symbolism and the use of the person of Christ as an emotive icon provided the authority for his view of liberty until the end of his life. It was what distinguished him from other socialists and communists of his time. He wrote, for example, in 1841 that communism produced collective liberty but individual slavery; Catholicism, collective certainty but individual slavery; Protestantism, individual liberty but collective anarchy. He believed that his understanding of religion combined the authority of collective certainty with individual liberty. It was doubtless for this reason that in 1843 he rejected the request of Arnold Ruge, Karl Marx's emissary, that he should edit the French edition of the early Marxist *Annales franco-allemandes*.[18] Engels and the Marxist establishment firmly rejected him and other utopians and idealists like him in favour of the economic realism which later became communist orthodoxy.

In the end, all this struggling seemed to achieve little. In the 1848 revolution he was a popular figure, was elected to the Constituent Assembly and worked on the drafting of a new constitution. But this was rejected in favour of a more conservative one which paved the way for the *coup d'état* of Louis Bonaparte in 1851. Lamennais retired from the scene and died a disillusioned man in 1854. In death, as in life, he made his impact by vivid drama: to avoid public demonstrations he was carried to the cemetery of Père Lachaise in darkness and buried in an unmarked grave.

History does not so much teach us lessons as require us to ask questions of our own time. A number arise from this sketch of one man's struggle. Is the existence of some authority an absolute prerequisite for the achievement of liberty? One of the difficulties of western liberal society is that it lacks that overarching sense of values which comes from such an authority. Lamennais still believed that it was possible to detect those values by means of the *sensus communis* and that in the end they were essentially religious. Perhaps the recrudescence of various types of authoritarian religion, alongside a mistrust of 'liberal' Christianity, points to the need to renew the search for an authority which (as for example in liberation theology) will be a more reliable context for true freedom.

A second question concerns the place of reason. Does apparently authority-free liberalism depend too heavily upon reason? Does it rely upon the consensus of reasonable people, which often means middle-class people who earn their money with their heads more than with their hands? Democracy requires discussion, where reason more than other human faculties has an advantage. Throughout his life Lamennais had a profound mistrust of human reason, which led him to be practically involved in the struggles of the people and to tap the roots of human emotions in imagery, particularly biblical imagery. Does the lack of one source of values deprive us of that necessary, non-rational imagery?

The third question arises from the fact that at every stage Lamennais' life was a failure. Does this suggest that in matters of social organization and individual liberty, we shall only ever travel hopefully, and never (in this life at least) arrive? The point of the two poles of authority and liberty is to keep the struggle going, to provide cause for hope. Is it the case that once we abandon the necessity of one or other of the poles, we abandon all possibility of a future for mankind? One of the striking features of Lamennais' life is that, through all its many changes he maintained the two poles, while for ever re-examining their true nature. Like him, we need constantly to be asking, 'What or whom do I really believe in as authoritative?' and, 'In what sense do I still want to be free, and to help others to be free?'

2 THEOLOGY AND HISTORY

Jesus and History

Morna D. Hooker

How much can we know about the historical Jesus? The fact that I am tackling this topic in a relatively short paper could, I suppose, be taken as implying that I am assuming that the answer will be 'Not very much'. It is one of the surprising facts of history that there is so little material that even claims to offer us information about Jesus of Nazareth; it can all of it be set out on a couple of hundred pages at the most – 99 per cent of it is to be found in our Gospels, and much of it is repetitive.

In spite of this dearth of material, popular theological discussion and preaching place tremendous emphasis on the figure of Jesus. Perhaps this is because so many people find the notion of God difficult. Those who have been encouraged by Don Cupitt to take leave of God find Jesus easier to grasp. But this appeal to Jesus puts the student of the New Testament in a dilemma. For what, in fact, do we *know* about Jesus? What was he really like? I have to admit that I sometimes find myself listening in some amazement to the confident appeal made by many Christians to the career and character of Jesus.

Where should we begin on our quest for the historical Jesus? Since the Gospels, which are our major source, were written by convinced Christians, the safest place might seem to be the references to Jesus in the pages of Roman historians. Unfortunately, these do not take us very far. There is a brief reference in Tacitus, writing at the beginning of the second century AD; another in Suetonius, who manages to get the name wrong, and refers to Chrestus; and the famous letter of Pliny to Trajan describing Christian worship, and that is all. Nor do Jewish writers help us much. The Jewish historian Josephus refers in one place to Jesus as 'the so-called Christ', but a more elaborate reference to Jesus in another passage, describing him as Christ and referring to his resurrection, is universally regarded as either a Christian interpolation or the result of Christian alteration of the original text. Several centuries later, in the Talmud, we find occasional references to Jesus and his disciples, of which the most illuminating tells us that he was put to death for sorcery on the eve of Passover. But if non-Christian writers tell us little or nothing about Jesus, we should not be surprised: indeed why *should* we expect them to refer to someone who at the time seemed to be of no significance whatever in the history of mankind?

This means that if we want to find out anything about the historical Jesus, the only documents that are going to be of any help to us are Christian ones. Our Gospels were written by committed men from a standpoint of faith; they are in fact propaganda. If we want to discover the truth about Jesus, we must realize that we are dealing with partisan documents. But what do we mean by 'truth'? 'Gospel truth' has been traditionally understood to mean that which is absolutely historically accurate; the phrase reflects the old belief that the Bible provides us with a body of objective truth standing over against men and women. Few theologians today would consider that definition to be a very good one; and yet the Church has been slow to recognize that the Bible does not provide us with that kind of truth – with objective historical data and incontrovertible 'facts'. Many Christians have tended to cling to the idea that the Bible supplies the facts, while the biblical exegete and preacher supply the interpretation, and have failed to recognize the extent to which interpretation is built into our Gospel records; they have failed to grasp that the Gospels themselves are the work of evangelists – of preachers; that any form of truth can be expressed only in terms that make sense to those who proclaim it; that truth and its expression are therefore bound up with the experience and understanding of those men and women who receive it and try to pass it on. The very word 'gospel' means 'good news', so that the idea of interpretation is built into the titles of these books. They are concerned with the significance that is given to certain events – they are good news. Gospel truth, then, will be about the truth of this good news, and not about historical and accurate details.

And yet the relationship between history and interpretation, between what happened and the significance of what happened, is of supreme importance. As an historian, the New Testament scholar is concerned with the relationship between the two. It is not surprising, then, to discover that a great deal of scholarly ink has been spilt in trying to work out the relationship between the Jesus of history – that is, the man who lived and died in Palestine – and the Christ of faith – that is, the person whom Christians worship as Lord.

It is perhaps as well to realize at the beginning that though this question presents us with the historical problem in an acute form, it is by no means unique. It should be no surprise to us to find that the New Testament does not provide us with 'pure history', since there is no such thing to be found anywhere. Historical evidence can never be 100 per cent certain – there is always room for ifs and buts. Try to find out on Monday morning who threw the first bottle on Saturday night, and you will discover how confused the evidence is, after only thirty-six hours. The historian always deals with probabilities, never with certainties. In one case the balance of probabilities may seem overwhelming, in another case 50:50, but always judgement and interpretation are involved. Subjectivity is built-in, both on the part of those who originally recorded an event, and on the part of those who, centuries later, try to assess their accounts. However impartial we try to be (and we do not always try very hard), we see things from our own viewpoint. And the more significant the figure, the greater the scope for disagreement, as comparative studies of Luther or Marx or Churchill will show.

But however great the difficulties, that does not prevent men and women from making the attempt. The material about Jesus may be scanty, but that did not keep nineteenth-century New Testament scholars from the pursuit of the historical Jesus. Indeed, it may be fairly said that the history of nineteenth-century Gospel criticism was the history of this quest. Literally thousands of lives of Jesus were published. Recognizing that the Jesus presented to us in the Gospels is not the historical Jesus, New Testament scholars nevertheless believed that it was possible to separate the two. All they had to do was to extract the beliefs of the Church from the material, and the real Jesus of history would be left. So one after another they analysed the Gospels, hoping to discover the real Jesus of Nazareth.

If we analyse the attempts of these men to discover the historical Jesus, we discover that the answers they gave to the problem were as numerous as the attempts. Such an analysis was in fact made by Albert Schweitzer, in his famous book, *The Quest of the Historical Jesus*. Schweitzer set out to demonstrate the inadequacies of all the 'Lives of Jesus' that had ever been written. He succeeded even more brilliantly than he expected, for his book demonstrated not only the failure of everyone else's attempt to discover the historical Jesus, but the failure of Schweitzer himself! Accusing other scholars of looking down a well and seeing their own reflections, he did no better himself; his own interpretation was equally subjective, equally dependent on presuppositions. It might have been thought that after this men would abandon the quest for the historical Jesus, since it had met with so little success, but the figure of Jesus continued to haunt not only scholars but writers of popular fiction as well; and still they depicted Jesus in their own image – they continued to discover the Jesus whom they expected. You may know the story told about one famous Cambridge New Testament scholar. Two dons were dining on high table one evening, and one remarked to the other: 'I see that T. R. Glover has just published his autobiography.' 'I hadn't heard that,' replied the other. 'Oh yes,' said the first, 'it's called *The Jesus of History*.'

Now the fact that everyone sees Jesus differently may tell us quite a lot about the relevance of the Gospel to everyone's needs, and the way that Jesus – as he is reinterpreted – speaks to men and women of every generation in every situation; but it does not really tell us a great deal about the Jesus of history. And part of our problem is that it is not only we, the readers of the Gospels, who interpret the material in terms of our own presuppositions and read the material through our own particular spectacles, but the writers of the Gospels also, who saw the material and wrote it down in terms that made sense to them; they, too, were wearing their own particular spectacles. It is not just that we impose *our* interpretation on the Gospels: interpretation is built in. The nineteenth-century authors of Lives of Jesus – and indeed the twentieth-century ones as well – have supposed that they could separate the Jesus of history from the Christ of faith. But all their investigations have served only to confirm that the two are firmly fused together. My scientific colleagues tell me that if iron and sulphur are mixed together it is a comparatively easy process to separate them again with a magnet. But once the two elements have been fused into iron sulphide, they are inseparable. In the Gospels, historical happenings and interpretation have been fused together in the accounts with which the evangelists present us, and most of the time it is impossible to prise them apart.

So what do we in fact *know* about Jesus? And just as important, how much do we *need*, as Christians, to know about him? There are various ways of tackling these questions. One is to dismiss the difficulties I have been outlining as largely imaginary: to maintain that the Jesus of history and the Christ of faith are, by and large, identifiable. This is really to allow little or no role to interpretation or response on the part of the disciples or the evangelists; to say that the gospel was, as it were, a pre-packed parcel delivered by Jesus from heaven to men – a message about himself, which he proclaimed and they accepted and passed on. It is, moreover, to suggest that the rules which apply to all other cases of historical reporting do not apply here; that here, and here alone, we have historical certainty. The possibility of error is excluded – because God has, as it were, provided a cast-iron guarantee that these documents are totally unlike any other documents. This answer seems to me to be vulnerable in two ways. First, it is vulnerable from the point of view of the historian who is being asked to handle this material quite differently from all other historical material; the only way that you can have historical certainty is by having prior faith that this material is, as it were, guaranteed. That means that Christians cannot really engage in dialogue about history with non-Christians, because they are playing the game with different rules. Secondly, this answer seems to me to be open to theological objections. For one thing, it doesn't really take the incarnation seriously; it refuses to allow that God takes risks; that he depends on human response, human interpretation of the Gospel; it supposes that the Gospel is not only pre-packed, but arrives in the pages of our Bible untouched by human hand (or mind). Moreover, it seems also to be unprepared to accept that *we* should take risks; it asks, not for faith, but for historical certainty. It is true that in the Fourth Gospel, Thomas demanded tangible evidence before he would believe; but Thomas was rebuked for his lack of faith.

An alternative approach goes to the opposite extreme, and says: we know very little with historical certainty, but this does not matter in the least. Faith does not depend on historical inquiry; it is response to the Gospel, and that remains true, whatever conclusions historians may reach. Pushing this view to its extreme, some have even argued that it would make no difference to faith were it to be discovered that Jesus never lived. Few go that far – certainly not Bultmann, the great exponent of this existential approach to faith. But since historical inquiry can provide props for faith, it must (so it is argued) be regarded as an enemy of faith. We do not know about Jesus – and we do not need to know.

The trouble with this kind of approach is that it cuts the link between the Jesus of history and the Christ of faith – or at least, if it does not actually cut that link, it leaves it so tenuous as to leave one wondering: but what *is* this Gospel to which I am asked to respond? Who *is* this Christ? It may be that everyone sees the figure of Jesus from a different angle – but is there *no* control which will enable me to say 'this picture is closer to the truth than that'? Is faith entirely subjective? Am I not being asked to respond to something real – and if so, does that reality have nothing to do with Jesus of Nazareth? It seems that we need some kind of continuity between the Jesus of history and the Christ of faith to make sense of the Gospel.

The second approach faces up to the uncertainties of historical research – and we have already said that we can never be 100 per cent certain about any historical happening, and that what we are dealing with is degrees of probability. But just as those who approach the problem in the first way, and who insist that history is important for faith, begin from an assumption that historical evidence in the New Testament is in fact thoroughly reliable, so those who approach it in the second way, and insist that history is irrelevant, appear to start from a prior conviction that faith must not be propped up.

The English are famous for seeking a sensible middle course; it may be more dull, but in the end it has more chance of being right! Faced with two extreme views, I opt for compromise. But where do we begin? The first thing to recognize is that the historical evidence offered us in the Gospels is primarily evidence for the faith of the early Christian communities and of the men who wrote those Gospels. And that is where we must begin. The first questions we ask, in reading the Gospels, should not be: 'What did Jesus do? What did he say?' but 'What did Mark or Matthew or Luke or John believe about Jesus? Why did they choose to tell their stories in this particular way?' By comparing the different ways in which a story is told or a saying is recorded, we may be able to ask questions also about the men and women who passed this material on before the evangelists wrote it down. In other words, we have to work backwards, from what we have (the Gospels) to what lies behind them – beyond the earliest groups of Christian believers – to the figure of Jesus who started it all off. What we need to do here is what we would have to do in any other historical investigation – asking why our various witnesses should interpret the evidence in the way they did, recognizing that in the course of years, as a story is told and retold, its form and substance will inevitably change, as men and women see different significance in the story. This kind of approach is what has come to be known as the new quest for the historical Jesus. The new quest differs from the old in recognizing the difficulty of separating the original happening from interpretation. Nevertheless, it insists that the quest for the Jesus of history is a proper one, and a necessary one. Even though in many cases we may not be able to answer the question 'What happened?' with any great confidence, we must look for evidence of continuity between the historical Jesus and the faith of the Church. It is one thing to demand historical props for faith, another to recognize that faith requires an historical basis. The relevance of the historical Jesus for Christian faith was summed up by Gerhard Ebeling, when he wrote: 'Where Christology is concerned nothing may be said of Jesus which does not have its ground in the historical Jesus himself.'

But what kind of picture of Jesus are we going to be able to draw? We must recognize straight away that it is likely to be an impressionistic one. Indeed, the more we insist on clarity – on finding evidence that suggests that the probabilities are overwhelmingly in favour of any particular detail or event – the more distorted our picture is likely to be, since the area in the picture that we are actually able to fill in will inevitably be smaller. Some scholars have applied very rigorous criteria to the words of Jesus, trying to sort out those that seem to be almost certainly genuine; unfortunately very few of the sayings pass these rigid tests, and we end up with a Jesus who apparently said almost nothing! We may do better to cast our net wider and include more material, recognizing that all the sayings will inevitably have been distorted to some extent, by being translated from Aramaic into Greek, by being transferred from one setting to another, by being passed on from one believer to another. We may end up with a somewhat fuzzy picture – but it may nevertheless be a fair one. So, too, with Jesus' activity. For example, the evidence for Jesus having performed healing miracles seems to be overwhelming. Here we have not only the evidence of the Gospels, but the accusations of Jewish opponents to Christianity, recorded in the Talmud, that Jesus was a sorcerer; a similar accusation is made in the Gospels, where the Jewish leaders accuse Jesus of healing men and women in the power of Satan. The interpretation given by the evangelists is, of course, very different, but that Jesus did perform cures seems beyond reasonable doubt. It is far less easy, however, to be confident about the details of any particular cure recorded in the Gospels. Some seem more straightforward than others, but we can never be as confident about any one particular story as we can about the general statement that Jesus performed acts of healing. In the same way, we may be far more confident in suggesting that Jesus spoke with great authority than in arguing for the authenticity of any particular saying.

I have said that the portrait of Jesus that we are likely to be able to draw will be an impressionistic one. But of course any portrait is an interpretation of its subject; the painter selects certain details, and presents the picture in a certain light, emphasizing details he considers important and ignoring others. How much more so when the portrait we are trying to recover is not a deliberate one, but one which lies concealed behind the work of many men who have painted their particular pictures, emphasizing or ignoring particular features according to their own situation or understanding of the Gospel and its relevance to their needs. In other words, our 'information' is not only blurred, it is selective.

The quest for the historical Jesus is important because basically it is a question about Christology. In asking 'Who was he?' we are concerned to know also 'Who is he?' Is the Christ of Christian proclamation recognizable in Jesus of Nazareth? Are they identical? Or are they so different that we must conclude that the Church has imposed its beliefs on to Jesus unjustifiably? Or can we find a valid link between them?

There was a time when any attempt to answer the question 'Who is Jesus?' began with Jesus himself, and with the questions: 'Who did he believe himself to be? Who did he claim to be?' In other words, we began with the so-called messianic self-consciousness of Jesus, with what he believed and thought and said about himself.

We have already seen that it is impossible to be certain what Jesus said; if that is so, how much more difficult it will be to have any confidence about what he believed or thought. But, it is sometimes asked, can the Church believe about Jesus what he himself did not believe? Can we proclaim him as Messiah if he did not believe himself to be Messiah? Can he truly be Son of God if he did not know himself to be such? Christian tradition has often assumed that the beliefs of the Church about Jesus and those of Jesus about himself must be identical for them to be valid.

One of the reasons for this assumption is, I suspect, belief in the divinity of Jesus. If he is divine, it is argued, then he must know everything – including his own identity. The problem of the relationship between the divinity and the humanity of Jesus is one that has occupied Christian theologians for two thousand years, and we can hardly tackle it here, in passing; but it is at least worth asking whether Christian emphasis on the divinity of Jesus has not sometimes swamped his humanity; whether a Jesus who knows everything, and who does not share our human situation to the full is not *less* than truly human.

And if we recognize Jesus as truly human, truly sharing our human situation, then we must certainly challenge the assumption that it is necessary to trace ideas back to the mind of Jesus himself in order for them to have any validity. What is the truth about Martin Luther? Is it the way he saw himself? The way the Catholic Church of the time saw him? The way the German peasants saw him? Or the way we assess him today, as we look back on what he did and on subsequent events? Though we may lack the detailed knowledge that some of those who experienced particular events may have enjoyed, we may sometimes feel that the benefit of hindsight more than makes up for what we have lost. How many of the Battle of Britain pilots realized what they were achieving? For them, it was simply a question of a war of nerves and skill against their opposite numbers in the Luftwaffe. It is for others to assess whether Churchill's judgement was correct, that never in the field of human conflict have so many owed so much to so few. If Christians use somewhat similar words to express their experience of what Jesus achieved, it may be that some aspects of the truth are clearer to us than they ever were to him.

In fact, it is easy enough to see that most of our traditional ways of expressing belief in Jesus use terms which are appropriate for believers rather than for Jesus himself. No one, I imagine, would suppose that Jesus thought about himself in the manner set out in the creeds drawn up at Nicea and Chalcedon; the language and ideas used by the Fathers of the Church were their way of understanding and expressing truth. Nor, I suppose, would we imagine that Jesus thought of himself in the way set out in the first chapter of St John – as the Logos of God; yet countless generations of Christians have found in that passage a supreme expression of the truth about who Jesus is. We do not need to trace these ideas back to the self-consciousness of Jesus in order to be able to say: 'Yes, this is true.'

But having said about the self-consciousness of Jesus in particular what we have already said about the life of Jesus in general – namely, that historical certainty is impossible, and precise knowledge not essential – I for one would still want to argue here, as elsewhere, that some kind of continuity between what Jesus believed about himself and what Christians believe about him is important. We do not need, and should not expect, identity; what we do need is an overlap; enough of a link to be able to say that the Church's judgement is an appropriate one, and has not been imposed upon the figure of Jesus. I doubt whether the best place to look for this kind of continuity is in titles or definitions – the places to which Christians have so often turned. These may not be important. But I think it would be difficult to maintain that the Church's judgement on Jesus were true if the Gospel evidence suggested that Jesus had no sense of mission – no consciousness of being sent by God, no sense of being obedient to God's will.

The Church has traditionally laid great emphasis on the titles of Jesus; on his use of the phrase 'the Son of man', on the confession by his followers that he was the Messiah. Even to mention these two terms just at the moment is to stir up a hornet's nest; most New Testament scholars have strong views about whether or not Jesus himself did use these terms – and if so what he meant by them: clearly this is the last place to look for historical certainty. Quite apart from the historical problems, however, there is something else to be said about this question of what terms or titles – if any – Jesus used to describe his own role. I remember cycling through Oxford one day some years ago, and finding myself confronted by a poster which informed me, in vivid lettering, that Jesus said: 'I am the Christ.' My immediate reaction was to protest, 'But he didn't! In so far as we can assess the historical evidence, it suggests that he did not do anything of the kind; others may have spoken about him in this way, but he did not make any such claims for himself.' My second reaction was to say: 'So what? Supposing Jesus *did* say such a thing – what difference does it make?' The term 'Messiah' might have meant something to first-century Jews. In so far as it means something to Christians, that is because two thousand years of tradition have made it a convenient shorthand summary of their beliefs. But to the non-Jewish non-Christian inhabitants of north Oxford, the announcement must have seemed total mumbo-jumbo. Terms which are useful and appropriate in one setting lose their force when they are transferred to another. Even if we could be certain what terms or titles – if any – Jesus used to describe his own mission, we might be no better off. Suppose, for example, that we decide that Jesus did use the phrase 'the Son of man' to describe his own role, which of us understands what *that* means? One can almost guarantee that whatever we may think it means we shall be wrong. And if we are at sea in trying to understand the background and meaning of this particular phrase, that is a useful reminder that many of the terms and ideas and images used in the Gospels might have made much better sense – and perhaps conveyed a different sense – to those who first read them.

I have said that the quest for the historical Jesus is basically a question about Christology. Christian faith focuses on the figure of Jesus. But of one thing we can, I think, be quite sure. And that is that for Jesus himself it was otherwise. His message was *not* centred upon himself, but upon God. Central in the accounts of his teaching in the Synoptic Gospels is his proclamation of the Kingdom of God. He proclaims the coming of God's Kingdom, and calls on men and women to respond to God's rule – calls on them to be obedient to God. Now of course if one were to begin with the Fourth Gospel, one would get a very different picture. Here, Jesus' teaching seems to be focused on himself – upon his own role, and on his relationship with his Father. The teaching of Jesus is summed up in the great 'I am' sayings. Instead of pointing us to God, Jesus seems to be pointing us to himself. Moreover, in John, all the controversies between Jesus and his Jewish opponents are explicitly Christological; the vital questions that concern everyone are: Who is Jesus, and are the claims that he makes for himself true? In the Synoptic Gospels, Jesus acts with great authority, but makes no explicit claims for himself; in John, we find him making explicit claims. What has happened is that in John we see more clearly than in the other Gospels the problems and concerns of the Christian community; the questions with which Christians had to grapple are brought out into the open – and so are their beliefs about Jesus. The language and terms used about Jesus reflect the debates that were going on between the Christian community and their Jewish opponents. So we drop in on arguments about whether Jesus was an imposter or someone sent from God; was he a lawbreaker or someone even greater than the lawgiver, Moses? Had Christian worship replaced the worship of Judaism – and if so, why? Answer – yes, because Jesus was the fulfilment of everything that the Old Testament had promised, God's final word to mankind. Everything that was once said about the Law or about the worship of God in the temple can now be said about him. These are the controversies and the beliefs that govern the language and the terms that are used. The great 'I am' sayings express the truth that the Christian community has discovered in Jesus. It is Jesus – not the Law – who provides the Way, the Truth and the Life. It is Jesus – not the Jewish leaders – who is the Good Shepherd. It is Jesus – not Moses – who offers the bread of life and the living water. It is Jesus who is the resurrection, going beyond anything that Moses ever offered.

So am I denying that these words are authentic? Not at all! But what do we mean when we use the word 'authentic'? It often seems to be assumed that we can only speak of 'authenticity' if we mean 'words actually spoken on some occasion by Jesus'. But this seems to me to be superficial. Jesus might have said a thousand times 'I am the Way' or 'I am the Good Shepherd' or 'I am the Lord', but this would not make him any of these things. The words might be 'authentic' in the sense that he spoke them, without ringing true to experience. It is only when I find that he *is* the way, only when he *proves* himself to be the Good Shepherd by laying down his life, only when men and women acknowledge him to be the Lord, that these words can properly be described as 'authentic', for then they are discovered to be true.

I have drawn a distinction between John and the Synoptics. But John's presentation of the Gospel is only the logical development of a process that is to be seen at work already in the Synoptics. The crucial difference is between Jesus himself and the Church. And the reason for that difference is neither an unwarranted leap of faith, nor some arbitrary shift in emphasis. Rather it is the world-shattering, mind-blowing experience of the resurrection. It is this that focuses Christian attention irrevocably on the person of Jesus and on what God does through him. How *can* the message of Jesus and the Church be the same, when everything that Jesus said and did is now seen in the light of the resurrection, from the perspective of Easter faith? It was by the resurrection – so runs one very early declaration of faith – that God proclaimed Jesus as His Son; it was by the resurrection – so runs another – that he was declared Christ and Lord. By the resurrection, what Jesus had said and done is affirmed as God's word to his world. This is why the proclaimer became the proclaimed; this is why the message of the Church cannot be the same as that of Jesus.

But is what the Church proclaimed true? Is its message legitimate? That is something that no amount of historical investigation can ever prove. It can only be tested by faith. At the end of the day, the quest of the historical Jesus can take us only so far along the road. The living Lord is encountered only by those who believe.

Is the New Testament Trustworthy?

Leslie Houlden

Trustworthiness is a more slippery quality than appears at first sight. We begin by focusing on the feelings and thoughts which we have about it. In relation to the New Testament, despite the general reference of my title, one matter is chiefly in mind when the subject is broached: the historicity of the Gospels. Did things happen as the record says, especially with regard to Jesus' birth, death and resurrection, and to his allegedly miraculous deeds?

The trustworthiness of these stories is far from being of merely academic interest (though it is certainly that, and has been for two centuries at least). It is a matter that occasions excitement and even alarm, because the feeling is widespread, among believers and non-believers alike, that in the trustworthiness of these accounts the Christian faith is at stake. There is often much unclarity about exactly how or why this is so, but nevertheless the feeling prevails that if the accounts are false, or even inaccurate in some respects, then Christian faith is in doubt. There is a general though often vague awareness that these matters have been called into question, even to the point of extreme scepticism (about, for instance, Jesus' very existence or the basic character and outline of Paul's career). There is a lack of assurance in knowing how much credence, if any, such sceptical opinions deserve. At the same time, there is a realization that in the transmission of stories, especially in another culture at a distant time, there is ample room for error and distortion to occur, perhaps accompanied by an inadequate aversion to the propagation of legend.

In relation to this mixture of feelings (for it is as such, rather than concepts, that they often present themselves), it is necessary to be aware of certain characteristics of the age and culture in which, like it or not, we live. First, we are peculiarly sensitive to the force of the question, Did it happen? Though a moment's thought and much that surrounds us tell us how foolish we are, we have high demands and expectations about factual accuracy in accounts that come our way. At one level, we know perfectly well that stories in our newspapers are biased, hurriedly assembled and incomplete, and liable to be targeted towards sales as much as accuracy; all the same we continue to be surprised and outraged when we discover them to be so. Our strong inner demand is for accuracy and truthfulness; and the unlikelihood and perhaps the impossibility of its being met does not deter us. The non-fulfilment of our demand touches a very raw nerve indeed.

An important and less ephemeral aspect of this side of our culture is the increased professionalism of historical inquiry and the heightened historical sensitivity which accompanies it. This is both cause and effect of the feeling about trustworthiness that we are considering. We expect the research to be thorough, the documentation to be full; and, where evidence is lacking, we do not thank the historian for simply making something up to fill the gap. At the same time, a moment's reflection tells us of the inevitability of bias, of the necessity of selectivity among the mass of evidence, and of the need to adopt a point of view. Here too our inner demand outruns and is at variance with our knowledge of the state of things.

In the period when these aspects of our culture (both in our practice and in our consciousness) have come to prominence, the Gospels have, not surprisingly, had at least their fair share of attention. A great deal of it has been directly occasioned by the factors that have been outlined, especially the pressure for accurate historical information – though some of the more interesting sides of the study of the Gospels, notably concern with their literary and theological character, have been quite free of them. Believers, both scholars and others, have come to them with the establishing of factual authenticity as their dominant interest. People indifferent or antipathetic to Christian faith have likewise often been almost violently motivated by the determination to show historical falsehood. On both sides, there has often been extreme sophistication and ingenuity; and so strong is the inner demand we have described that neither side has lacked its disciples, its bandwagons, and its ripples of notoriety.

With these features of our ethos before our minds, realizing how irrationally they may affect us, we turn to the terms in which the trustworthiness needs, as a matter of sober fact, to be examined. A number of factors spring immediately to mind.

In the first place, we must avoid the many-shaped trap of anachronism. In particular, we must not impose upon the New Testament writers the demand for full and accurate historical knowledge which we, in our time and place, happen to feel so powerfully. We must do them the courtesy of taking them on their own terms. In this case, courtesy coincides with common sense and with accuracy of focus. In relation to the Gospels in particular, it is necessary to 'hear' them, as far as we can, in the way their writers intended us to hear, and not to ask of them what they had no intention to provide.

Suppose, for example, that in the stories of Jesus' birth in the Gospels of Matthew and Luke, the writers simply did not reckon to provide simple, literal history, but some other form of statement, perhaps identifiable if we look into the conventions of their time, then we are simply going down a blind alley if we take them as simple, literal history. In other words, trusting the New Testament involves understanding those who wrote it. That includes refraining from insisting that they conform to our view of what is proper in the writing of historical accounts – in terms of meticulous research, plain conformity to what is discovered, conformity too to standard and accepted conventions of historiography.

In the second place, we must simply accept certain plain facts about the Gospels and not suppose that these writings could have somehow transcended the conditions in which they came into being. That means, for example, taking seriously their relative lateness in relation to the life of Jesus which they describe. Even if they had been written by eye-witnesses, that lateness would necessarily carry with it certain effects. As the earliest of them, the Gospel of Mark, was composed (we suppose, though the detail of the matter scarcely affects the argument) about forty years after the events it recounts, there has inevitably been a process of development. Simple experiments with a roomful of people will demonstrate the propensity of stories to develop, gaining new content and fresh meaning, within narrow limits of time and place; how much more, then, over a period of some years and considerable distance. It is not, we should note, that all 'truth' is thereby lost – it may indeed be enhanced and deepened in the process of interpretation – but it is certainly modified, and the objective of 'plain' accuracy is not necessarily kept solely in view.

Another plain fact about the Gospels is their variety, even in handling the same material, as is the case with the first three Gospels over much of their length. There is indeed evidence for tenacity of verbal form in the transmission of matter, especially sayings, in some rabbinic circles in the Judaism of the period shortly after the time of Jesus. But there is also ample evidence, again in Judaism, for the ready adaptation of stories and teaching, in response to new needs, fresh pressures and developing theological perception. There is indeed no call to go further than the first three ('Synoptic') Gospels themselves to see, in episode after episode, that process at work; sometimes by way of broad and striking changes, more often by the altering of small details which are not necessarily less significant for their smallness. Studied carefully, they reveal the differences of outlook and theological interest between the various evangelists and open up to us distinct 'worlds', each inhabited by one of them and each representing, no doubt, a distinct and specific circle of life and thought in the early church. Whether one regards these differences as big or small, significant or insignificant, is a matter for the individual to decide. It depends largely on the purposes one has in mind, and, as we have seen, on the nature of one's almost intuitive 'demands'.

In relation to this perception of divergence, we note that the character of the Gospels as *theological history* has become ever clearer in recent years. Once that is absorbed, some of the steam in the demand for plain history is surely bound to be dispersed. 'Plain history' (we have already seen as much) is simply not what these writings ever set out to give. They are accounts of the tradition concerning Jesus, written in terms of and in the light of faith in him. The stronger and the more deeply pondered that faith, the more inevitable it was that it marked the way in which the tradition was presented, even in respect of the smallest details of the wording. What lies behind this realization is the elementary point that in relation to these documents, as to any others, one simply has to ask about the conditions of their formation. This is, of course, something equally true of the most thoroughly and 'objectively' researched example of present-day historical writing. Every writer (including, naturally, the writer of this very article) brings his whole self, his heredity and his educational and cultural formation, to every act of self-expression, including those, such as pieces of writing, which, having acquired fixed form, are easily open to the scrutiny of others.

It is also worth recognizing certain rather humdrum limitations that apply to the Gospels. Their brevity means that they contain the merest fraction of Jesus' acts and teaching. Selectivity, with its rigorous pruning, has been slashingly at work here – therefore, once again, so has the force of the writer's viewpoint. In the process of selection, and already at the stage of oral transmission before ever the writing was undertaken, we must allow for the loss of many of the precise original settings in which deeds were done and sayings uttered. And change of setting entails change of meaning – as anyone who has told the same joke or delivered the same address to different audiences knows well, often to his discomfiture. Again, Jesus' teaching was almost certainly given in Aramaic, and the Gospels are written in Greek. There has been translation from the one tongue to the other, once more necessarily entailing interpretation. Any translator knows that simple equivalence is either misleading or unattainable, and that differences not only of language itself but also of underlying culture obtrude upon the task problematically.

Many of these points have at first sight a negative and perhaps depressing effect in terms of the quest for trustworthiness. But it is worth reflecting, once more, on the degree of stringency one requires. As we have seen, that requirement could reach such a pitch that it is, literally, impossible to fulfil, given the sheer facts of human communication and of the process of writing. And at a level of less intensity, one may rest content with trustworthiness in the Gospels as far as certain general thrusts are concerned, though even these are not immune from the general conditions we have been pointing out, while accepting fluidity of tradition with regard to details. There is the 'good news/bad news' dictum which, not undeservedly, is beginning to acquire the force of a proverb: we probably know a great deal about Jesus from the Gospels, the trouble is we cannot be wholly sure what it is.

On the other hand, in one important area, relevant knowledge has been increasing on a significant scale: our knowledge of the circumstances in which Jesus lived and died and in which the Christian movement began. Here numerous discoveries of epigraphical or archaeological kinds and the sharpening of perspective with regard to both Jewish and Greco-Roman institutions have made possible ever more intelligent guesses about how things must have been. The probabilities have thereby been narrowed. It is worth examining two examples to illustrate these matters in a little more detail. Both concern subjects where trustworthiness is a matter of particular sensitivity in relation to Christian belief.

First, the stories of Jesus' birth in the Gospel of Matthew. We have seen that the proper question to ask concerns the working of the evangelist's mind. It is futile to ask at the outset, 'What happened?', for our access to the event lies through the screen of Matthew's mind. (In this case, there is also the narrative in Luke 1–2, but the principle is identical.) It is clear that he is dependent upon a method of using passages from the old Jewish scriptures which strikes most people now as strange and mechanical. Those passages are viewed not at all in their original contexts, but as sheer verbal statements capable of use to illuminate the relevant incident in Jesus' infancy. Behind this procedure lies an assumed theological conviction: that God's purpose, finding its goal inevitably in Jesus, was plainly foretold, even necessitated, in the ancient writings. The generally neglected genealogy, obviously important to Matthew (otherwise, why its prominence?), makes the point with even more relentless and monotonous force. (One may be convinced of that by the discipline of reading it over aloud and intently: one enters an alien world, and the effect is salutary.)

But then there is the question (as trust in Matthew's historical accuracy wanes): Why was his attention drawn to those particular passages of scripture, in the midst of such abundant choice, if elements in inherited tradition did not prompt him? If trustworthiness is still one's concern rather than Matthew's meaning at the time of writing, one has then moved some way backwards towards events

– though not all the way, and only in the light of Matthew's no doubt axiomatic way of using scripture. At a certain point in the process, it is of course necessary to be courageous enough to admit ignorance. That may be as much a religious as a scholarly decision, and it raises deeper religious issues than merely the trustworthiness of the New Testament.

We move to the opposite end of the story, to the narratives of the resurrection in the Gospels. Focusing on the material in the Gospels of Mark and Matthew, we face striking differences of content and ethos. Not only does Mark's 'young man' become 'an angel', but apart from his central message, his behaviour is quite different, for it is he who rolls away the stone from the tomb and then seats himself upon it. Most strikingly, the guard of soldiers, so prominent in Matthew, and almost dominating the whole chapter, is not only omitted from Mark but very positively absent. Or rather (as we must see it, for Matthew is almost certainly secondary and used Mark as his source), this element is added by Matthew to the story he inherited. And as far as ethos is concerned, Mark's quiet encounter, with only the young man and the woman involved, gives place to an event of apocalyptic drama and cacophony, inescapably impressive. Matthew's story was developed further in the Gospel of Peter, written perhaps a few decades later, and the dramatic circumstantiality of the account was increased; to the point of including a description of Jesus' emergence from the tomb in the presence of the awe-struck soldiers and escorted by two angels who had entered the tomb for that purpose. We are confronted by a process of development in the telling of a story. The changes were, however, not occasioned by pure imagination; nor is it likely that the later authors were in possession of additional information – clearly, their accounts do not supplement Mark's, they contradict it. It is matter of different theological 'atmospheres', motives and needs. Mark conveys a sense of modest, bare, yet effective testimony to the fact of the resurrection of Jesus. Matthew seeks to give more impressive authority for the claim, and, especially, to quell accusations from the ill-disposed that the disciples of Jesus simply stole the corpse. The Gospel of Peter seeks to quell all doubt and to answer all questions.

Here again it is illuminating – and part of the truth we need to trust – to recognize the range of factors present in the stories before us. These factors are all aspects of the movement of history and belief in early Christianity. That movement was, not surprisingly, particularly creative in relation to those episodes in the story of Jesus which were more important for faith.

There is, as we conclude, an issue which is both theological and, more intimately, religious. How much does the trustworthiness which we demand really matter? Christianity is a historical religion, we repeat, and hear repeated as if it were some clear and irrefutable claim, and that seems to make a high degree of historical reliability in its origins a strong requirement. It is, however, worth reflecting more soberly on the nature of Christian allegiance. That allegiance involves a response to the total gift of Jesus, as the one from God; a response necessarily drawing upon our varied capacities to respond, so that we, in our individuality, become part of the 'statement' that ensues. There is no final, objective picture of Jesus to which all must adhere: each adheres as he or she alone can, out of the given (the term is serious) conditions. And that response has a necessary character as faith, in the sense of a kind of abandonment. That does not mean sheer irrationality, flying in the face of all evidence, or accepting anything with credulity; it means a generosity of heart and mind, a giving of allegiance to a cause, in trust and exploration.

There is then a question of what exactly we ought to want to trust the New Testament for. It may be that mere historicity (itself in so many ways something of a will-o'-the-wisp) is not the appropriate demand for us to feel, if Christian theology or Christian allegiance is our primary interest. The bond between Christian belief and historical factuality, so long taken for granted and yet itself imperfectly dwelt upon, needs candid consideration before we decide what character it should bear. The object of Christian trust is never less than or other than God himself. And as far as the New Testament is concerned, then its purpose and use are to further that well-being in relation to God which he wills for us. It does not itself contain or bestow that salvation, but, in ways more varied and subtle than we are often ready to recognize, is an agent of that salvation. It is a witness, rather a collection of witnesses, an agent of response, essentially like our response, to him who lies behind it and is mediated to us through its words. The issue then becomes: can we range ourselves alongside it in making the faithful response?

3 THEOLOGY AND GOSPEL

St John's Gospel and Religious Truth

Barnabas Lindars SSF

Truth is an important word in the Fourth Gospel. We may recall the famous words in the prologue: 'The Word became flesh and dwelt among us, full of grace and truth' (1.14). Looking further on in the Gospel we find that it has a moral side to it. When John wants to speak of the opposite of doing evil, he does not say 'doing good' but 'doing what is true' (30.20–21). Moreover, truth is something that can be learned from Jesus, and there is a promise attached to it. Jesus says, 'If you continue in my word, you are truly my disciples, and you will know the truth, and the truth will make you free' (8.31–32).

With such statements as these before them, many readers of John's Gospel expect it to be specially concerned with conveying deep truths of religion, which they can use to solve their own religious uncertainties or to deepen and strengthen their own Christian spirituality. John's Gospel is different from the others. It is less factual and more concerned with ideas, and it uses words like life and light and truth which have a philosophical ring. But those who come to it with the expectation of gaining light on these things are often disappointed, because it does not really deal with them in an abstract or theoretical way. It is not a treatise on prayer or doctrine or philosophy.

So we have to let John make his point in his own way. I want to suggest that he does have an important point to make, which can be valuable to people today in their quest for religious truth. What he had to say arises out of the life and death and resurrection of Jesus, which is the subject of his book. But the way in which he presents it is specially geared to the needs of a group of people whose social conditions and intellectual outlook were not only very different from ours today, but different also from those of other groups in early Christianity, and from the audience of other New Testament books. We shall not get the best out of John unless we can think ourselves back into the situation in which the Gospel was written. The effort is worth making if it leads to deeper understanding. John's message is not merely dictated by his own individual approach to the traditions about Jesus, but is in response to people for whom his approach is meaningful and illuminating. The thing which makes them different is the sort of religious aims which they have. It is what they are looking for in religion. If Jesus is presented as the answer to their religious needs, then it is their needs which we must try to understand.

What I propose to do is, first, to spend some time looking at the different kinds of religious needs which were met by the preaching of the Gospel in the New Testament period. This will lead to the conclusion that John's audience consisted of Christians drawn from a Jewish milieu which had a strong sense of the mediatorial role of the Law of Moses in the approach to God. I shall then show how John presents Jesus over against this Law-centred spirituality in such a way as to make personal relationship between believers and God through Christ the primary category of religion. It is here that religious truth for John is located. Finally, I shall attempt to indicate what this has to offer for the quest for religious truth today.

The audience for the Fourth Gospel

The Gospel of John has a definite religious aim, and this is concisely expressed in well-known words in 20.30–31, the original ending of the book: 'Now Jesus did many other signs in the presence of the disciples which are not written in this book; but these are written that you may believe that Jesus is the Christ, the Son of God, and that believing you may have life in his name.' So what is offered is 'life'; but that can have any number of meanings in religious discourse, and we shall need some more information to fix the parameters.

Let us look first outside the Fourth Gospel to see some of the ways such an offer might be understood in New Testament times. We can think first in a broad way of the pursuit of the good life. In the ancient world there were many wandering religious teachers, who went among ordinary people teaching the good life. Vermes, in his book *Jesus the Jew*, quotes traditions of rabbis in Galilee around the time of Jesus, such as Haninah ben Dosa and Honi the Circle-Drawer, who were much respected gurus and famed for working miracles. Gerald Downing has recently pointed to the similarity of the Cynic teachers in the Greek-speaking world. Jesus' itinerant ministry in Galilee has something in common with this kind of teacher, providing a deeper and more challenging outlook to people whose religion is conventional and whose economic situation is never easy. It is easy to see the sayings of Jesus in the Sermon on the Mount in this kind of setting.

The miracle stories of the Gospels also contribute to this impression. Morton Smith, in his book *Jesus the Magician*, has shown how such stories reflect the aims of people both in Judaism and throughout the Greco-Roman world who wanted divine help for their daily well-being. The magical papyri from Egypt invoke gods or demons on the assumption that particular spells or incantations are likely to be effective to produce different results, such as cure of diseases or protection against misfortune. They use all sorts of divine names, borrowed from any culture, including the names of angels like Michael or Gabriel and biblical names for God such as Iao (i.e. Yahweh) and Sabaoth. There is something similar to this in the references to Beelzebub and the demons in Mark 3.22. It is of course a superstitious level of religion, implying the supposition that there is some mysterious relation between the hundreds of gods or demonic beings on offer, as it were, in the religious market and the cosmic forces which control human experience.

It is not to be supposed that such perceptions of Jesus can bring us to the core of his message or to the group of people who carried it forward after his death and became the Christian Church. Jesus not only spoke in timeless proverbs and exercised a healing ministry, but he had a Gospel to give which related to the particular hopes and yearnings of the Jewish people of his time. Many Jews were, as Luke says of Simeon in Luke 2.25, 'looking for the consolation of Israel'. They resented the rule of Herod Antipas in Galilee and hated the Roman regime in Judea, and the vicissitudes of their history in the century before them had produced a great longing for the righteous rule of God foretold in messianic prophecy. The *Psalms of Solomon*, composed shortly after 50 BC, express hatred of the Hasmonean rulers and horror at the intervention of Rome in their affairs, and beseech God to send the Messiah of the house of David, and these hopes are reflected in the Dead Sea Scrolls and in the Targums. The expectations in these documents are not uniform, but in different ways they express the longing for divine intervention. And this is what Jesus proclaimed in his Gospel of the Kingdom of God. He does not promise a Messiah, but the coming of God himself in mercy to the poor. The day is near when wickedness will be overthrown and God's rule will be established permanently. The apostles added to this basic message the claim that Jesus himself, risen from the dead and exalted as Messiah, would be God's agent for judgement and mercy on that day.

cf Moltmann

Christianity made its way as a movement in Judaism among people who wanted better things. It was not intended to overthrow the Jewish Law, but rather to confirm it (cf. Matthew 5.17). But the emphasis in Jesus' teaching on the state of the heart as the real criterion of readiness for the coming of God opened the way to take the Christian message beyond the confines of Judaism to the Gentile world. Here too there were people ready to respond to the Gospel because it met their religious needs. Paul is the great champion of the view that Gentile converts should not be subject to the Jewish Law, because the essence of the Gospel is God's saving grace. Though the people to whom Paul preached belonged to many different social groupings, as Wayne Meeks has shown in his study of them in *The First Urban Christians*, we can get some idea of the religious aims from Paul's description of the Thessalonian converts in 1 Thessalonians 1.9–10: 'You turned to God from idols, to serve a living and true God, and to wait for his Son from heaven, whom he raised from the dead, Jesus who delivers us from the wrath to come.'

These all too brief remarks about the audience of Jesus and of the leaders of the early Church are, I hope, enough to show that with John we move into a different world. In his Gospel the miracle stories are retold only because they serve a deeper theological purpose. There is very little teaching in the form of sayings of a proverbial type. The most striking difference from the Synoptic tradition is that the Kingdom of God is never mentioned except in one saying (John 3.3, repeated in verse 5), which is clearly a variant of a traditional saying of Jesus (cf. Matthew 18.3). Elsewhere the expression 'life' or 'eternal life' is always used where the Kingdom of God might be expected.

It seems, then, that John's audience is much more sophisticated than those who first responded to the Gospel. They are not waiting for divine intervention to bring in a better world order, like many of those who first received the message. They are not seeking Jewish faith without the Law, like many of the Gentiles to whom Paul preached. They are interested in eternal life, and this suggests a timeless approach to religion. Instead of pinning faith on a coming event, a future manifestation of glory for which they must be always ready, they are interested in the possibility of a meaningful relationship with God in the present. John does not deny the future event, but he takes care to place all the emphasis on its meaning for the present. So in 5.24 he makes Jesus say: 'He who hears my word and believes him who sent me, has eternal life; he does not come into judgement, but has passed from death to life.'

In his original conclusion in 20.31 John summed up the Gospel as the offer of life. We have now seen that this implies a different concept of the religious aim from other presentations of the Gospel. John takes back the future event of resurrection and judgement into the present. The Christian life is present enjoyment of the conditions

that belong to the future. It is even possible to dispense with the
idea of the future altogether, as a relic of the earliest Gospel which
can and should be discarded. In that case only the present, timeless
relationship with God is meaningful to these Christians.

So now we are faced with the further question, what sort of people
are likely to find that John's apparently timeless Gospel meets their
religious needs? This question has received a number of answers in
modern scholarship. I will mention three of them.

First there is the view espoused by the very influential scholar
Rudolf Bultmann that John's readers are dualists likely to be
attracted by Gnostic teaching. According to this view the divine
life is totally distinct from the created order and fundamentally
incompatible with it. What is then needed is a mediator, sent down
from the divine order, who can provide the means for the impri-
soned soul to escape from the trammels of the flesh and ascend to
the divine life. Teaching of this kind is characteristic of Gnosticism,
which probably began as philosophical sects on the fringe of Judaism
and came under Christian influence in the second century. It is
well known that Bultmann regarded the Fourth Gospel itself as a
Christianized version of a Gnostic treatise. But though there are
numerous words and phrases in John which can be taken to support
this theory, Bultmann himself was aware that John does not presuppose a thoroughgoing dualism. In two particular ways John affirms
the value of the created order as the vehicle of God's saving acts.
There is first the incarnation, the fact that 'the Word became flesh'
(1.14) in the person of Jesus, and second the real death of Jesus on
the cross, which is the act in which God is glorified and the salvation
of the world is accomplished (1.29; 12.31–32; 13.31, etc.). Thus, in
adapting the Gospel, John does not go so far as to open the door to
people who despise the flesh and regard religion as a way of escape
from it.

Second, we can think of a quasi-Gnosticism which does not presuppose an ultimate dualism of this kind. This does not deny that
the created order belongs to God, but thinks in terms of a hierarchy
in which the mental life has the highest value. Philo the Jew of
Alexandria, who was a contemporary of Jesus, is an excellent example of this. He regards the soul as the high priest of the personality.
Contemplation is the true end of mankind. The very name Israel,
which, he says (using a fanciful etymology), means 'man seeing
God', shows that the Jewish people are specially privileged from
this point of view. The Hebrew scriptures, specifically the Law of
Moses, enshrine the revelation of God, and so provide the knowledge of the truth. However, this knowledge is not always to be
found in the surface meaning of the text, and Philo indulges in

elaborate allegorical exegesis to extract what he regards as the genuine spiritual meaning of the Law.

Philo takes us much nearer to the religious aims of the readers of the Fourth Gospel, but John makes no use of Philo's kind of allegorical exegesis and does not expect his readers to be familiar with it. Moreover, there are features of John which ally him more closely to Palestinians rather than Alexandrian Judaism. This has been increasingly recognized since the discovery of the Dead Sea Scrolls, which show a number of contacts of thought and expression with John. Our third view is that of H. Odeberg, writing before this discovery but to some extent anticipating it. He suggested that John was commending the Gospel to people who can best be described as mystics. The verb 'to see' plays an important role in John. Jesus promises to Nathanael sight into heaven (1.51). Later he says to Philip, 'He who has seen me has seen the Father' (14.8). However, in the end the concept of sight is rejected. The risen Jesus says to Thomas: 'Blessed are those who have not seen and yet have believed' (20.29).

Can we find another clue to the religious aims of John's readers? I should like to suggest that we should look at what John opposes, the kind of contrasts which he makes in order to bring out his own positive teaching. Recent work on John takes seriously the special feature of disputes between Jesus and the Jewish authorities, which form the bulk of the discourses and are quite unlike what is found in the Synoptic Gospels. J. Louis Martyn has shown that they reflect the disputes between Christians and Jews late in the first century, when Church and synagogue had almost reached breaking point. When we look at John from this point of view, we can see that what John opposes is reliance on the Jewish Law. But this is not at all a matter of legalism, corresponding with the popular (though not entirely correct) stereotype of Pharisaism. It is rather a Law-centred spirituality, and to that extent reminds us of Philo. For these Jews the Law is loved and valued as the highest expression of the wisdom of God, and in their willing performance of its precepts they make the nearest approach to a loving relationship with God. What John has to offer is a much closer relationship with God through Jesus, who replaces the Law as the true mediating agency between humanity and God. For these Jews there is no direct sight of God (1.18; 5.37). But Jesus is 'the way, and the truth, and the life' (14.6).

This leads to the conclusion that the aim of the Fourth Gospel is to present Jesus as the means of entry into a personal and loving relationship with God. This is what is meant by the offer of 'life in his name' (20.31). It applies in the present, so that the believer has indeed passed from death to life, but its fullness belongs to the 'last day' (6.40). The religious truth of the Fourth Gospel is bound up with the cogency of this claim. We must now see how John makes this point, and then consider what he has to say to us today.

Jesus and the Law

John writes for Christians who are drawn from Jews who have what I have called a Law-centred spirituality, and they are under constant pressure from their fellow Jews who have not embraced the faith and accuse them of leading the people astray (cf. 7.12). This is the classic Jewish accusation against Jesus, known from rabbinic sources. It means persuading people to be unfaithful to the Law. John's readers share in the same accusation and similarly incur persecution (15.18 – 16.4). John aims to support them by reinforcing their faith. But what he has to say is also the message which would bring the opponents salvation, if only they would hear it.

In proposing his Jesus-centred spirituality in contrast with the Jewish Law-centred spirituality, John consciously takes up the values which these Jews attach to the Law and argues that the true fulfilment of them is to be found in Jesus alone. I hold that this scheme is far more pervasive in the Fourth Gospel than is commonly realized, and that it provides the key to understanding the structure of some of his most important arguments.

The point is made explicit at the beginning of the Gospel in the prologue: 'For the law was given through Moses; grace and truth came through Jesus Christ' (1.17). Behind this statement is the wisdom poem of Sirach (Ecclesiasticus) 24, which I am persuaded is the most important item in the literary background to the prologue. In this poem we see God's wisdom as his agent in creation. But she has not only 'made the circuit of the vault of heaven' (5), but also made her 'dwelling in Jacob' and been 'established in Zion' (8; 10), just as in John's prologue the Word of God, through whom 'all things were made', 'came to his own home', though in his case 'his own people received him not' (John 1.3, 11). But then the Sirach poem goes on to claim that God's wisdom is actually embodied in the Law of Moses, which provides an inexhaustible fountain of divine knowledge like the rivers of paradise (Sirach 24.23). Similarly in John God's Word, which is personified as the Son of God, is incarnate in the historical Jesus, and he contains all the 'grace and truth' ('steadfast love and faithfulness', Exodus 34.6) which was proclaimed but only partially seen when God revealed himself to Moses on Mount Sinai at the giving of the Law (John 1.14). Thus a very high doctrine of the Law as revelation, or, one might say, as the supreme vehicle of religious truth, is matched by a surpassing claim with regard to Jesus himself. In both cases the Law and Jesus act as a screen in front of God who is invisible. But this is not a barrier, but a mediation of invisible God in a form apprehensible to mankind.

Another example of this contrast comes in the conversation of Jesus with Nicodemus, who is represented as an accredited teacher of the Law (3.10). Jesus says that the religious desire to 'see the kingdom of God' (3.3) is not attainable by human effort, but requires a sort of birth from above, i.e. the action of the Spirit of God. This being so, the agent of this action must also come 'from above', and Jesus, as the one sent by God, must also have a heavenly origin (3.31–36). However, in the middle of the argument Jesus suggests that anyone who seeks the divine truth might think it necessary to go up to heaven itself in order to bring it down (3.13). The point is that this would seem to be the only thing possible, unless there is a mediating agent. That John is referring to the Law as a possible mediator becomes obvious when we pick up the allusion in this verse to Deuteronomy 30.12, where Moses mentions the possibility (or rather impossibility) of going up to heaven to fetch the Law. By contrast Jesus is the Son of Man who has come down from heaven, and he will reveal God, not in the form of Law, but in the act of being lifted up on the cross (3.14). How this surpasses the limited revelatory capacity of the Law is then declared in these unforgettable words: 'For God so loved the world that he gave his only Son, that whoever believes in him should not perish but have eternal life' (3.16). It is at once evident that the concept of the mediating agent has been raised to a level where the only form of expression that is sufficient is the category of personal relationship.

John refers again to Sirach 24 in the great discourse on the bread of life in Chapter 6. The formal contrast is between the heavenly manna in the wilderness (Exodus 16) and Jesus as the true bread from heaven. But when he says, 'He who comes to me shall not hunger, and he who believes in me shall never thirst' (6.35), there is clearly a contrasting allusion to wisdom's claim that 'Those who eat me will hunger for more, and those who drink me will thirst for more' (Sirach, 24.21), which immediately precedes the identification of wisdom with the Law. In this connection we have independent evidence for a spirituality of the Law as nourishment for the soul, for the manna miracle is so interpreted both in Philo and in the Jewish Midrash. This explains the otherwise unexpected quotation in John 6.45 from Isaiah 54.13, 'And they shall all be taught by God'. This appears to abandon the metaphor of food, but actually it comes from a passage which leads into an invitation to 'come, buy and eat' (Isaiah 55.1). For Christians John says that they should 'eat the flesh of the Son of man and drink his blood' (John 5.55). This surely refers to the eucharistic celebration of the death of Jesus which

reveals the Father's love. It is this above all which provides the true
nourishment of the soul.

As a final example we may note the way in which the language
of Jesus in the discourse attached to the account of the Last Supper
reflects the language of Deuteronomy about the Law. Deuteronomy
constantly exhorts Israel to love the Lord and to keep his commandments. So Jesus says, 'If you love me, you will keep my commandments' (14.15). But if we ask what his commandments are, we find
that they are not specified. There is only one commandment in
John's presentation, and that is the command of love. This of course
goes back to the Jesus tradition, in which Jesus quotes from Deuteronomy the *Shema*, the command to love God, which has always
been recited by Jews (Deuteronomy 6.4; cf. Mark 12.28–34). Hitherto
the love of God has been mediated through the Law. With Jesus it
comes into its own as an intimate personal relationship. Jesus
explains that it is participation in his own relationship with the
Father. 'If a man loves me, he will keep my word, and my Father
will love him, and we will come to him and make our home with
him' (John 14.23).

Thus for John the essential difference between the Law and Jesus
is that the Law is impersonal, and to that extent places a barrier
between the faithful and God, whereas Jesus is a person who is
himself in such close relationship with God that those who love him
are brought with him and in him into his own loving relationship
with God. This is why the response of faith in John is always
expressed with the dynamic phrase to believe *into* Jesus, i.e. to
entrust oneself to him.

It would be very easy to conclude that the cardinal point of John's
contrast between Jesus and the Law is the incarnation. Just as the
wisdom of God was embodied in the Law, so the divine Word was
made flesh in Jesus Christ. It can then be supposed that all that is
necessary for salvation is to believe into Jesus and so to be joined
with God. Raymond Brown, in his intriguing study of *The Community
of the Beloved Disciple*, has argued that that is precisely what some of
John's readers thought he meant. But these people are regarded as
heretics in the First Epistle of John! The trouble is that, because they
partake of the divine life, they regard themselves as beyond the
reach of sin. They see no virtue in the humanity of Jesus, because
the whole point of believing is to be joined to his divinity and so to
experience the new birth that comes from above.

What these Christians fail to understand is the crucial importance
of the cross. The death of Jesus is necessarily a human act. To John
it has the character of a sign. It signifies something indispensable.
'As Moses lifted up the serpent in the wilderness, so must the Son
of Man be lifted up' (3.14). The reference is to the bronze serpent

of Numbers 21.9, which is referred to as a 'token, or sign, of deliverance' in Wisdom 16.6. It is because of its value as a sign that John insists that the death of Jesus must be by crucifixion (12.32; 18.32). It signifies the lifting up of Jesus through human death to the divine glory. It is the supreme example of obedience, because Jesus nerves himself to accept it only because it is his Father's will. So he says: 'When you have lifted up the Son of Man, then you will know that I am he, and that I do nothing on my own authority' (8.28). Jesus thus lays down his life of his own volition, as the Good Shepherd who gives his life for the sheep: 'No one takes it from me, but I lay it down of my own accord' (10.18). Thus the cross reveals the total union between the human Jesus and the heavenly Father, so that he can say, 'I and the Father are one' (10.30). It is the ultimate application of a universal truth, which nevertheless people are all too slow to learn, and the heretics addressed in 1 John are refusing to face and accept. This is the fact that 'Unless a grain of wheat falls into the earth and dies, it remains alone; but if it dies, it bears much fruit' (12.24). It is therefore true for the disciples too. They too must learn that 'greater love has no man than this, that a man lay down his life for his friends' (15.13). It is something that has to be both received and given. The disciples know that 'God so loved the world that he gave his only Son' (3.16), and in response they give themselves to follow his example (13.15). So long as we are in this world, participation in the divine life involves following Jesus along the way of the cross (12.26).

This is the Jesus-centred spirituality which John sets before his readers. Jesus is presented as the enabler of a personal relationship between humanity and God. Jesus surpasses the Law as a mediating agency, because instead of being a static statement of rules and precepts Jesus is the focus of a dynamic relationship which can be described only in terms of love.

Religious truth today

This was the religious truth which John found so deeply meaningful to himself and sought to convey to his readers. It was formulated in the light of the special needs of the educated Hellenistic Jews from which the Johannine converts were drawn. It marks a special development in the history of early Christianity. It is a creative response to the problem of commending Christian faith in a milieu which was significantly different from the earliest community.

At the same time it is basically faithful to the original tradition. John's idea of the loving relationship between Jesus and God is directly dependent on the *Abba* spirituality, Jesus' direct and intimate address of God as Father, which is attested in the Lord's Prayer and in the Gethsemane story (Mark 14.36). John has given it a cosmic, timeless undergirding by seeing Jesus as the Word of God, personified as the Son of God who is 'in the bosom of the Father' (1.18) and actualized historically in the human Jesus. But he has filled out the picture with the essentials of the life of Jesus, seeing his miracles as the works of God which he does as an obedient Son, and conveying the essence of the moral teaching of Jesus in the love command. Both the works of Jesus and his teaching culminate in the cross, which is the point where the reality of the Father and Son relationship reaches its deepest and most poignant expression.

In his account of the death and resurrection of Jesus, John introduces an anonymous character called 'the disciple whom Jesus loved' (13.23; 19.26; 20.2; 21.7). It is unnecessary to go into the question who this is meant to be historically. The important thing is his function in the Gospel. In my view John intended him to be one with whom each reader could identify. In other words the Beloved Disciple is intended to be yourself. He is one who is close to the heart of Jesus and understands him. He is permitted to know that Jesus must be betrayed by one of his closest friends. He, like the mother of Jesus, stands beside the cross. He is the first to reach the empty tomb, but he needs no resurrection appearance because he believes.

The religious truth which John conveys is not a philosophical argument for the existence of God, or any other aspect of epistemology, but a deep and satisfying account of how religion may be expressed. Jesus in John's presentation is both the model and the means of a personal and loving relationship with the ultimate reality which theists refer to as God. The point remains valid, even if we find the traditional approach to the doctrine of God unacceptable. The necessity of a personal relationship for the highest form of religion arises from the fact that God is personal as much as from the fact that we ourselves are personal, and have to be so to be fully human. John's readers were drawn from Jews who had a strong sense of a personal God, but a profound sense of his holiness and transcendence made it necessary to focus on the Law as the mediating agent. For us today the barrier is more likely to be the paralysing doubt whether God can be fitted into our scientific account of the universe at all.

At this point John's Jesus is available as the mediator of personal relationship with ultimate reality, however that is conceived in philosophical terms. He is the human embodiment of the Word of God. In his life and teaching and death and resurrection, he is the model of personal response to God as Father. He is also the means of a personal kind of relationship with God, in spite of all uncertainties.

This is achieved through the Johannine concept of faith which, as we have seen, is a dynamic quality of 'believing into' Jesus in the sense of entrusting oneself to him. So the effort of making Jesus the focus of our life draws us into his own relationship with God as Father. This is done not only by individual commitment, involving the will and the imagination and the practice of private prayer, but also by fellowship with other followers of Jesus in the liturgy and the common life of the Body of Christ.

John presents Jesus as the Word made flesh, who is therefore full of grace and truth of God. To follow Jesus is to 'do what is true' in a religious sense. Jesus also says: 'If you continue in my word, you are truly my disciples, and you will know the truth, and the truth will make you free.' Because the response to God through believing into Jesus is necessarily a matter of personal relationship, it is a fully human response, and it is therefore the truth of the human side in the bond with the divine which we call religion. But this bond is not slavery but freedom, because it constitutes the full flowering of our nature, in so far as we are conformed to Christ crucified. 'So', says Jesus, contrasting the functions of a slave and a son, 'if the Son makes you free, you will be free indeed' (8.36).

Interpreting the Sermon on the Mount

Graham Stanton

In 1629 John Donne, the poet and Dean of St Paul's, made a bold claim about the Sermon on the Mount. 'All the articles of our religion, all the canons of our Church, all the injunctions of our princes, all the homilies of our fathers, all the body of divinity, is in these three chapters, in this one Sermon on the Mount.' While Donne overstated his case, no other short section of the Bible has been more prominent in theological discussion and controversy, and in the general life of the Church.

In our modern secular society the Sermon's influence continues. Many men and women who have little or no contact with the Church are confident that the Sermon contains clear ethical teaching for all men of goodwill – though they may have given the matter little thought. An opinion poll would quickly uncover a hazy knowledge of the contents of the Sermon, but strong support for the proposition that if only everybody lived by the teaching of Jesus in his Sermon on the Mount, the world would be a better place.

Once those who claim that the Sermon contains clear ethical teaching for all men and women of good-will begin to read Matthew 5–7 carefully, they quickly discover that some verses in the Sermon are difficult to understand, some seem quite unrealistic, some are impossible to carry out literally today. Interpretation of this influential and apparently simple passage is far from easy.

In this short article I hope to show that interpretation of the Sermon raises a whole series of fascinating questions. Of course it is possible to read and reflect on the Sermon without a knowledge of the historical and theological issues at stake. But, as with a Beethoven string quartet, some knowledge of the original historical setting and structure of the Sermon, as well as of the variety of ways it has been approached over the centuries, greatly enhances our appreciation.

Simply for convenience we shall first of all set out some of the most important theological, exegetical and historical questions which arise in interpretation of the Sermon. By exploring these often difficult questions, we may gain fresh insights into this familiar passage. We shall then sketch out some of the main ways these chapters have been interpreted down through the centuries. The history of the interpretation of the Sermon warns us that there is a risk that our own theological convictions may blind us to the intention of the text, but it also encourages us to find our own ways of allowing the text to speak powerfully today.

The term 'the Sermon on the Mount' goes back to Augustine. His important commentary on Matthew 5–7 *De Sermone Domini in monte* was probably written between 329 and 396. In spite of Augustine's enormous influence on many later Christian writers, these three chapters were not generally referred to as 'the Sermon on the Mount' until the sixteenth century.

Since the beginning of the twentieth century most writers have accepted that the evangelist Matthew compiled the Sermon from various sources: Jesus did not 'preach' Matthew 5–7 as a sermon. But even in recent decades many have paid only lip-service to the fact that the Sermon is the first of the evangelist's five discourses. The Sermon is often taken without further ado to be a summary of the ethical teaching of Jesus. As we shall see, it is important to distinguish between two ways of approaching the Sermon. On the one hand it is a composition of the evangelist Matthew which contains some of his own distinctive emphases. On the other hand, behind these three chapters of Matthew are some sayings of Jesus which can be appreciated fully only when they are read in the wider context of sayings of Jesus from other parts of the Gospels.

The serious student of Matthew 5–7 soon discovers that interpretation of these chapters involves a large number of issues, some of which are theological, some ethical, some historical and some exegetical. They may be divided into five sets of overlapping questions.

(i) Does Jesus simply interpret or clarify the Law of Moses? Or does he present radically new teaching? Is Jesus portrayed as the 'new Moses' who 'goes up on the mountain' (Matthew 5:1) in order to present on a 'new Mount Sinai' a 'new law' for a 'new people'?

Matthew 5:17 is often taken as the preface to the central section of the Sermon which runs from 5:17 to 7:12. But what did Jesus mean when he said, 'Think not that I have come to abolish the law and the prophets; I have not come to abolish them but to fulfil them'? This verse bristles with difficulties. Jesus clearly rejects any suggestion that his coming overturns the 'law and the prophets', but what is meant by 'fulfilling' them? Does Jesus set forth the real intention of the Law? Or does he confirm or establish the Law? The latter suggestion is often supported by linguistic arguments based on the force of the Aramaic word which Jesus may have used, and by an appeal to 5:18–19. These two verses seem to underline the continuing importance of the law: 'not a letter, not a stroke will disappear from the law' (NEB). In the next section of the Sermon (5:21–48), however, Jesus seems to contrast his teaching with that of Moses. Six quotations of the Law are followed by the solemn phrase 'but I say to you'. In some cases Jesus seems to strengthen the teaching of the Law (5:22, 28, 34); in others, he seems to overturn the teaching of Moses (5:39, 44 and perhaps 32).

(ii) What is the relationship between Matthew 5–7 and Paul's Gospel of grace? Is the Sermon (as 'Law') intended to make the reader or listener aware of his need of 'grace'? Or does the Sermon *presuppose* God's forgiveness and acceptance of the sinner and therefore set out demands for true discipleship? We shall return to these questions in our discussion of Luther's interpretation of the Sermon.

(iii) To whom is the Sermon addressed? To men and women in general, or to those committed to the way of Jesus? The text itself is ambiguous at this point. The introduction and conclusion (5:1 and 7:28) imply that the Sermon was addressed to the crowds, but 5:2 notes that 'when the disciples had gathered around him Jesus began to address them'. While many parts of the Sermon seem to set out an 'ethic of Christian discipleship', the final verses of the whole Gospel imply that the teaching of Jesus is to be part of the message taken to 'all nations' (28:18–20).

(iv) Is the Sermon a *code* of ethics to be followed in every detail? Or does it set out principles or attitudes on which conduct is to be based? Are all parts of the Sermon to be interpreted literally, as some have claimed? Or do some sayings (such as 5:22, 39, 43) contain hyperbole? Many writers have urged that the harsh demands of the Sermon can be understood and obeyed only if they are taken to portray 'the attitude of heart' appropriate for a 'member of the kingdom'.

(v) To what extent are individual sayings dominated by the expectation (either of Jesus or of Matthew) of the approach to the end-times (i.e. eschatology)? For example, does Jesus commend a casual attitude to food and clothing in 6:25ff. because of the approach of the end-times, or simply because this is the right attitude regardless of when the end-times come?

Is every petition of the Lord's Prayer (6:9–13) to be interpreted eschatologically? On this approach, when we pray, 'Give us this day our daily bread', we are not asking for the basic necessities of everyday life, but requesting a partial anticipation of the 'feast of heaven' – the 'bread of heaven'. Does the petition 'lead us not into temptation' concern the time of testing expected in the end-time, or everyday temptations?

The modern interpreter of the Sermon will quickly find that his interpretation of individual sayings or groups of sayings will be determined by his answers to all five sets of questions. These questions have been discussed for nearly two thousand years, though some have been more prominent than others in different periods of Church history.

The first commentary on the Sermon was probably written by Origen in the middle of the third century, but only a short fragment of it has survived. The two most important expositions of the Sermon in the early Church were written by Chrysostom and Augustine at the end of the fourth century. Both the influential Church Fathers insisted that the Sermon was the perfect pattern for the life of all Christians. In his homilies on the Sermon Chrysostom attacked the heretical views of Gnostics and Manicheans. He rejected their view that the body is evil and the mind and spirit are good; 5:29 taught that it is the 'evil mind' which is accursed, not bodily organs such as the eye and hand. Chrysostom also refuted 'those heretics who say that the old covenant is of the devil'; the sayings of Jesus do not repeal the old law, they 'draw out and fill up its commands'.

Augustine also grappled with the relationship of the Sermon to the Law of Moses. The Manichean Faustus had claimed that 5:17 was a saying neither of Jesus nor of Matthew; someone else had written it under Matthew's name! In his *Reply to Faustus* Augustine stressed the continuity of the 'old Law' and the 'new' more strongly than was usually the case in the early Church. In his own exposition of the Sermon, however, he emphasized sharp discontinuity by distinguishing between the 'lesser precepts given by God through his holy prophets and servants to a people who still needed to be bound by fear' (i.e. to Israel before the coming of Christ) and 'the greater precepts given through his Son to a people now ready to be freed by love'. Augustine is not the only interpreter who interpreted 5:17–48 in different ways either in different contexts or at different points in his life. Augustine may have been inconsistent, but the issue is still with us today. To what extent and in what ways is the ethical teaching of the Old Testament still important for Christians? Do we retain the parts which find an echo in the teaching of Jesus, and ignore or reject the rest?

In the thirteenth century, Thomas Aquinas also stressed the discontinuity between the old Law ('the law of bondage' i.e. the Old Testament) and the new Law ('the law of liberty', i.e. the New Testament, especially the teaching of Jesus), but without conceding that the latter contradicted or abrogated the former. He used the analogy of the tree (the new Law) which is in a sense contained in the seed. Aquinas also introduced a distinction which was to become very influential in Catholic thought. In addition to the *commandments* of the new Law which are necessary in order to gain salvation, there are also optional *counsels* which 'render the gaining of eternal bliss more assured and expeditious'. The latter are intended for those Christians who strive for perfection; they are based on poverty, chastity and obedience and are therefore primarily for those who join the religious life. This distinction is hardly hinted at in interpretation of the Sermon in the early centuries, though it may be implied by the harsh saying of Jesus concerning the renunciation of marriage: 'let those accept it who can' (Matthew 19:11–12).

Luther, Zwingli and Calvin wrote extensively on the Sermon. They all insisted that Matthew 5–7 represents the true interpretation of the Law of Moses which had been obscured by Judaism; on the whole they emphasized the continuity between the 'Law of Christ' and the 'Law of Moses' more than their Catholic opponents. They rejected the use made of the Sermon by radical Anabaptist groups who claimed that the ethical teaching of Christ was a clear development beyond the law of Moses, parts of which have been abrogated. Anabaptists claimed that the Sermon should be interpreted literally and that Christians should therefore never use violence (Matthew 5:39), never swear oaths (5:34), and never hold office as a judge or ruler (7:1). Their literal interpretation of the Sermon led them to opt out of secular government completely.

In a series of sermons on Matthew 5–7 (and in other writings), Luther developed his well-known doctrine of the two realms, the secular and the spiritual. The Christian lives in both spheres. In the spiritual sphere (i.e. within the life of the Church) the Christian must obey all the commands of the Sermon; in the secular sphere, natural law or 'common sense' must prevail. In his remarks on Matthew 5:38–42 (the use of violence and compulsion), for example, Luther claimed that most interpreters failed to distinguish properly between the Kingdom of Christ and the kingdom of the world. In these verses

> Christ is not tampering with the responsibility and authority of the government, but he is teaching individual Christians how to live personally, apart from their official position and authority . . . A Christian should not [use violence to] resist evil; but within the limits of his office, a secular person should oppose firmly every evil.

For Luther a 'secular person' included Christians participating in the secular realm.

Luther also discussed the Sermon in terms of 'Law' and 'Gospel'. In some of his writings he emphasized that the Sermon is the 'Law of Christ' that makes people aware of the Gospel of God's grace through Christ: 'we are not able properly to fulfil one tittle out of our own strength . . . but must always crawl to Christ.' But in other passages Luther stated that the Sermon is not just the accusing Law that points to sin: it is also 'Gospel'. This is especially true of the beatitudes (5:3–12). Christ 'does not press but in a friendly way entices and speaks: "Blessed are the poor." '

By referring in different passages in his writings to the Sermon both as 'Law' and as 'Gospel', Luther confused some of his later followers. Many Lutheran theologians have stressed that the Sermon is the Law that makes us aware of our sinful natures and of our need of Christ's forgiveness. But some Lutherans (notably J. Jeremias) have claimed that the demands of Jesus in the Sermon are preceded by 'Gospel', i.e. by his proclamation of the Kingdom and by his encouragement to his disciples to share his own sense of sonship.

In his comments on Matthew 5:21, Calvin noted that 'we must not imagine Christ to be a new legislator, who adds anything to the eternal righteousness of his Father. We must listen to him as a faithful expounder.' Calvin partially anticipated eighteenth- and nineteenth-century discussion of the sources of the Sermon in his recognition that Matthew 5–7 is 'a brief summary of the doctrine of Christ . . . collected out of his many and various discourses.'

All the various approaches which we have just sketched can be found in modern discussions of the Sermon. Twentieth-century scholarship, however, has added two new issues: the extent to which the Sermon reflects the views of Jesus (or of Matthew) concerning the end-times (eschatology) and the extent to which Matthew the evangelist has shaped the traditions he has incorporated into Chapters 5–7.

In 1892 Johannes Weiss published a short but influential discussion of Jesus' proclamation of the Kingdom of God. Jesus expected that the Kingdom would shortly be ushered in through a cataclysmic divine intervention. In 1901 Albert Schweitzer developed this approach even more vigorously. Both writers believed that the ethical teaching of Jesus was intended as a preparation for the short period before the end ('interim ethics'); the sayings of Jesus were not intended to be used by later generations, as most readers of the Sermon down through the centuries had simply assumed. Thus most of the issues with which earlier interpreters of the Sermon had grappled were declared to be irrelevant.

Weiss and Schweitzer raised in an acute form the relationship between the ethical teaching of Jesus and his proclamation of the coming Kingdom. Discussion of this issue has to range far beyond Matthew 5–7 and consider all the relevant sayings of Jesus.

In 1902 B. W. Bacon published one of the first discussions of the Sermon in English which attempted to reconstruct its earliest attainable form. He concluded that in the original form of the Sermon Jesus spoke as a prophetic interpreter of a new Law; Jesus did not lay down rules, but opened up principles. These conclusions were hardly novel, but in his isolation of the 'intrusive additions' of Matthew, Bacon paved the way for later redaction critical studies. Bacon claimed that Matthew has supplied 'neo-legalistic touches' in verses such as 5:16 ('good works')' 5:18–19; 5:32 (the 'exception' to no divorce); 7:12b. The original Sermon of Jesus is not legislative (as Matthew seems to have regarded it) but prophetic.

Since 1945 interpretation of the Sermon and of Matthew's Gospel as a whole has been dominated by redaction criticism. This approach underlines the extent to which the evangelist himself is responsible for the shaping of Chapters 5–7. In the last few years fresh approaches to the interpretation of the Sermon have drawn on structuralism (A. Kodjak and D. Patte), literary criticism (J. D. Kingsbury and R. A. Edwards), and even political theology (S. Van Tilborg). But for the foreseeable future, discussion of Matthew's intentions in Chapters 5–7 is likely to be based on redaction criticism.

Most scholars accept that Matthew has drawn on an earlier version of the Sermon in Q, a collection of sayings of Jesus which Luke also used. Matthew has expanded the Q version of the Sermon (now found in Luke 6:20–49) by including a number of other Q traditions and also further oral traditions to which he had access. Redaction criticism has confirmed that Matthew is more than a compiler. In all five discourses the evangelist has rearranged and reinterpreted the sayings on which he drew. He often elucidates them with extra phrases or even (on occasion) with whole verses which he himself has composed. The following may be noted as examples: 5:10, 13a, 14a, 16, 20; 6:10b and c, 13b; 7:12c, 19, 20, 21. In many places Matthew's own distinctive vocabulary and emphases are evident. For example, the five important references to 'righteousness' (5:6, 10, 20; 6:1, 33) are all redactional additions made by the evangelist himself.

Several scholars, notably M. D. Goulder, have attacked the Q hypothesis which has been almost axiomatic for nearly all recent interpreters of the Sermon. But most scholars are not convinced by attempts to argue that Luke had radically reinterpreted Matthew's Sermon by preserving only a much truncated version of it (Luke 6:20–49), and by placing other parts of Matthew 5–7 in quite different contexts in his Gospel.

In recent years several proposals concerning the structure of the Sermon have been made. Some have suggested that the beatitudes are a 'table of contents' for the whole Sermon. In his excellent commentary (not yet translated from the German) U. Luz (1985) has claimed that the Sermon has been built symmetrically around its centre-piece, the Lord's Prayer, 6:7–15. The first section, 5:3–16, corresponds to the last section, 7:13–27; the second section, 5:17–20, corresponds to 7:12; 5:21–48 corresponds to 6:19–7:11 (these two passages are identical in length); and 6:1–6 corresponds to 6:16–18. Although the theory is not completely convincing (the correspondence between 5:21–48 and 6:19–7:11 is forced), there is little doubt that Matthew does intend 5:17–20 to introduce the central section of the Sermon, and 7:12 to conclude it: both passages concern fulfilment of the Law and the prophets.

The first half of the Sermon is carefully structured. It opens with the beatitudes and the salt and light sayings in 5:1–16; 5:17–20, on the Law and the prophets, follows and introduces the central section of the Sermon which ends with the same theme at 7:12. In 5:21–48 there are six antithesis, all with the same structure: 'You have heard it said of old [i.e. in scripture, by Moses] . . . but I say to you.' Chapter 6:1 introduces three paragraphs on almsgiving, prayer, and fasting (6:2–18), all of which have exactly the same structure.

But what about the second half of the Sermon? Chapter 6:19 to 7:11 has puzzled interpreters. This part of the Sermon seems to be a rag-bag of sayings, only some of which are loosely related to others. G. Bornkamm has offered a novel solution: this part of the Sermon is a 'commentary' on the Lord's Prayer. Chapter 6:19–24 expounds the first three petitions of the Lord's Prayer, 6:9–10; 6:25–34 then works out the implications of the bread petition, 6:11; 7:1–5 is an exposition of the forgiveness petition, and 7:6 takes up the theme of 6:13. Bornkamm's ingenious explanation has not convinced other scholars, but he has shown just how strongly the whole section 6:5 to 7:11 is dominated by the prayer theme.

Some of the themes Matthew emphasizes in the first of his five discourses are also prominent elsewhere in the Gospel. For example, in 5:20, one of the key verses which Matthew himself has almost certainly composed, disciples are told that their ethical conduct must exceed that of the scribes and Pharisees; in 5:48, a related verse, they are told to be perfect or whole-hearted. In 6:1–18 their conduct is contrasted starkly with that of the 'hypocrites' (6:2, 5, 16) whom the reader naturally assumes to be none other than the scribes and Pharisees of 5:20. These same points are developed in Chapter 23. The crowds and disciples are urged not to follow the example of the scribes and Pharisees (23:2–3) who are then referred to explicitly as 'hypocrites' six times. There is even some verbal correspondence between 6:1, 5 and 16 on the one hand, and 23: 5 and 28 on the other. Both in Chapters 5 and 6 of the Sermon and in Chapter 23 the evangelist used the scribes and Pharisees as a foil: disciples of Jesus are called to 'superior' ethical conduct.

For Matthew, the Sermon is but one part of his attempt to set out the significance of the story and teaching of Jesus for the life of his own community. The Sermon is the largest and most impressive of the five discourses in Matthew, but it must not be separated from the rest of the Gospel.

In the verses which immediately precede the Sermon, Matthew provides the interpreter with an important theological clue. Jesus announces the 'good news of the kingdom' (4:17, 23) and calls Peter, Andrew, James and John into radical discipleship which involves renunciation of their occupation and of their family ties (4:18–22). As in the Sermon which follows, and as in the Gospel as a whole, grace and demand are linked inextricably. The Jesus of Matthew's Sermon is the Son of God (3:17, the baptism of Jesus, and 4:1–11, the temptations) through whom God is acting for mankind; it is his demanding teaching which is to be central in the life of the community and in its disciplining of the nations.

In the past the Sermon has often been removed from its present setting in Matthew and treated as a convenient summary of the teaching of Jesus. By reading the Sermon as part of Matthew's Gospel we are able to see how the evangelist intended his first readers to approach these chapters. But this important principle of interpretation does not resolve all the difficulties. Many verses in the Sermon still puzzle us. Is there a man who had not committed adultery 'in his heart' by looking on a woman with a lustful eye (Matthew 5:28)? What are the pearls which are not to be thrown to the pigs (7:6)? Difficult parts of the Bible often provoke us to think about issues we might otherwise have avoided.

It is a mistake to suppose that we cannot understand the Sermon without the assistance of an expert. We do not need to be musicians to be profoundly moved by a piece of music; nor do we need to be art historians in order to appreciate a work of art. At the very heart of the Sermon we find one of the most radical and demanding of the sayings of Jesus, a saying which sums up the ethos of the Sermon and which is as relevant today as it was in the first century: 'You have learned [from scripture], "Love your neighbour, hate your enemy." But what I tell you is this: Love your enemies and pray for your persecutors" ' (Matthew 5:43–44).

For further reading

In recent years four commentaries on the Sermon on the Mount have been published. They all include verse-by-verse comments and also some discussion of wider issues. All four can be used with profit both by the general reader and by those who with some knowledge of modern New Testament studies. R. A. Guelich's commentary is the most substantial; the other three are medium-sized paperbacks.

R. A. Guelich, *The Sermon on the Mount: a Foundation for Understanding*, Word, 1982.

H. Hendrickx, *The Sermon on the Mount*, Geoffrey Chapman, 1984.

J. Lambrecht, *The Sermon on the Mount*, Michael Glazier, 1985.

G. Strecker, *The Sermon on the Mount: an Exegetical Commentary*, T. and T. Clark, 1988.

4 THEOLOGY AND SPIRITUALITY

Making Sense of Prayer

David Conner   *Valuable*

I want in this paper to describe something of what prayer means to me and of the way in which I have tried to make sense of it.

It has become something of a cliché to describe life as a kind of journey. Clichés, however, become clichés only because they have been overused, and they have been over used only because they have been found to have been so useful. So, cliché or not, life is a kind of journey. We begin our journey without thinking about it. Indeed we cannot even think about it. We are pushed out of the womb and on to the road without the equipment for conscious thought as we later come to understand it. We simply travel. Most of us are lucky enough to be fed, watered, sheltered and loved but, sometimes gradually and sometimes all at once, something strange and unwelcome begins to dawn upon us. Everything is not quite as it was. The age of unreflective innocence has passed. We are now aware of what it means to be a human being. That awareness brings with it a twinge of fear or unhappiness. The process is what we call 'growing up' and, in a funny kind of way, we are doing it all the time. We cannot remember, as we look back, quite when it started, but we know with increasing certainty as we get older that we carry around inside us a sense of being lost on our journey through life. It is hard to describe. John Betjeman, in his poem *Norfolk*, looks back on his innocent childhood and asks: 'When did the devil come?' How did it arrive, this time of 'Unkept promises and broken hearts'? Dylan Thomas, in his lovely poem *Fern Hill*, reflects upon that time of innocence, now long lost, when:

> . . . as I was young and easy in the mercy of his means,
> Time held me green and dying
> Though I sang in my chains like the sea.

Though it is hard to describe, the poets have a go at describing it for us, this sense of being lost on our journey. For some of us it hangs around as a sort of pervading anxiety, about the future, about the family, about death. For others it colours our lives by flooding them with a sense of being alone, lonely, isolated, hollow inside. Others of us experience it as a kind of impotence in the face of possible virtue, that inability to perform what, for some reason or other, we believe to be right. It is expressed through the story of Adam and Eve and their exile from Paradise. It is something of what those of us who are religious (or *Christian*-religious) mean when we talk of the Fall and of a sense of sin.

Usually, however, we are led on, coping or half-coping with everyday life, carrying our lostness with us. None the less, though we might know that we are lost, quite commonly, every now and then something happens. All at once some of us experience what I have only ever been able to describe as a kind of surge of energy arising within us and, for a fleeting moment, we no longer feel out of tune with our surroundings and with ourselves, but rather at one with them, for a moment *whole*. What is more, however short-lived the experience, that surge of energy reverses all that has so far diminished us and we sense, just for a second or two, that we are bigger people, more loving people, more generous and courageous. The experience soon dies but, just for that moment, we think that we might have glimpsed something of life's possibilities, had a taste of journey's end, felt and imagined something of what it might mean to have arrived. You might say that, buried within us, there is a kind of homing instinct which, once in a while, is awakened.

Such moments are not usually associated with dramatic or special situations. When they happen, they occur in the course of our ordinary lives. We simply remember some of them more than others because of clusters of associations which gather round them. At any time it can seem that energy is surging through, ready to be released maybe by a piece of music, perhaps by a piece of poetry or a story, possibly by a lovely sight, sometimes by a smile, a kindly gesture, absolutely anything. I am describing something of what Ian Ramsey used to mean when he spoke of those 'disclosure situations', moments when life comes alive and things begin to take on depth. Humanistic psychologists have talked of 'peak' experiences. You might have your own label for them.

Of course, within a fleeting moment, the experience has gone. It is as if, as soon as thought is brought to bear upon it, it evaporates. Yet it has made a difference to us; it has made us just a little thirstier. We cannot help but reflect upon it, try to make some sense of it. As we do so, it seems to some of us that that surge of energy of which I spoke did not just arise within us, a product of our own minds and bodies. It *was* ours, certainly it was; it was part of us. The more we ponder it, however, the more it sometimes seems as if that energy had its source somewhere beyond us, much further back somehow than our own minds and bodies. More than that, it can feel as if that energy, independent of us in its origin, was moving us, trying to shape us and to mould us. We were the objects of its work even though, in a real sense, it was us! It can feel as if that energy was a kind of breath passing through us, ruffling our leaves as it went.

When that is the case, we want to give some account of that 'beyondness'. Some of us talk in terms of a collective unconscious pool of energy that can erupt within us, given the right conditions. That seems to make some sense. After all, when we try to grapple with such rich experience, we have to use 'as if' language, the words of metaphor; we have to paint some kind of picture. But it is at this point that some of us begin to find religious language more useful and expressive, and we begin to talk about the Spirit of God. We say that ordinary, everyday experiences might be experiences of God himself doing his best to irrupt into our lives and drive us homeward on our journey.

The picture that develops is of God as Spirit, ever-present within the fabric of creation, pressing upon the world, seeking to shape it and to form it and to direct it towards its destination, and finding opportunities to break through in, as it were, felt spurts of energy. Many human beings experience these irruptions from time to time but, beyond that, find it hard to say very much. They can seem rather random and, though they can be experienced as powerful and real and though they can seem to change lives, it is impossible to find any *entirely* satisfying formula that accounts for their occurrence or God's operation within them.

For most of the time, of course, life is not coloured by such good experiences, such consolations. Mostly it is a matter of being left with that thirst I spoke of, a longing for something richer and better. Those of us who have begun to use religious language might by now be calling it God's Kingdom or heaven or some such thing. Yet sometimes it can dawn upon us that the very thirst we feel, the very yearning, is the quieter operation of this same Spirit within us (our own spirit yet also not quite ours – seeming to come also from beyond us) feeling after God. It is a kind of deep calling to deep or, you might say, God himself praying inside us. His Spirit and our own spirits are inextricably bound together in a creative process.

None the less, even though we might feel that this is going on, we can also feel that there is something hard inside us resisting the operation of the Spirit. It is as if our personalities are somehow twisted and obstruct the easy flowing of the Spirit. Maybe the resistance is a kind of fear, a reluctance to let go and to allow ourselves to be driven by the Spirit. Whatever it is, the Spirit does not get through. It is as if God's prayer, his attempt to urge the world onwards towards a goal he has in mind for it (a goal we glimpse however partially in those odd experiences of unity) for the most part hits solid rock and dissipates. What ultimately causes the rock to be so hard, either in the whole created order or just in us human beings, we cannot be sure. The answer to the problem is to do with why the world, and we, should be 'fallen' in the first place; it depends on what account you choose to give of the origin of sin. Yet it is experienced as reality; it is more than some fanciful idea, some theory that we like to play around with.

Whatever the answer to that knotty little problem, we might by now have arrived at a kind of understanding of prayer. It is not so much something that we do; it is rather the total operation of God's Spirit working within the universe and us, struggling to make it all into something that we just occasionally taste in part, something that we dream of and imagine and yet we know lies far beyond our wildest dreams and our most fanciful imaginings.

Where does that leave us? The truth is that it leaves us all in different places. For me, and for a number of people I come across, it leaves us wanting (in spite of that resistance that I spoke of) to find some way of co-operating with the Spirit, of opening out to the Spirit, of allowing ourselves to become more fluent channels of the Spirit's operation. Of course we have a hunch that even this desire is, in the end, the Spirit's doing. Be that as it may, we know we want to *do* something.

That is just where prayer, as it is conventionally understood, comes in. For the practice of prayer is exactly that; it is practising. It is engaging in exercises in order to discover a way of being more naturally and lastingly open to the activity of the Spirit. In a way it is like practising the piano. We do it in order to be able to play the concerto more accurately and movingly on the night. So it is with prayer. We do it in order to live the rest of the time more openly, more available to the Spirit. As with practising the piano, sometimes the activity takes off and we find ourselves 'performing', so in prayer we find it sometimes actually takes off and merges into the real thing. That can be marvellous! But the less it does so, the more we know we need to go on practising. There has to be a discipline about it, but the discipline cannot be cold; it must arise out of a genuine desire that the performance should be good. A basic thirst to be at one with God and open to his Spirit is essential.

What then might this practising involve? Again, it depends on who you are and where you are. But I have a few observations to make.

If *you* want to be open to the working of the Spirit, if *you* want to become a channel of the Spirit's operation, then you must find some way of getting down to *you*. Honesty is fundamental and yet, I have to say it, very often it is the first casualty of religious practice. It is so easy to go into the practice of prayer already covered up and smothered by some holy religious image that we already have of ourselves. But God cannot work through me, with me allowing him to work through me, until *I* open up to Him. The first stage of the life of prayer must always be the quest for truth about ourselves. That is not an easy business. It can be painful too. Yet, if it is *me* I want God to be working through, to heal, restore, redeem and make, then it is *me* that I must offer to Him. It is me with all my anger and frustration, me with all my frightenedness and weakness, me in all my incompleteness. Self-knowledge and self-confession is the beginning of the practice of prayer. I suppose, if we have come to think of God as Truth for some reason or other, then it is clear that he cannot work through a lie. Perhaps that is why repentance seems to be the start of so much of our religion. Maybe that is also why the psalms, with all their earthiness and openness and honesty, have been found throughout the ages to have been such useful aids to prayer. Out of all our confusion at least we can invite this only half-known God to come into our *real* lives.

However, there are always subtle allurements to stop our being honest. One is particularly active so far as Christians are concerned. I suppose you might say that Christians are people who have dis-covered Jesus to be the one whom they believe to have been most open to the operation of God's Spirit. His story has moved them and awakened in them some recognition of what it might be to be at one with God himself, fully a channel of his working. So much is this the case that Christians are happy to say that he *is* God; here the human spirit and the divine Spirit have become totally at one, entirely coalesced. Therefore it is not in the least surprising that Christians should use the Gospel story as a source of inspiration and of guidance in their lives of prayer. But (and here is the problem) too often Christians anticipate the goal of all their praying and think that they must be *like* Jesus. They have a sort of fantasy of themselves as Jesus clones. So, in the end, their prayer is little more than the chance to gather up the strength to imitate Jesus. This too often means that they try to short-cut the process. They do not start from where they are because they are too eager to be somewhere else, and someone else. In other words, the confession-repentance-honesty attitude goes by the board. Furthermore, they presuppose that God *wants* them to be like Jesus. It might be that God wants them to be *themselves* as Jesus was *himself*. It might be that Jesus' openness to the Spirit would have, in all respects, the same result. Perhaps God wants more variety within his universe. We cannot anticipate the end product.

A similar allurement which often discourages honesty stems from the view that the end-product of prayer would be a life of peace and tranquillity. There are many books on prayer which seem to suggest that the whole purpose of prayer is the reduction of stress and that the whole enterprise is to do with calming down. Of course, those glimpses of the future we might have had from time to time in the context of 'peak' religious experiences often speak of a kind of harmony, and no doubt all our theological picture-painting of the end-product includes a sense of equilibrium and harmony. But to pretend that harmony can be achieved by *me* in the next few minutes is ridiculous. To attempt to discover some sort of personal tranquillity in a world which is torn apart and bleeding seems to me to be quite selfish and nothing whatever to do with the love which, we might have found reason to believe, is the best way to describe the character of God's Spirit. The gentle voice and slightly spaced-out manner that prayers are tempted to assume is usually no more than affectation. It is, quite simply, dishonest and must therefore act as a blockage to, rather than a release of, God's Spirit in our lives. Who can tell what the result of that release would be?

It sounds, I know, as if I am on something of a hobby-horse, but I will take just one more look at this allurement to dishonesty. It is the idea that if we pray enough, we shall, as they say, 'grow'. What seems to have happened is that people who are interested in spiritual matters have simply adopted the humanistic psychological model of growth towards freedom and the enriching of inter-personal relationships and so on, and have given it a spiritual twist. Once again, apart from the fact that there is little evidence that people really do achieve that goal, it presupposes that we have in the back of our minds some ideal image of ourselves, some personal model which we are working towards. I have said enough to suggest that that is a mistake. We cannot tell in advance just where each individual will be driven.

So far I have simply suggested that prayer is the activity of God's Spirit in the world; that the practice of prayer is the practice of opening up to the operation of the Spirit; that a fundamental rule must be the rule of honesty because it is *me* I am wanting God to work through; and that there are a number of common allurements which might look very spiritual but which prevent us from being honest all too often and therefore prevent us from entering into prayer.

When we set aside some time to practise getting more in tune with God, we are automatically expressing a little bit of faith. It might not be quite of the force to move mountains but we would not be there at all if something inside us was not suggesting that this might be a proper thing to do. The motivation of course might be more powerful than this. At any rate, some faith is present.

In the context of faith, we simply try to be ourselves and to acknowledge ourselves. It seems to me that, immediately we try to be ourselves, we come up against our *needs*. We discover that, for the most part, underneath the coping layer, we are in a helpless (if not hopeless) mess. Out of that realization that we are needy creatures arises quite naturally the childish desire to *ask*; to ask for help; to ask for forgiveness; to ask for healing. We find ourselves, rather to our shame very often, crying out in the dark. We find ourselves talking to God.

This can be alarming to us. We have been brought up to think in terms of development and success in all our work. This has often affected the way in which we think of prayer. Too many people have laughed at those old ideas about prayer and have told us that of course prayer is not 'saying prayers'; it is not talking to God. It is something far more sophisticated than that. So, when we find ourselves simply asking for help, we feel we must be pretty underdeveloped creatures. We are tempted to go off after a whole range of more polished 'techniques'; and they abound.

It is, however, possible that this simple asking, this simple crying out that we might find ourselves engaged in when we are ourselves before God, *is* the essence of prayer. Possibly, at that moment the little part of the creation that is *us* is brought into a right relationship with the creator upon whom we are entirely dependent. Perhaps that is why Jesus is reported as having said: 'How blest are those who know their need of God; the kingdom of heaven is theirs' (Matthew 5:3).

What seems to happen when people open up as needy creatures before God is that they are, in some way or other, changed. It need not be dramatic but it is usually to do with being given a sense that they are accepted, acceptable and somehow cherished, just at the point that all pretence evaporates. We can see where that might lead. It might lead to the expression of thanks and adoration in prayer. It might also lead to a changed attitude to other people and to the world around us: compassion (in the real sense of that word) might become a realler possibility. At the point of need God might squeeze into this fallen world and begin to move it and to change it.

That must be left open-ended just for now. But here I do want to make just two more points. The first is this. Though we are, so I believe, all needy creatures, and to that extent have much in common, we are, at the same time, all different from one another. We have different personalities, different histories, and so on. In other words, the material that God has to work on takes different forms. Consequently, we would not expect us all to follow the same course. There is something entirely unpredictable about it. We do not know where we shall be led. That can be rather frightening because we like to have our lives tied up and sorted out well in advance. So there is always a temptation to extrapolate from experience nice neat theories and then to allow the theories to take over. That is a kind of idolatry. It can only be avoided by a constant return to that honesty of which I have spoken and to an acknowledgement of need which brings one chunk of the created order into a right relation to the creator; after that it is a matter of holding our breath!

The second point is this. There is no evidence that people who pray set out on a smooth journey by which they become better and better, more loving and caring and virtuous as the days go by. The process is more complicated than that. We are part of an intricate system of relationships within which we shall get hurt, have awakened old hostilities, regress from time to time. Each individual will only be 'saved' in the end when everything is saved. That is why prayer is always, you might say, 'social' and never individual. It would be horrible if it bred a small and élite group of the virtuous. Thank God it does not. For reasons which we cannot grasp fully, saints and sinners are inextricably bound together, part of each other. As God prays through us and moves us, so we become increasingly involved in a creative tumble which can take its toll. Of that it is hard to make much sense because we are too mixed up in it. Yet it can feel right and we can know within ourselves a kind of integrity, a sense of being ourselves and of being alive. This can provide us with the desire and the necessary courage to go on praying. The cross of Jesus is, however, for Christians a warning that, if we remain open to God's Spirit, we might be driven to the point where we cannot make sense of it at all.

This realization that we are all part of each other encourages me none the less to go further in my attempt to make some sense of prayer. My emphasis on honesty as the starting point for this activity has possibly given the impression that I believe prayer to be ultimately an individual enterprise. This impression would be mistaken; it is more mysterious than that. Whenever we come before God in prayer, it is as if we bring with us, in our hearts and minds and bodies, our families and friends, our neighbours and colleagues, everybody and everything to which we are, maybe at the deepest of levels, connected. We cannot help it. There is a strange and surprising unity in everything. When we pray we are the creation's representatives and, in our prayers, we give utterance to the deepest yearnings of creation itself, its longing for redemption. The fundamental neediness that we discover when we face our real selves is the fundamental neediness that is shared by everybody and everything that exists. The basic dependence upon God which we confess when we confront our neediness is the same dependence that is common to the whole of creation. That calling-out to God to answer our needs is a calling-out to God that lies (albeit muffled) at the heart of all. To put it another way, in our prayer we give voice to God's prayer, prayed within everything that he is making, as he seeks to draw and to direct the world towards the destination that he has in mind for it. Real prayer is never the activity of an individual. An individual can be the occasion of the uttering of the prayer – the prayer that is the prayer of all that is.

It is for this reason that all prayer can be understood as a kind of intercession. Since all those who pray are representatives of the creation, in every prayer the whole creation, in however small a manner, is opened up to God and drawn a little more into the orbit of his love. Sometimes this will be done quite consciously, when someone prays with a particular person or need in mind. Perhaps, the more we confront and acknowledge our own needs, and the more our compassion is thereby developed, the more conscious and frequent this activity will become. However, conscious or not, it is happening in every prayer that is felt or uttered. No person can ever pray as a self-enclosed, encapsulated individual. In an age when individualism is often highly prized, that is easy to forget. Yet a significant strand in the Christian tradition, with its emphasis on body, community and some kind of mystical co-inherence, challenges us always to break free of the individual mould and to understand ourselves always as belonging to a greater whole. Heaven, our destination, is usually thought of as harmonious. It is the Fall that speaks of separation and fragmentation. In our prayer and worship it is heaven that we stretch towards and perhaps begin to realize.

Our prayer is not, then, a private occupation so much as our public responsibility. As we come to see ourselves as occasions of a giving voice to the Spirit's longing within all that exists, vehicles of intercession through which everything is drawn more within the orbit of God's love, we begin to feel not only a desire to pray but a proper sense of obligation too. Prayer, you might say, becomes our work. An appreciation of this undergirds an emphasis, in some Christian circles, on the recitation of the Daily Offices. This is not an aspect of private devotion. It is the Church's prayer. It is intended to be said publicly for that reason, and the congregation is invited to participate. Yet it is said publicly for another reason too. The bell is tolled not only to summon the faithful to their prayers but to remind those beyond the Church's walls that prayer is being offered on their behalf. The Church is the representative community.

Orare est laborare

Perhaps we have now arrived at the point where we can see that prayer is most appropriately expressed within the context of public worship. In such worship it is signalled as a corporate activity, the body giving voice to the Spirit's yearnings. For many of us it is the Holy Communion that is *the* focal point of all our praying. In the offering of bread and wine *everything* is offered, lifted up to God for him to bless, change and make. The praying community brings with it the concerns, needs and aching aspirations of the creation of which it is a part. The Church is not a heavily-guarded bastion separated from the world. It *is* the world – the world as it stretches out towards its maker for healing and redemption. The bread and wine are symbols of that world and, offered, they become symbols of that world's deepest needs and longings. When they have been blessed they are returned to us. We kneel or stand around the altar and, receiving broken bread and poured-out wine, commit ourselves to participating in all they represent, to sharing the world's burdens. In that act of receiving we are reminded of our corporate task and of our necessary rootedness in all that is. The blessed bread and wine will always be returned until all has been redeemed. It will be redeemed when all of it has been taken up and offered. So the cycle of our praying is encouraged to continue.

Of course, my having homed in on the Holy Communion has led me to consider Christ who is re-membered at its heart. In the life and death and resurrection and ascension of Jesus Christ we see the whole history of the universe focused and in miniature. Everything is being created to enjoy a final unity with God, that journey's end of which we have sometimes had a tiny taste. In Jesus the creation has at last attained its destiny. He is its final representative. In being most open to the operation of the Spirit, and in being most eloquent in giving voice to the Spirit's prayer, he has made the final break-through. In him the created order has finally opened on to heaven. As we pray, yearn and stretch towards God, offer ourselves (in all our neediness) and offer all that is to him for healing and redemp-tion, so we catch hold of Jesus' coat-tails and become integrated into his movement. That is why, in the Holy Communion, our offering and the offering of Jesus somehow coalesce. That is also why, so Christians have come to believe, all prayer, all offering, is prayer to God the Father, through Jesus Christ, and in the self-same Spirit who inspired him.

If Christ, however, is truly our representative, his work cannot be complete. To consider it so would be to return to, and entrap him within, the individualistic model that, in this paper, I have tried to guard against. There is much within the Christian tradition to suggest that his work continues. The most obvious is that part of the tradition which sees the Church as his body continuing, here on earth, his redemptive work. Perhaps more mysterious is the idea, rooted in the fact that the Risen Lord still bore the marks of his crucifixion, that his suffering continues until the end of the world.

Maybe the most sublime is the idea that he is the high priest who 'always lives to make intercession' for us (Hebrews 7.25), that prayer continues to be offered by him until all is redeemed. As our high priest he is our representative.

All Mine and Seen So Easily: the Inclusive Vision of Thomas Traherne *Loveby*

Ronald Blythe

There is a tradition of certain literature having to bide its time, of having to lie low until the day of its understanding. But no first-class work need ever do this and if we discover it long after it was written, that is either because changes in the language made it inaccessible (the Anglo-Saxon and Medieval poets) or simply because it got lost. Considering their fragility, it is puzzling to realize that books and manuscripts are among the most numerous of ancient human artefacts. The late blazing-out of Thomas Traherne's light from one of those tempting barrow-loads of junk in Farringdon Road in 1895 is high among the incidents of great finds. It was then that William Brooke tugged forth two handsomely bound old manuscripts, one folio, one octavo, and was blinded by what he took to be a previously unknown collection of the writings of Henry Vaughan, at that moment the most light-drenched poet known to the Victorians. There was no signature, only a luminosity which had to belong to the author of 'They are all gone into the world of light', and a vision of childhood as bright as that of the man who had influenced Wordsworth's *Intimations of Immortality*. Others confirmed Brooke's supposition and a sensational new volume of Vaughan was well on the way to publication when Brooke discussed his find with his friend Bertram Dobell, soon to be the founder of the celebrated Charing Cross Road bookshop, who remembered something. Brooke had once shown him some poems he had copied from an anonymous book of devotions in the British Museum – and now they were reading these poems, set down in a beautiful hand, again. They rushed to the Museum and found that *A Serious and Pathetical Contemplation of the Mercies of God* was the work of the 'Private Chaplain to Sir Orlando Bridgeman', Keeper of the Great Seal to Charles II.

Sir Orlando's chaplain was a young man from Herefordshire, a country clergyman who died aged thirty-six, a master of the Affirmative Way, Thomas Traherne. When his *Poems* appeared in 1903 and the glorious *Centuries of Meditations* in 1908, they overthrew, or at least made unsafe, a whole range of private and public religious attitudes. Nor could the agnostics escape, for even if one was indifferent or sceptical of his philosophy, none, having once encountered them, could get away from his voice and his art. Traherne seduces for God – one critic-victim went so far as to call him 'a devout hedonist' – and his language is at its almost unbearably magnificent in the often, but never too often, quoted passage towards the beginning of *The Third Century*. The writer is recalling himself as a little boy in mid-seventeenth-century Hereford:

> The Corn was Orient and Immortal Wheat, which never should be reaped, nor was ever sown. I thought it had stood from Everlasting to Everlasting. The Dust and Stones of the Street were as Precious as GOLD. The Gates were at first the End of the World, The Green Trees when I saw them first through one of the Gates Transported and Ravished me; their Sweetnes and unusual Beauty made my Heart to leap, and almost mad with Extasie, they were such strange and Wonderfull Things: The Men! O what Venerable and Reverend Creatures did the Aged seem! Immortal Cherubims! And yong Men Glittering and Sparkling Angels and Maids strange Seraphick pieces of Life and Beauty! Boys and Girles Tumbling in the Street, and Playing, were moving Jewels. I knew not that they were Born or should Die. But all things abided Eternaly as they were in their Proper Places. Eternity was Manifest in the Light of the Day, and som thing infinit Behind evry thing appeared: which talked with my Expectation and moved my Desire. The Citie seemed to stand in Eden, or to be Built in Heaven. The Streets were mine, the Temple was mine, the People were mine, their Clothes and Gold and Silver was mine, as much as their Sparkling Eys fair Skins and ruddy faces. The Skies were mine, and so were the Sun and Moon and Stars, and all the World was mine, and I the only Spectator and Enjoyer of it. I knew no Churlish Proprieties, nor Bounds nor Divisions: but all Proprieties and Divisions were mine: all Treasures and the Possessors of them. So that with much adoe I was corrupted; and made to learn the Dirty Devices of this World. Which now I unlearn, and becom as it were a little Child again, that I may enter into the Kingdom of GOD.

Whatever the 'dirty devices' the growing Traherne may have picked up they must have very soon been dropped, and less out of guilt than out of the need to have both hands free to clasp something infinitely more exciting – natural and spiritual Happiness, or Felicity, as he sometimes called it, and always in capitals. He repudiates both the facile Christian optimism and the exquisite religious melancholy of his age. Sir Thomas Browne, who outlived him by a few years, had become the doyen of the latter by means of a similarly irresistible prose-carrying-off-the-honours-of-poetry style. 'Certainly there is no happiness within this circle of flesh,' wrote Browne, 'nor is it in the optics of these eyes to behold felicity. The first day of our jubilee is death.' Among a thousand other things, Browne was an archaeologist, a sifter of the dust. Traherne's investigations could have been in obedience to that apocryphal saying of Jesus, 'Look with wonder at what is before you; penetrate the present depth.' It actually takes nerve to write, as Lewis Thompson[1] did during a lifetime dominated (and yet undominated) by two world wars that: 'I don't believe in misery; my nature is the fact that Joy is the norm.'

Traherne's Herefordshire 'Orient and Immortal Wheat' was trampled into mud and blood during the Civil War, and, later, not even the decencies of his employer Sir Orlando Bridgeman would have sheltered him from the disgusting life led by Charles II and his court. Time has dealt picturesquely with the famous whores, but what of the man who allowed the Primate of All Ireland to be hanged, drawn and quartered at Tyburn for a faith which was openly practised in the royal chapel? Is Traherne no more than his age's most ecstatic escapist, its most dazzling Other Lifer? Or does his philosophy teach that, on the whole, we are more entertained than horrified by faithlessness, cynicism and cruelty? Nor was living with the good Keeper of the Great Seal in fine houses in London and Teddington the cloistral bliss it might have seemed, for the rowdiness of Lady Bridgeman and her sons was a legend. Yet, from childhood on, Traherne lived 'above it', as it were. Was this because he had no choice – because he was, like many artists, unable to descend to it? His trouble, if one dare call it that, was that he was spellbound at being alive – doubly alive in Nature and in Christ, and his insistence was that others should be spellbound too. Why be tied in any other way? he asks. 'For the man whose hands are free everything is a gift,' said Lewis Thompson. Early on, probably when he was made Rector of Credenhill, a tiny parish in his own Herefordshire, Traherne made up his mind never to be shackled.

> When I came into the Country, and being seated among silent Trees, had all my Time in my own Hands, I resolved to Spend it all, whatever it cost me, in Search of Happiness, and to Satiat that burning Thirst which Nature had Enkindled, in me from my Youth. In which I was so resolut, that I chose rather to liv upon 10 pounds a yeer, and to go in Lether Clothes, and feed upon Bread and Water, so that I might hav all my time clearly to myself: then to keep many thousands per Annums in an Estate of Life where my Time would be Devoured in Care and Labor. And GOD was so pleased to accept of that Desire, that from that time to this I hav had all things plentifully provided for me, without any Care at all.

Thomas Traherne was born in 1637, an apparently poor boy who was given a chance by a rich relation. The family roots were in Lugwardine, a place-name derived from the Welsh for light and brightness. Both he and his brother Philip were educated at Oxford and it was during their long stay at the university that they must have met the woman who was so profoundly to influence their lives. For Philip married her niece and Thomas sent her, piecemeal, the poems and meditations which, due to her careful binding, were to stay safely between covers for over two hundred years until, giving them the title *Centuries*, Bertram Dobell was to launch them on an astounded literary scene. The recipient of Traherne's intensely beautiful fragments was Susanna Hopton, a contentedly married lady ten years his senior who, after various trials and errors, had found a Rule by which to live not unlike that practised by the Herberts at Bemerton and the Ferrars at Little Gidding. It was into this austere and intellectual Anglicanism that Thomas Traherne poured his gratitude and bliss, his sacred sensuality and a Platonic Christianity, some of which seemed to rise like the Thames from sparkling springs in an English shire. Reading his *Centuries*, one suspects that they were not so much written for Mrs Hopton as the necessary capturing on the page of at least some of that joy which the companionship of the Christ and the sights in the meadows and fields incessantly filled him, and of which he had to tell someone. One cannot imagine any bishop approving the Rector of St Mary, Credenhill's spiritual advice to Susanna Hopton. 'Pious, ingenious Tom', is what the Master of Balliol called him when he heard of his death.

Traherne remained at Credenhill for six years in what has gener-ally been accepted as a state of solitude sandwiched between four sociable years at Oxford and the remainder of his brief life in the wild London of the Restoration and at nearby Teddington. But since a village is the last place where anyone is left alone, particularly so scrupulous a clergyman as Traherne, one realizes that his second achievement of never allowing society to disrupt his seclusion is no less exciting as a condition of his Rule than its primary requirement that happiness was to be pursued 'both in a natural and transcen-dent way'. John Bunyan taught that pilgrimage should not take us further than the familiar path to work, to the shops, etc. Traherne teaches how to live with others. 'Why should we not retire to adore Him?' He recommended 'A meditating inward eye' ('They flash upon that inward eye/Which is the bliss of solitude', Wordsworth, who could never have heard of him, was to put it.) 'And what Rule do you think I walked by?' Traherne writes to his friend Susanna. 'Truly a Strange one, but the Best in the Whole World. I was Guided by an Implicit Faith in Gods Goodness: and therefore led to the Study of the most Obvious and Common Things . . . Air, Light, Heaven and Earth, Water, the Sun, Trees, Men and Women, Cities, Temples &c.' Like Julian of Norwich's hazel-nut, which existed because God loved it, and William Blake's grain of sand, there was nothing which did not have its place in eternity 'and in God's Esteem'. Certainly the human body, naked, is its Creator's icon, marvellously provident and most beautiful. And, it should be added, not usually the subject of religious contemplations in the 1660s. 'O how Divine / Am I! . . . I am his Image and his Friend.' But, 'You never know yourself until you know more than your Body.' His meditation upon the ruined flesh of the executed Christ would seem to contain terrible information from Tyburn, London's theatre-like gallows. It is heart-breaking:

> Is this He that was transfigured upon Mount Tabor! Pale, Withered! Extended! Tortured! Soyld with Blood and Sweat and Dust! Dried! Parched! O Sad! O Dismal Spectacle! . . . What is here but a Heap of Desolations! A Deformed Carcais! A Disfigured Countenance! A Mass of Miseries; and silent Footsteps of Innumerable Sufferings! . . . Can this be an Entertainment!

The solitude of his Lord amid Palestinian crowds, and particularly when surrounded by his family and friends, and overwhelmingly at death, entranced as well as awed Traherne. Yet in imitating this aspect of the Christ one had to guard against such dangers as 'negative contentment' and 'seeking all one's bliss in one's self alone'. Like the young Buddha, 'We must not live as if there were no sickness and death in the World' and must always remember that 'A quiet mind is worse than poverty Unless it from enjoyment spring'. Warnings against introversion are frequent; one had to love Another. Even 'brutish love' was a 'sympathy of bodies'.

The inordinate amount of love which men directed towards money and possessions puzzled Traherne. He doesn't so much moralize over materialism as record his own bafflement that his contemporaries, with the loveliness of this world and the next in some kind of natural conjunction before their eyes, do not see the pointlessness of what they pursued. Mrs Hopton and he, of course, and it has to be said, were outside the mid-seventeenth century's version of the rat-race. Traherne, George Herbert, Andrew Marvell in his masterpiece *Upon Appleton House*, and Abraham Cowley (who could have been Traherne's hero), as well as many intellectual ladies who turned their houses into retreats for the Spirit, unapologetically practised the art of keeping one's head down. 'He has lived well who has laid well hidden,' said Cowley. Christ had certainly shown himself (epiphany) but there were the hidden years, and the frequent secret solitarinesses of the public years. His Affirmative Way took in all the flowers, creatures, weather and earthly scenes through which he had passed, and so should ours. We had to possess landscape, and not those 'superficial toys Which in the Garden once were hid. Those little new Invented Things . . . Which all our Happiness destroys.' Traherne also discovers that knowing how to use solitude clarifies the brain, which is a very necessary thing for a scholar, for 'To think well is to serve God in the Interior Court'. Traherne's interior court was the English countryside, still one of the most magical places on earth to be alone in. 'Wants here may be seen and enjoyed . . . You must want like a God, so that you may be satisfied like God . . . His wants put a Lustre on his Enjoyments . . . Be sensible of your Wants.' His gratitude for being born to walk under trees and through pastures, and by streams, like the Christ, is infinite: 'It is an irresistible Joy that I was raised out of Nothing, to see and Enjoy this Glorious World.' What a mercy it is that we 'are permitted to Breath and be Diverted'.

But the central law or recommendation of his Rule, happiness, he finds unteachable. Susanna Hopton and all his subsequent pupils are given the Authorized Version of the King James' Bible, especially David's poems, and an idling ramble from Herefordshire to Middlesex as clues to where they might not so much discover it, for this must surely be in God, as *naturally* enjoy it. As God is 'the Life and Soul of the Universe', so in this 'ample Territory of Field of Joys' must he be 'an Immediate help'. One must learn how to possess the earth – 'He who thinks the Heavens and the Earth are not his, can hardly use them.' Traherne offers a corrective to what we should be greedy and acquisitive about, which are those natural, and thus spiritual riches which provide humanity with its environment. The more one gets of nature, the more one gets of God, and of his Son, the natural lover and friend, and the redeemer of the *world*, let it not be forgotten.

Traherne's shire-fed solitude frequently took him to the edge of the map, the spot where geography ends and a further scenery begins to suggest its reality, a vista usually fatal to language – what Traherne in his brilliant poem *Shadows in the Water* describes as 'A *Seeming* somewhat more than *View*', and St Paul says that we all get glimpses of, although 'through a glass, darkly'. Both writers had begun to peer into what they came to see as the ultimate reality when they were children, the apostle via a murky Roman mirror, Traherne via a puddle, and grew up to accept 'A Film . . . that stood between'. What was being reflected? Surely not a temporal Eden, blissful though it was. So it had to be St Paul says 'wait and see'. Traherne says, 'speculate, dream, imagine' – it is a saint's and poet's right. If nature is the reflection of paradise, and happiness here but the shadow of happiness there, then what a prospect! 'All mine! and seen so easily!' Rivers continually provide his dark glass. Is that in *Shadows in the Water* the Thames at Oxford, London or Teddington?

O ye that stand upon the Brink,
Whom I so near me, throu the Chink,
With Wonder see: What Faces there,
Whose Feet, whose Bodies, do ye wear?
I my Companions see
In You, another Me.
They seemed Others, but are We;
Our second Selvs those Shadows be.

Of all the Play-mates which I knew
That here I do the Imagine view
In other Selvs; what can it mean?
But that below the purling Stream
Some unknown Joys there be
Laid up in Store for me;
To which I shall, when that thin Skin
Is broken, be admitted in.

The thin skin was broken about the beginning of October 1674, exactly when nobody knows. Traherne's master Sir Orlando had died in the June of that year, and both of them were buried in Teddington parish church, the poet under the lectern. Two densely-argued published works, *Roman Forgeries* and *Christian Ethicks*, had earned him the epithet 'learned', and his personality a reputation which nobody could quite put into words. Like George Herbert, he was regarded as certainly more than 'Reverend'. Many of his writings passed to his brother Philip, the Rector of Hinton Martell, Dorset, who extensively 'corrected' them. Susanna Hopton lived on into the eighteenth century, dying at Hereford when she was eighty-two, and treasuring the manuscripts which her young mentor had sent her, and whose incandescence so astonished the literary world just before the First World War. Stylistically, Traherne is, like the very greatest religious writers, a master of the art of repetition; philosophically, the most loving of inclusionists. And in as absolute a way as any Christian could be, a source of human gratitude.

Part II
THEOLOGY THINKING OUTWARDS

5 THEOLOGY AND THEOLOGIES

Still Chosen?

Anthony Bayfield

Some years ago I led services on Yom Kippur – the Day of Atonement – for a Jewish community in Surrey. Rosh Hashannah (the Jewish New Year) and Yom Kippur are two days on which the majority of Jews will identify with the community by attending synagogue. Since, for the rest of the year, British Jews are much like British Christians and like having a place of worship not to go to, most Jewish communities have opted for buildings which serve their normal week-by-week needs but which are therefore often not big enough for the bumper gate on Yom Kippur. North-west Surrey was no exception and in the year in question had borrowed the local Methodist church. This was extremely convenient, since it had no conspicuous Christian symbolism – no stained glass, a small, fortunately portable altar and only a discreet notice on the pulpit, visible solely to the officiant, which declared: 'Sir, remember we would rather see Jesus.' I had my doubts in that regard about the three hundred or so assembled Jews but otherwise all was fine – or almost so.

That year, autumn had come early (in June, as I recall) and by October it was cold outside. Our Yom Kippur service began at 10.30 a.m. and lasted until nearly 8.00 p.m. A long, long day of sitting and contemplating and fasting – no food or drink since early the previous evening. People feel the cold on Yom Kippur. To be truthful, Molesey Methodist church was as cold as only a church can be. We did not need Rabbi Lionel to be blue.

In the middle of the afternoon a lay reader, a man called David Sigaloff, came forward to the reading-desk to relieve me for a spell. He surveyed the huddled masses yearning to be warm and said: 'Now I know what it means to be God's frozen people.' It was actually more than a good quip. It was a remark suffused with the dimension of corporate feeling and purpose, the hint of ruefulness, the tinge of self-deprecation and the subliminal reference to persecution that characterizes Jewish humour. And to justify that claim we need to look at the complex of feelings which Jews experience when the concept of 'chosen people' is raised.

Biblical origins

The author of the Book of Deuteronomy wrote: 'For you are a people consecrated to the Lord your God; of all the people on earth the Lord your God chose you to be His treasured people.' (7:6). That particular verse is a helpful one for a number of reasons. It uses the Hebrew verb, *bachar*, 'to choose', and links it with the important phrase *am segullah*, now translated as a treasured people (which, incidentally, used to be translated as a 'peculiar' people, and those of us who have chosen to be full-time servants of the Jewish community tend to think that 'peculiar' was probably a better translation!). Chosen, by God, from all the people on earth to be his treasured people. That confronts us unmistakably with the concept.

Deuteronomy, according to many scholars, was not written until the seventh century BCE but the chosen people idea is even earlier than this first formal expression of it. For the idea is indissolubly linked with the idea of covenant which undoubtedly pre-dates Deuteronomy. Abraham encountered God, was singled out by God. A covenant was cut, struck, made. Abraham would walk before God; God would be with Abraham. The covenant was renewed and extended at Sinai with all of Abraham's descendants. Israel was chosen for partnership and her partner became the God of Israel. That idea of covenant has been central to Jewish thought and theology for three thousand years. When a Jewish baby boy is circumcised his father declares: 'Blessed are You, Lord our God, King of the Universe, who makes us holy through doing Your commands, and commands us to bring our sons into the covenant of our father, Abraham.' On Friday night both in our homes and in our synagogues, we sanctify, set apart and set aside the ensuing twenty-five hours for a special purpose, for the Sabbath and, as we make *kiddush*, as we sanctify the day ahead, we assert that we do so *ki vanu vacharta v'otanu kiddashta mi-kol ha'ammim* – because You chose us to be holy among all peoples. Chosenness, treasuredness, convenant are indeed integral both to biblical thought and later liturgy.

But let us stay, for the moment, with the Bible. And let us, without in any way indulging in unnecessary apologetics, ask 'Why?' And here the Bible is unequivocal: Why? Out of love. Why? For obligation. Once again it is the Book of Deuteronomy which expresses the thinking most succinctly: 'It is not because you are the most numerous of peoples that the Lord set His heart on you and chose you – indeed, you are the smallest of peoples: but it was because the Lord loved you . . .' (7:7–8) Not because of numbers or any other factor denoting any kind of superiority. Nowhere in the Hebrew Bible is there the remotest suggestion of group superiority, let alone group superiority as the reason for election. It is not suggested that Israel was bigger, stronger, cleverer, more endearing – not even more righteous or more faithful; the choice is a matter of love or, if you prefer the term, grace. Nor does the choice bring with it any suggestion of privilege – not special protection, certainly not special dispensation for transgressions. The reverse. The consequence of election is obligation. 'You have I known,' says Amos, 'therefore I will visit upon you all your iniquities' (Amos 3:2).

The prophet Deutero-Isaiah makes explicit the ultimate purpose of election: to be a witness, to be a prophet, to be a light, to testify to the absolute need to establish justice, to create a society of righteousness, to bring about that world of peace and harmony which so much of prophetic literature gives us a glimpse of. To work for the turning of swords into ploughshares and spears into pruning-hooks (Isaiah 2:2), to pursue social equity, to speak peace. And even to suffer in the process, (Isaiah 52:13); chosenness is about that.

Every Sabbath Jews read from the Torah, the Five Books of Moses. Every Sabbath the reading is prefaced with a blessing: 'Blessed are you Lord our God, King of the Universe, who has chosen us from among all peoples and given us your Torah, Your teaching.' What is that teaching about? About duty, responsibilities, assuming the yoke of the Kingdom of Heaven. It is about commandments, given in love and intended to bring about *tikkun olam*, the repairing of the world. Chosenness is central to biblical Judaism. But chosenness was about duty not privilege, obligation not superiority.

Rabbinic literature

We call the Mishna, the Talmud and the Midrash, those records of debate, discussion and exegesis which stem from the first five centuries or so of the common era, rabbinic literature. In rabbinic literature, the rabbis continue to emphasize the concept of chosenness, though voluntary acceptance of the covenant of Sinai plays a prominent part in their thinking. Many of the liturgical references to chosenness stem from this period – the Friday night kiddush, the blessing before the Torah, both of which I have already quoted. Indeed there is a marked emphasis on, a definite reassertion of, the doctrine which reflects a dramatic development in the climate in which the rabbis lived and their literature evolved. That dramatic development was the emergence of Christianity.

The challenge of Christianity

What those who bridle at the Jewish concept of chosenness so often ignore or overlook is the Christian concept of election. As Ellen Umansky puts it:

> The Christian concept of election is rooted in the self-identification of the early church as the true Israel. While acknowledging that the Jewish people had originally been the chosen of God, early Christian theologians insisted that those Jews refusing to acknowledge Jesus as their Messiah could no longer claim the status of divine privilege. Viewing Israel as a community of the faithful rather than as the biological descendents of Abraham, Paul declares that 'not all who are descended from Israel belong to Israel' (Rom. 9:6). His contention here, as elsewhere, is that the concept of election, though once referring solely to the Jewish people, the Israel of the flesh, had been superseded by a new concept referring to those Jews and Gentiles who, by accepting the church's teachings, can justifiably claim to be the true Israel of the spirit.[1]

Paul declared a new convenant; he declared the covenant at Sinai superseded, he argued that Torah could no longer lead, of itself, to salvation. Suddenly there was the assertion of an Old Testament (the very word 'testament' means 'covenant') and a New one – with all the triumphalism that the use of those terms implies.

'How odd of God to choose the Jews.' It's a curious and bitter irony that the use of the phrase 'chosen people' as a taunt and a reproach and a sneer should emerge out of a society rooted in a religion which believes equally emphatically in chosenness and adds to it an imperialism which is not characteristic of Judaism! But more of that in a moment. First let me continue tracing the development of the concept of election in Judaism. What we can now see is that what rabbinic Judaism was doing was reasserting chosenness in the face of dramatic counter-claims from emergent Christianity. And it may well be that references to 'Who has chosen us from among all people' in the Torah service and at kiddush only came into being as a forcible restatement of belief in the face of Pauline denial and dismissal.

The Medieval period

As we have seen, biblical Judaism makes no claims to special merit or special talent on the part of Jews. Special obligation, yes, but special virtue, no. In the Middle Ages we find, for the first time, an exception. This is to be found in the writings of Judah Halevi. Halevi was a Spanish Jew of the late eleventh century. A great poet, he also wrote a book called the *Kuzari* in which, characteristically in an age of disputations, he argued the case for Judaism as against Christianity and Islam. According to Halevi, Jews have a special religious faculty, a unique soul. Halevi goes on to argue that Jews are the beneficiaries of special, supernatural providence. It is highly significant that Judah Halevi lived at the very end of the Golden Age of Jewish life in Muslim Spain, at the time of the Christian reconquest, when the Middle Ages were closing in on the Jews and the road to Inquisition and expulsion, to ghetto and pogrom was beginning to open up. Halevi's view of the Jew as having a special religious soul is isolated and almost unique. In certain mystic circles, in Kabbalistic literature, one could later find echoes of Halevi – the claim that only the souls of Israel are from God, while the souls of others are base material or *ke lippot* (shells). Given the precarious position of the Jew in Medieval Europe such claims were a means of making bearable, if not intelligible, the continued oppression of the Jewish people. As Lou Silberman puts it: 'The more the Jew was forced to close in on himself, to withdraw into the imposed confines of the ghetto, the more he tended to emphasize Israel's difference from the cruel gentile without.'[2] These aspirations to superiority and exclusivity never entered the liturgy and are nowhere to be found in significant Jewish thinkers other than Halevi. In Maimonides, for instance, the greatest Jewish thinker of the Middle Ages, even the doctrine of election itself plays only a marginal role. And with the political emancipation of the Jews in the period following the French Revolution, the very idea of Jewish specialness is itself challenged.

Salvation and race

Before we look at modern Jewish reactions to the concept of chosenness, there are one or two aspects of Judaism we ought to examine. Judaism does not teach that there is no salvation outside the synagogue. At the climax of the Book of Jonah, the people of Nineveh repent and are saved. They do not convert to Judaism. God is God of the whole world: 'Are not you and the Ethiopians all the same to Me, Children of Israel? – It is the Lord who speaks' through Amos (9:7). As the rabbis put it, perhaps echoing Galatians 3:28: 'I call heaven and earth to witness that whether it be Jew or non-Jew, man or woman, manservant or maidservant – only according to their deeds does the spirit of God rest upon them.'[3] Chosenness and possession of the sole route to salvation are not synonymous.

That in turn explains why Judaism is not a missionary religion in the same way that Christianity and Islam in one case have been and in the other case is. Christianity taught that there is no salvation outside the church; no one comes to the Father except through the Son. Islam, too, is a religion of election and has tendencies to religious imperialism. Indeed, Islam and classical Christianity have much in common in this regard. As Henri Atlan writes of Christianity and Islam:

> These two civilisations have adopted the God of Israel but have taken Him, if one may dare say so, too literally, regarding Him as the only legitimate God of the entire planet . . . These two monotheisms each claimed election by the God of Israel for itself, distorting its image so much that they became the only two socio-cultures that claimed universality by divine right, justifying and sanctifying everyone's conversion by fire and sword.[4]

A close friend of mine, Sister Margaret Shepherd, is a member of the Sisters of Sion, a Catholic order devoted to building good relations between Christians and Jews. Her work has been featured on television where she stated categorically that she did not seek to convert Jews since, post Vatican II, it was no longer an article of Catholic faith that a Jew needed to be converted before he or she could be saved. Although she is right and Vatican II was a landmark in the de-imperializing of the Church, Margaret was inundated with letters and callers accusing her of heresy: the old covenant has been revoked and only the new promises redemption. The need to hang on to that imperial exclusivity dies hard.

Judaism does not seek to convert the whole world. But neither is it the property of some superior racial group. Jews are not a race and have never been. Conversion to Judaism is always available to those who seek it. It has been frequent at many periods in the past and is a common feature of life in Britain and America today. However, some years ago, the American journal *Commentary* posed a list of theological questions to a range of American Jewish theologians. In referring to the issue of chosenness, *Commentary* added: 'How do you answer the charge that this doctrine is the model from which various theories of national and racial superiority have been derived?'[5] Respondents pointed out that Jews are not a race, that conversion is an ever-present possibility, that there is no assertion of superiority (*pace* Halevi), and that any idea can be distorted and abused. But the very question reflects Jewish sensitivity and nervousness. Chosenness has been caricatured by anti-Semites: it did fuel monstrous calumnies such as the Protocols of the Elders of Zion. 'How odd of God to choose the Jews' does carry a sting. And Toynbee infuriates when he writes: 'The most notorious historical example of idolization of an ephemeral self is the error of the Jews . . . they persuaded themselves that Israel's discovery of the One True God had revealed Israel itself to be God's chosen people.'[6] The idea of chosenness has been used as a stick with which to beat and decry Jews. Hence the complex feelings I referred to earlier.

At this juncture, I think one further word of clarification is called for. Chosenness does not lead Jews to wish to make all people Jews in order to save their souls. Chosenness has nothing whatsoever to do with claims of superiority – racial or otherwise. There is nothing exclusive or excluding about Judaism. But it would be true to say that Jews have felt themselves to be special, set aside for a particular purpose, entrusted with a unique set of teachings. These ideas are, indeed, wrapped up in the concept of chosenness. What we now have to ask is whether those ideas have any validity for Jews today. Do they express anything which Jews would still claim for themselves? How do Jews talk about chosenness in the second half of the twentieth century?

Responses to chosenness

Abandon the concept
One contemporary Jewish response is to abandon the concept of chosenness altogether. A Conservative rabbi, Harold M. Schulweis, has argued that the claim is an 'aristocratic conceit'[7] which demeans all other people. He sees chosenness as going beyond specialness and positing a claim of exclusive possession of truth. He concludes: 'Judaism . . . now has an opportunity to make a major moral contribution to the world by pioneering the rejection of all religious claims to exclusive divine revelation, its own included.'[8] Mordechai Kaplan, the founder of the Reconstructionist movement within Judaism, likewise eliminated all reference to chosenness from Reconstructionist liturgy.[9] Though, since Reconstructionism rejects traditional theism, this is something of a special case, nevertheless, the sensitivity and modesty of this position is impressive. But leaving aside the question of its historical and theological truth, one wonders whether Schulweis and Kaplan are correct in assuming that chosennes is *per se* a claim to exclusiveness and the conceit they seek to reject. Judaism does not claim an exclusive monopoly on truth. Is a feeling of specialness *ipso facto* conceit?

Radical modification

A second school of thought responds to the same anxiety that Kaplan and Schulweis feel by opting for what one may term radical modification rather than abandonment. Jacob Agus, another Conservative rabbi and biblical scholar, argues that chosenness should be regarded as a metaphor for the vocation which each people, each culture, is called upon to fulfil:

> We ought to be a chosen people, as example, not exception. We call
> upon all faiths so to universalize their sense of being covenanted as
> to recognize that other faiths offer similarly holy, even if not identical,
> doctrines and commitments. Perhaps we may induce other religions to
> follow our example and renounce their claims to exclusive possession
> of the 'Keys of the Kingdom'.[10]

The great merit of Agus's position is that it emphasizes the Jewish rejection of possessing exclusive truth, recognizes the value of the religious mosaic, and points to the key agenda issue of twentieth-century religious thought: How do the world religions accommodate each other's insights without resorting to some kind of bland and uncritical relativism – every path to God is equally profound and equally valid? One of my own personal quests is to work out a theological position which enables me to respond to the central truths of Christianity in a sympathetic and unpatronising way without compromising my own Jewish faith. That is an enormous task, since at the heart of the relationship between Judaism and Christianity is much apparent mutual denial – Messiah, not Messiah; resurrection, no resurrection; Old Testament, New Testament, and so on. The truth-claims which religions make, especially where they conflict, present a fascinating area for thought and discussion, not just for those engaged in dialogue. Perhaps Agus begs the question, leaves the real work still to be done. Indeed, Rabbi Lord Jakobovits manages to say, in the same essay, the following:

> Yes, I do accept the chosen people concept as affirmed by Judaism in
> its holy writ . . . In fact, I believe every people . . . is chosen . . .
> Maybe the Greeks were chosen for their unique contribution to art and
> philosophy, the Romans for their pioneering services in law and
> government, the British for bringing parliamentary rule into the world,
> and the Americans for piloting democracy in a pluralistic society.[11]

But do note the secular nature of the other instances of chosenness. On the very next page of the essay Jakobovits adds: 'As a practising Jew, I obviously consider Judaism the only true religion.'[12]

Agus's radical modification is interesting. However, it raises theological questions of great importance but does not solve them. What is the value of sharing chosenness if it does not also lead beyond closed assertions of the one true faith? And does it also, I wonder, do justice to the unique and moving experience of Judaism over nearly four thousand years?

Choosing rather than chosen

A third contemporary response to the concept of chosenness is to modify the word – moving from chosen to choosing: 'not half so odd that we chose God.' There is some support for this approach in early rabbinic literature. While in one famous Midrash (rabbinic commentary on a biblical passage) God holds Sinai over the heads of the Jewish people until they accept the Torah[13] – chosenness as an involuntary fact; in another Midrash God hawks the ten commandments round the peoples of the world and only the Jews are prepared to take on this burden[14] – choosing as a voluntary response. Much of rabbinic literature seeks to emphasize this voluntary acceptance and it leads to Zangwill's epithet 'a choosing people'.[15] As Eisendrath would have it, Israel chose to be witnesses to the truth of ethical monotheism and speak out for justice and righteousness.[16] 'Israel was not chosen, it was a volunteer in the service of God,' says Max Routtenberg. Israel chose to accept the Torah; any and everyone else can so choose, says M. D. Tendler, an orthodox scholar.

George Steiner utilizes this insight in a way I find particularly helpful. Wrestling with the problem of theodicy and the suffering of the Jews in the twentieth century, and their apparent abandonment by God, Steiner writes:

> God suffers gusts of murderous exasperation at the Jews, towards a people who have made Him a responsible party to history and to the grit of man's condition. He may not have wished to be involved: *the people may have chosen Him, in the oasis at Kadesh, and thrust upon Him the labour of justice and right anger. It may have been the Jews who caught Him by the skirt, insisting on contact and dialogue.* Perhaps before either God or living man was ready for proximity.[17]

That choosing is part of the glory and tragedy of Jewish history seems to me to be axiomatic. That there is only choosing, and no being chosen, denies the clear voice of tradition.

Obligation and service

Perhaps the most popular and widespread response to the concept of chosenness is to reaffirm what we have already stressed, namely that the choice did not denote privilege but obligation, not superiority but service. Remember the blessing before the reading from the Torah on Shabat morning. This school translates that blessing 'who chose us from among all people *by giving us* the Torah'. Chosenness is about a regime of commandment and duty. Thus Eliezer Berkowitz can write: 'The people that God chose became the Jewish people as a result of their taking upon themselves the task and responsibility for the realization of Judaism.'[18] Jews were chosen for special responsibilities, not special glory;[19] Judaism is 'a teaching of service and a service of teaching',[20] 'a statement of moral aspiration'.[21] 'There were', says David Greenberg, 'many tribes who walked the same desert . . . but one was chosen by God to be catapulted across the horizon of history to write its flaming message indelibly upon the hearts of men'[22] – a message of brotherhood, of social concern, of justice and of love.

This interpretation of chosenness is not a modern one; it runs, as we have seen, right the way through Jewish history. It is interesting that this understanding of chosenness is still so popular in the late twentieth century. For chosenness, as we have seen, is related to covenant and, when Jews accepted the covenant, they could never, as Irving Greenberg has pointed out, have been expected to take on a burden which was to lead to Auschwitz. The Jew today may well ask of God a question: chosen for service, yes; but chosen for such humiliation and such suffering – what gives anyone the right to ask that of us, still less the right to impose it upon us? And yet reaffirmation there is. So Chaim Potok can write: 'We [still] choose to be chosen . . . We choose to be the bearers of a tradition which we feel enhances human existence. It is an assumption of responsibility, not superiority.'[23] Which leaves one gigantic question – why you? By what right do you set yourselves up as a light to the nations, as teacher and guide? Why should God choose you for this mission as you claim?

Singling out

And that question I cannot answer. I can only say this. I look back upon the history of the Jewish people – the fact of the declaration 'The Lord is One,' the fact of Torah (Jewish teaching), the fact of the prophetic writings, the fact of giving birth to Christianity and Islam, the fact of endurance, the fact of our pursuit by history even to this very day – and I cannot but be aware of an existence touched by God and in that sense special. Not exclusively, not uniquely, but undoubtedly. And touching implies a deliberate act, a divine choice. What Emil Fackenheim calls a singling out, not an accident. It has nothing to do with race and there is no claim to exclusivity in the designation. As Fackenheim says: 'Christianity shares with Judaism the scandal of a singling-out God' and he who singled out Israel did so 'not for the sake of Israel only but for the world.'[24]

I know that my existential defence of chosenness fails to answer all the questions and solve all the problems, especially if you are not a theist and see Jewish survival in terms only of the strength of group identity and the power of self-delusion. For by rooting my response in Fackenheim's singling-out I rely, in the last analysis, on a mystery. But there, for me, it must rest. As Arnold J. Wolf once wrote:

> The doctrine of the chosen people is a mystery, not a problem. It must be lived out, not explained away. It is irrational, implacable, incommensurate with Jewish character or competence. It entails no pride but condemns to recurrent humiliation. It is in no way self-serving. It is not a Jewish idea but only our interpretation of historic fact. That is why it is so easy to caricature chosenness. The sacred is only a step from the absurd.[25]

Christian and Muslim Perspectives on Jesus in the Qur'ân

Neal Robinson

There are a number of passages in the Qur'ân which mention Jesus explicitly or refer to him obliquely. If we piece these references together we obtain the following picture. Jesus, whose name is invariably spelled 'îsâ, was the Messiah, a spirit and a word from God. He is described as illustrious in the world and in the hereafter and one of those brought near. He was conceived by a virgin whom God preferred above all the women of creation and into whom he breathed his Spirit. By God's permission he performed a number of miracles including creating birds from clay, healing the blind and the leper and raising the dead. On another occasion he complied with the disciples' request and asked God to send down a table spread with food for them to eat. Yet for all that, Jesus was only one of a series of prophets and a servant on whom God showed his favour. He was most emphatically not the Son of God, nor did he tell mankind to treat him and his mother as deities. The main thrust of his message was that the Children of Israel should worship and serve God who was his Lord and their Lord. He received a revelation called the Gospel and he brought good tidings of one whose name would be Aḥmad. He apparently expected his disciples to engage in *jihâd* for he summoned them to be 'helpers' in God's cause. The disbelieving Jews plotted against him and subsequently claimed that they had put him to death. In fact they neither killed him nor crucified him; it appeared so to them but God raised him into his presence and there is not one of them who will not believe in him before his death.

Although I have omitted a lot of the details, I am confident that most Christians and Muslims would acknowledge that this is a fair summary of what the Qur'ân says about Jesus. Yet if they were to begin to discuss the meaning of the Qur'anic statements I have no doubt that the dialogue would quickly flounder because of unexamined presuppositions about how the questions should be tackled. Western Christians generally assume that modern 'critical' scholarship is more objective than classical Muslim exegesis. For many

Muslims, on the other hand, the classical commentaries are virtually sacrosanct because they enshrine the normative interpretation of the Qur'ân which is based on tradition. In this essay I shall first suggest that there are in fact several Christian approaches to the subject and that it is important to distinguish between them. Then I shall examine the Qur'anic representation of Jesus from the standpoint of classical Muslim exegesis, indicating that this approach has an inner logic which is rarely appreciated by Christians. In my concluding discussion I shall argue that the avowed scholarly objectivity of the so-called 'critical' approach advocated by Christians is in fact largely illusory. I shall also argue that classical Muslim exegesis is much less cut-and-dried than it appears.

Four Christian approaches to Jesus in the Qur'ân

Christian writers have produced a substantial body of literature about Jesus in the Qur'ân. A complete survey is beyond the scope of this study. Instead I shall attempt to delineate the four principal approaches which Christians have adopted.

The polemical approach
The earliest Christian writings about Islam were polemical. The polemicists' treatment of the Qur'anic representation of Jesus was part and parcel of their attempt to undermine Islam by exposing Muhammad as a fraud. They alleged that the Qur'ân gives a distorted account of Jesus and of Christian beliefs about him, that it is inconsistent, that it contains some palpable errors, and that Muhammad derived his information from heretics or from Jews who were hostile to Christianity.[1]

We learn from a famous Muslim man of letters called al-Jâhiz, that in the ninth century Christians flatly denied that they had ever believed secretly or publicly in the divinity of Mary. In the same period al-Kindî (died *c.* 820) stated that the Qur'ân's insistence that God had not acquired a son was wide of the mark if aimed at Christians for this was not what they taught. Another alleged distortion was the prediction of the coming of Ahmad. Christian polemicists denied that Jesus had made such a prediction and resisted the Muslim suggestion that Ahmad (i.e. Muhammad) was none other than the Paraclete mentioned in St John's Gospel.

The supposed inconsistencies occur in the Qur'ân's statements about the divinity of Christ and his death on the cross. John of Damascus (died before 753?) was well aware that the Qur'ân repudiated the Christian claim that Jesus was the Son of God but he mockingly pointed out that other passages which called him 'word' and 'spirit' implied that he was divine. A few decades later the Nestorian Catholicos Timothy I (died 823) was called to account by the Caliph. When asked for his reaction to the Qur'ân's disavowal of the crucifixion (4:156), Timothy politely indicated two other âyas (3:55 and 19:33) which seemed on the contrary to assert the reality of Jesus' death.

Potentially more damaging is the polemicists' claim to have pinpointed palpable errors in the Qur'ân. I shall mention only the most famous of these. First there is the statement that nobody had been called John before Zechariah's son (19:7). Already in al-Jâḥiẓ's day Christians were arguing that this was based on a misunderstanding of Luke 1:61 where we read that there was nobody in Zechariah's family who bore that name. Second, a ninth-century Christian theologian called Nicetas of Byzantium noted the oddity of Mary's being described as the 'Sister of Aaron' (19:23). He concluded that Mary, whose name in Greek and Arabic is Maryam, had been confused with Miriam the sister of Aaron and Moses. Third, in the seventeenth century Maracci argued that Muḥammad called Jesus 'îsâ because he confused him with Esau.

The alleged distortions, inconsistencies and factual errors were evidence enough for the polemicists that the Qur'ân was not a revelation from God. Some of them suggested more mundane sources from which Muḥammad might have derived his information. John of Damascus said that Muḥammad was casually exposed to the Christian scriptures and that after supposedly encountering an Arian monk he formed a heresy of his own. Others identified the monk as Baḥîrâ who is mentioned by Muḥammad's biographer. Al-Kindî claimed that Muḥammad's informant was a Nestorian called Sergius who deliberately set out to use him to corrupt the Arabs. He also stated that the Qur'ân echoes the false accusations made against Christianity by early Jewish converts to Islam. Maracci revived this latter view and suggested that the Jews called Jesus Esau out of hatred for him and that Muḥammad took the name from them in good faith.

The assimilative approach

Christian apologists who engage in dialogue with Muslims frequently attempt to narrow the gap between Christianity and Islam by propounding a Christian interpretation of the Qur'ân.[2]

There are of course a number of important details on which the Qur'ân seems to be in agreement with the New Testament. These include the blessedness of Mary, the virgin birth, the description of Jesus as Messiah, servant and prophet, and the assertion that he performed miracles and was raised into heaven. Yet even if all of these supposed agreements were to command common assent they would hardly detract from the problems posed by other passages which apparently deny the divinity of Christ and the reality of his death on the cross. Christian apologists attempt to reinterpret those passages in the light of the Qur'ân's more positive statements.

As regards Christ's divinity they argue as follows. In attributing to Jesus miracles such as creating living birds and raising the dead the Qur'ân implies that he exercised divine prerogatives. Moreover by asserting the virgin birth and referring to Jesus as God's 'word' and 'spirit' and 'one of those brought near' (3:45) the Qur'ân implicitly proclaims the Incarnation. For if Jesus were simply called 'one of those brought near' the implication would be that he was an embodiment of one of the spirits who stand in God's presence (cf. 4:172). But since he is also called 'word', he differs from the other spirits in not being a reality exterior to God but in some sense God himself. Furthermore, according to the Qur'ân, God breathed his spirit into Adam and commanded the angels to prostrate themselves before him (eg. 2.34; 15.28 ff.). Since it is not lawful to fall down in obeisance to any but God, Adam must originally have been a divine being although of course he soon lost the divine spirit through sin. As the Qur'ân elsewhere compares the creation of Jesus to the creation of Adam (3:59), Jesus is likewise divine but unlike the first Adam he remained sinless and is still a legitimate object of worship, which is why God raised him into his presence. In view of all this, those statements in the Qur'ân which apparently deny Christ's divinity must be interpreted differently. In fact many of the passages which deny that God has ever acquired a son make no mention of Jesus. They were probably originally directed against Arab paganism rather than against Christianity. The remaining passages were presumably directed against localized heresies spawned by semi-Christianized Arabs who mistakenly supposed that Mary was God's consort and that Jesus was their son, a notion which is as abhorrent to orthodox Christians as it is to Muslims.

A similar strategy is used in discussing the crucifixion. Christian apologists take their lead from the polemicists and emphasize that according to the Qur'ân Jesus himself spoke of his death (19:33) and God told him that he was going to 'recall' him (3:55, i.e. cause him to die). Therefore, so the argument goes, 4:157 cannot possibly be a denial of Jesus' death on the cross, but rather a denial of the Jews' claim that *they* killed him. This denial is well founded historically (because it was the Romans who carried out the execution) and also theologically sound (because the real reason for Jesus' death was that it was in accordance with God's will).

The ecclesiastical history approach

Christian historians often seek to throw light on the Qur'ânic representation of Jesus by reference to the contemporary Christian background. This approach involves the study of Eastern Christianity and its penetration into Arabia, the impartial evaluation of the evidence concerning Muḥammad's contacts with Christians and the scouring of ancient Christian writings in search of parallels to the Qur'ânic material.[3]

Orthodox Christianity did not appeal to the Arabs because they associated it with Byzantine imperialism. Nevertheless two major 'heresies' – Monophysism and Nestorianism – were diffused by the Christianized and semi-Christianized tribes in the north and were also actively propagated by missionaries. Moreover, Mecca controlled the trade which passed up and down the western fringe of Arabia and was thus in direct contact with Monophysites and Nestorians in Syria and Southern Arabia as well as with Christian towns and monasteries along the caravan route. Monophysism and Nestorianism survived the rise of Islam and for that very reason they are comparatively well documented. We should, however, almost certainly presume the presence in Arabia of other heresies which have vanished virtually without trace.

The evidence concerning Muḥammad's personal contacts with Christians is patchy. Al-Kindî's Nestorian monk Sergius is a figment of his imagination. Baḥîrâ, the other individual favoured by the polemicists, is mentioned in a Muslim legend which serves to show how Muḥammad was recognized as a prophet by a person who was well-versed in the Christian scriptures. It is disingenuous to use such a legend to indict Muḥammad of fraud. To do so is rather like citing St Mathew's story of the wise men as proof that Jesus was instructed in oriental magic. The same holds true of Muslim traditions about Muḥammad's contacts with his wife's cousin and with a Christian bishop whose sermons he heard at Ukâz. These men *might* have had a decisive influence on him but there is no evidence that they did. We are on more solid ground with accounts of early Muslim dealings with Abyssinia. Muḥammad encouraged eighty-three of his companions to seek refuge there in 615 CE. We may infer that he thought that they would be temporarily safer in a Monophysite Christian country than they were in pagan Mecca. In 622 CE Muḥammad himself left Mecca and settled in Medina where he seems to have been more favourable towards the Christians than to the Jews who constituted a third of the population. During the last years of his life, when he held the reins of power, he made many treaties with neighbouring Christian tribes and with Christian rulers from further afield; for example, the ruler of Najrân in Southern Arabia sent an impressive embassy including Christian scholars who were allowed to use the mosque for prayers. It is conjectured that during this period Muḥammad's attitude towards Orthodox Christianity hardened because his adoptive son Zayd was killed in a skirmish with Byzantine troops.

The quest for ancient Christian parallels to the Qur'anic Jesus material has yielded some positive results. For instance the miracle of the birds is mentioned in the *Gospel of Thomas* and the apparent fusion of Mary with Miriam is in keeping with the Syrian Church's typological exegesis of the Old Testament. Much more debatable is the degree to which the Qur'anic representation of Jesus can be 'explained' by reference to Nestorianism and Monophysism. The Qur'ân accuses Christians of regarding Mary as divine; is this an echo of Nestorian opposition to calling Mary the Mother of God? The Qur'ân speaks of *the* Gospel; is this because the Nestorians and Monophysites rejected the four Gospels in favour of a single Gospel harmony? The Qur'ân claims that Jesus predicted the coming of one whose name would be Aḥmad or 'more highly praised'; does this reflect speculation among Monophysite monks that the Paraclete was yet to come? The Qur'ân seems to deny Jesus' death on the cross; should this denial be linked with the beliefs of the Julianists – Monophysite extremists who held that Christ's body was incorruptible? These explanations are plausible but they are not conclusive. The influence of Gnosticism, Jewish Christianity and Manichaeism are also distinct possibilities. According to the Gnostic *Apocalypse of Peter*, the person who was crucified was a substitute who came into being in Jesus' likeness. Jewish Christians known as Ebionites and Elkesaites revered Jesus as a prophet but denied that he was divine or that his death had saving significance. They had their own gospel and like the Muslims they abstained from wine and performed elaborate ablutions before prayers. Manichaeism was an eclectic religion which owed much to Jewish Christianity. Its founder Mani taught that Jesus was a prophet but denied that he was crucified. He believed that the Paraclete had not been effectively revealed until he himself experienced his first vision. Moreover some Manichees used the *Gospel of Thomas* which consists exclusively of words of Jesus and which like the Qur'ân comprises 114 sections!

The Muḥammad-centred approach

In recent years some Christian scholars have recognized Muḥammad's religious genius and have been led to suppose that his theological vision played an important role in moulding the Qur'anic Jesus material.[4]

The Qur'ân presents itself as a discourse which God addresses in the first place to Muḥammad but which Muḥammad is charged with relaying to a wider audience. The material about Jesus is an integral part of this discourse. Consider the following statement which interrupts the account of the annunciation. It describes how lots had previously been cast to determine who should be Mary's guardian: 'This is the tidings of the Unseen which We reveal to you. You were not with them when they cast their reeds [to decide] which of them should have charge of Mary. You were not with them when they disputed' (3:44).

The implication is that the narrator – God – observed the events in question and that the story revealed to Muḥammad is thus the true version of what happened. The revelation of the 'true' version of past events serves to put the record straight and to settle disputes between the various sects of Jews and Christians (see e.g. 18:9–30; 4:157). It also serves to authenticate the prophetic ministry of Muḥammad.

A second way in which the Qur'anic representation of Jesus authenticates Muḥammad's prophetic ministry is by describing him and Jesus as two of a kind. Like Muḥammad, the Qur'anic Jesus is called a 'prophet', 'messenger' and 'servant' of God. Jesus is said to have received a revelation called the Gospel just as Muḥammad subsequently received the Qur'ân. Jesus' teaching and the teaching of the Gospel are referred to as 'wisdom', 'right path', 'guidance', 'light' and 'admonition' – terms which recur as descriptions of the Qur'anic message. The central thrust of the Gospel was the same as that of the Qur'ân – the summons to serve and worship God. Moreover, Jesus reputedly practised ritual prayer (ṣalât) and almsgiving (zakat) (19:31), which are the two fundamental religious obligations of Islam. It should therefore come as no surprise that the Qur'ân urges the believers to fight at Muḥammad's side on the grounds that in so doing they will be following the example of Jesus' disciples who accepted the challenge to be helpers in God's cause (61:14).

Despite the Qur'anic stress on the affinity of Jesus and Muḥammad, there is no attempt to deny the virgin birth or the miracles which seem to Christians to mark Jesus out as different. Even here, however, there are some interesting correlations. Like the Prophet's wives Jesus' mother was secluded by a 'curtain' (33:53, cp. 19:17) and like his only virgin bride she was the victim of 'a tremendous calumny' (24:16, cp. 4:156). Like Muḥammad's revelations, Jesus' miracles were 'signs' (2:99, cp. 3:49) which were 'sent down' (2:97, cp. 5:112) 'by God's permission' (2:97, cp. 3:49).

There are no statements about God raising Muḥammad into his presence (4:158) or about it 'appearing' to his enemies that they had killed him. There are, however, some tantalizing similarities in what is said about Jesus and Muḥammad in respect of their mortality. The Qur'ân tells us that Muḥammad's critics mocked him for needing to eat food but it says that Jesus had had similar needs (25:7, cp. 5:75).

Like Muḥammad, Jesus was only a messenger, and messengers had passed away before him (3:144, cp. 5:75). Both men were victims of plots against their lives and God plotted on their behalf (8:30, cp. 3:54). Finally, God 'recalled' Jesus, and Muḥammad is made to face the possibility that the same might happen to him (3:117, cp. 40:77, 13:40, 10:47).

Traditional Muslim exegesis

Christians who write on the subject of Jesus in the Qur'ân sometimes refer to Muslim interpretations but rarely seem to grasp the principles of Muslim exegesis. This is not surprising because it is a specialist field and only fragments of the classical commentaries are available in translation. Nevertheless, in the interests of Christian-Muslim dialogue it is imperative that Christians take the Muslim exegetical tradition seriously.[5]

The type of exegesis favoured by the majority of Sunni Muslims is called *tafsîr bi-ʄl-ma'thûr* (commentary by tradition). It comprises explanations of the Qur'ân which can be reliably traced back to a sound source. According to Ibn Kathîr (died 1372), whose commentary is extremely popular among Arab Muslims and among Muslims in Britain who come from India and Pakistan, there are only three sound sources. He lists them in order of importance as the Qur'ân itself, the Ḥadîth, and the interpretations which can be traced back to the Companions. However, he recognizes that many commentators also refer to a fourth source, the interpretations advocated by the Successors. Finally, he sees no harm in commentators drawing on their expertise in technical matters such as Arabic philology, provided that they do not produce interpretations which are at variance with tradition.[6]

Taking my lead from Ibn Kathîr, I shall therefore discuss each of these five sources in turn. Wherever possible I shall select examples that have a bearing on the interpretation of those aspects of the Qur'anic representation of Jesus which have attracted the attention of Christian scholars.

The Qur'ân
For orthodox Muslims the Qur'ân in its entirety is a revelation from God. Specific statements therefore have to be interpreted in accordance with the general tenor of the overall message. Let us see how this works out in practice.

We noted earlier that Christian apologists sometimes suggest that God's commanding the angels to prostrate themselves before Adam (2:34, etc.) is a pointer to the divinity of Christ the second Adam.

This suggestion would be ruled out immediately by anyone who was familiar with the Qur'ân's emphasis on the unity of God and its repeated warnings against associating any other being with him. How then should we understand the angelic prostration? Although Muslims are not allowed to prostrate themselves before mortals this custom was permitted in pre-Islamic times. The Qur'ân itself tells us that Joseph's parents fell down prostrate before him (12:100) but they did so out of respect and as a greeting; there is not the slightest hint that they were worshipping him. The angelic prostration must have been of that kind (TIK I:135).

One more example will suffice, namely the Qur'anic references to Jesus as God's 'word' (3:45; 4:171). There is no distinction between upper and lower-case letters in Arabic and we have seen that Christian polemicists and apologists often argue that these passages should be understood in the light of orthodox Christian teaching about Jesus as the Incarnate Word of God. Ibn Kathîr will have none of this. The Qur'ân warns believers against people who seek dissension by concentrating on ambiguous passages (3:7). In commenting on this âya (TIK II.6) he says that this is what Christians are doing when they stress that the Qur'ân calls Jesus God's Word but neglect to mention that it also states clearly that he is only a servant on whom God showed his favour (43:59). How then should we understand the title 'word'? According to him the child Jesus was a word from God in the sense that he owed his existence to God's command, the creative word transmitted to Mary by the angel Gabriel. That is to say, the interpretation of 3:45 is given in 3:47, 'God creates what He wills. When He decrees anything He only says to it "Be!" and it comes into being' (TIK II:459).

The Ḥadîth

The Ḥadîth are the sayings of the Prophet Muḥammad. They cover almost every conceivable aspect of the life of the Muslim community and only a very small proportion of them are directly concerned with the exegesis of the Qur'ân. Muslim scholars were well aware that many spurious Ḥadîth had been put into circulation by story-tellers who pandered to popular taste and by sectarian groups. By the time Ibn Kathîr wrote his commentary, however, the wheat had ostensibly been separated from the chaff and six collections had achieved canonical status. The two most important are those compiled by al-Bukhâri (died 256/870) and Muslim b. al-Ḥajjâj (died 261/875). All the Ḥadîth in these two collections are regarded as indisputably authentic because in every case the text of the saying is supported by one or more unbroken isnâds – chains of guarantors which reach back to the time of the Prophet. All the guarantors in the isnâds can be identified and are known to have been reliable, of sound memory and of orthodox belief. The other compilers included many Ḥadîth whose isnâds did not quite meet these stringent conditions. Some of them are deemed to be of only 'fair' authority but none the less good enough for establishing points of law. Still others are regarded as 'weak'; they cannot be used for legal purposes but may none the less be used for exhortation. The three examples which I shall give are all of the first grade. For the sake of brevity I shall omit the isnâds.

From early times Christian polemicists have supposed that the Qur'ân confuses Mary with Miriam. From the perspective of traditional exegesis this matter can be resolved by reference to the following authentic Ḥadîth which Ibn Kathîr cites from the collection of Muslim:

> Mughîra b. Shu'ba said, 'The Messenger of God (The peace and blessings of God be upon him!) sent me to the people of Najrân. They said to me, "Do you [Muslims] not recite [in the Qur'ân] 'O Sister of Aaron' [19:28]?" I said, "Yes, indeed." They said, "And do you know what [period of time elapsed] between Moses and Jesus?" So I returned to the Messenger of God (peace and blessings up upon him) and informed him. He said "Did you not tell them that [the Jews] used to give [their children] the names of their prophets and the pious persons who lived before them?" ' (TIK IV:453)

Christian apologists frequently emphasize the high esteem which the Qur'ân has for Mary. There can be no denying the Qur'ân's assertion that God preferred her above all the women of creation, but this is relativized by another authentic Ḥadîth which puts Mary on the same level as Muḥammad's first wife:

> 'Abd Allah b. Ja'far reported that he heard 'Alî say in Kûfa that God's messenger (peace be upon him!) said: 'The best of the women of her [time] was Mary daughter of 'Imrân and the best of the women of her [time] was Khadîja daughter of Khuwaylid.' (TIK II:37f.)

My final example has a bearing on the interpretation of the Qur'anic statement about the crucifixion. The sequel to that statement runs as follows: 'There is not one of the People of the Scripture who will not believe in him before his death, and on the Day of Resurrection he will be a witness against them' (4:159).

Christian apologists, who claim that the Qur'ân does not deny the crucifixion, assume that 'before his death' must mean before the death of the Scripturist. The classical commentators, on the other hand, insist that it means before Jesus' death. In their view Jesus has not yet died and all the People of the Scripture will eventually believe in him when he returns. As proof they invariably cite this Ḥadîth which occurs with slightly different wording in five of the six canonical collections, including those of Bukhârî and Muslim:

Abû Hurayra reported that God's messenger (peace be upon him!) said, 'By Him in whose hand is my soul, it will suddenly happen that Jesus Son of Mary will descend amongst you as a just judge. He will break the crucifixes, cause the pigs to perish, suppress the poll tax and make wealth so abundant that no one will desire any more. One prostration will be preferable to him to the whole world and all that is in it.' (TIK II:436)

The interpretations of the Companions

When neither the Qur'ân nor the Hadîth throw any light on an exegetical problem the commentator should turn to the transmitted sayings of the Companions of the Prophet. A dozen or so Companions, including the first four Caliphs, are said to have concerned themselves with Qur'anic interpretation. However, the Companion whose name occurs most frequently in the classical commentaries is Muhammad's young cousin, 'Abd Allah Ibn al-'Abbâs (died 687). I shall give two examples of explanations attributed to him, again leaving out the isnâds to save space.

I mentioned earlier that Christian polemicists frequently allege that the Qur'ân mistakenly states that nobody had been called John before Zechariah's son. Those who make this allegation assume that the âya in question means: 'O Zechariah! Behold We bring you good news of a boy whose name is John. We have not before constituted anyone of the same name as him' (19:7).

The word *samîy*, which I have translated 'of the same name', occurs only twice in the Qur'ân – here and at 19:65. In both instances Ibn al-'Abbâs took it to mean 'similar'. He said that what is meant is that there had never before been a boy similar to John in the sense of being born to an aged father and a barren mother. Isaac was not like him because although the Qur'ân says that his parents were old it does not say that either of them was infertile (TIK IV:440, 474).

My second example concerns the crucifixion. We have seen that some Christian apologists argue that the Qur'ân does not in fact deny Jesus' death on the cross. However, according to Ibn al-'Abbâs the key clause 'it appeared so to them' (*shubbiha lahum* – 4:157) means that the Jews crucified someone else on to whom God had projected Jesus' 'likeness' (*shabah*). Here is the first part of his comment:

When God desired to raise Jesus to heaven twelve men who were Jesus' companions were in a house. Jesus came out to them from a spring in the house and his head was dripping with water. And he said, 'One of you will disbelieve in me twelve times after he has believed in me.' Then he said 'Which of you will have my likeness projected upon him and be killed in my place and share my exalted rank?' A youth who was the youngest of them in years stood up and said, 'I will.' Jesus told him to sit down. Then he repeated his request and the youth again stood up and said, 'I will.' Jesus said 'Yes you are the man.' The likeness of Jesus was projected on to him and Jesus rose to heaven from a skylight in the house. A search party came from the Jews and they took his likeness and killed him and crucified him.

This report, together with the Ḥadîth about Jesus' return, are decisive for the traditional Muslim understanding of the crucifixion. From this standpoint it is quite clear that God's statement that he was going to 'recall' Jesus (3:55) cannot mean that he was going to cause him to die on the cross.[6]

The interpretations of the Successors

The Successors are the pupils of the Companions. Ibn Kathîr regarded them as a distinctly lower-grade source. He held that it was permissible to take them into account but not compulsory to do so. Furthermore, if the Successors disagreed over the correct interpretation then none of them was to be treated as authoritative. I have therefore chosen an example where there is no evidence of the Successors having disagreed. It is taken from the voluminous commentary of Abû Ja'far al-Ṭabari (died 923).

Christian apologists have sometimes argued that the description of Jesus as one of 'those brought near' (3:45) implies his pre-existence because the same word (*muqarrabûn*) is used of the angels (4:172; 83:21). In fact there are eight occurrences of the word in the Qur'ân. Of the other five, two refer to Pharaoh's wizards (7:114 and 26:42) and three refer to believers who will be brought near to God at the resurrection (56:11, 88; 83:28). It is surely in this latter sense that the word is applied to Jesus because he is described as 'illustrious in the world and the hereafter, and one of those brought near'. This at any rate is how it was understood by Qatâda b. Di'ama (died 736) and Rabî b. Anas (died 756) who are the only Successors whose comments on the subject have been transmitted.[7]

Informed opinion

Ibn Kathîr was implacably opposed to speculative exegesis so he can hardly have approved of the many philosophical discussions in the commentary by Fakhr al-Dîn al-Râzî (died 1209). Nevertheless he saw no objection to commentators drawing on their expertise in more directly relevant disciplines such as philology provided, as I have already indicated, that their views did not clash with tradition. The following example from Râzî meets that criterion.

Christian apologists sometimes claim that when the Qur'ân affirms that Jesus created living birds (3:49; 5:110) it implies that he was doing something usually done only by God. The exegesis of these âyas is extremely complex and here I am concerned only with one small part of it: the meaning of the verb *khalaqa*. Râzî follows the philologist Ibn al-Anbâri (died 328/940) in arguing that it does not mean 'create' in the full sense of the world. He first draws attention to several other âyas in which the verb or its derivatives are used to denote human activity. These include:

This is only a creation (*khuluq*) of the men of old. (26:137)
You create (*takhluqûna*) a falsehood. (29:17)
This is nought but an invention (*ikhtilâq*). (38:7)

He then suggests that the verb means to 'determine', 'arrange' or 'measure'. In support of this, he cites ancient poetry and non-Qur'anic expressions. For instance the poet Zuhayr said:

Thou indeed cuttest what thou hast determined (*khalaqta*).
Some of the people determine (*yakhluqu*) then do not cut.

Râzî's readers would have known that this was the seventeenth line of a twenty-three line poem by the celebrated pre-Islamic poet, Zuhayr b. Abî Sulmâ, in which he eulogizes Ḥârim Ibn Sinân. The meaning is that, unlike others, Ḥârim executes his plans. The non-Qur'anic expressions which Râzî adduces include: *khalaqa 'l-na'ala* which means 'he fashioned a sandal'; *khalâq*, 'a portion', i.e. a measured amount; and *khalîq* 'suitable', i.e. endowed with a measure of worthiness.[8]

Concluding Discussion

One reaction to my survey of the Christian approaches to the subject might be to dismiss the first two as regrettable aberrations while holding on to the third and fourth as viable. This would be an oversimplification. The polemicists' version is undeniably narrow and distorted but they occasionally make interesting observations – observations which it would be all too difficult to make with the eyes of faith. The apologists are overingenious, and at times rather naive, but their assumption that the Qur'ân is less anti-Christian than its Muslim interpreters maintain is not in itself implausible. On the other hand, if the first and second approaches cannot be so lightly dismissed, nor can the third and fourth be so readily approved. Although advocates of these two approaches attempt to treat the data impartially the actual agenda for their research has grown out of the polemical concerns of their predecessors. The ecclesiastical history approach tests the polemicists' assumption that Islam is a Christian heresy. The Muḥammad-centred approach arguably has its roots in the polemicists' allegation that Maḥammad was a fraud. A further complication is that modern studies of Jesus in the Qur'ân are sometimes eclectic, combining elements drawn from more than one approach.[9] Then there is the work of Kenneth Cragg

which is really in a class of its own. A former research student of
Zaehner and unashamedly a Christian apologist, Cragg offers a
profoundly Christian reading of the Qur'ân without attempting to
argue that it actually affirms the Incarnation or Jesus' death on the
cross.[10] All in all, it is hardly surprising that Muslims are suspicious
of Christians who write scholarly studies of Jesus in the Qur'ân!

My account of traditional Muslim exegesis may have given the
impression that the classical commentators have left little room for
manoeuvre and that they have tied up most of the loose ends. That
this is in fact the case is often assumed by Muslims. It is, however,
an assumption which should not be left unchallenged. There are at
least three grounds for questioning it. First, the notion of any text
– even a sacred text – having a single meaning, is one which it is
very difficult to reconcile with modern linguistic theory. Moreover,
the evidence preserved by Ṭabari suggests that in the pre-classical
period there was greater openness towards the possibility of a plu-
rality of meaning. Second, although the classical commentators
rarely refer to Christian polemic, the early interpreters probably had
it in mind when they developed their approach to the Qur'anic
Jesus material. Third, it is arguable that Ibn Kathîr's hierarchy of
authorities turns the historical development of exegesis on its head.
That is to say that interpretations attributed to the Successors are
more likely to be authentic than those attributed to the Companions,
and that the latter are more likely to be authentic than those
attributed to the Prophet. For instance, there are accounts of the
crucifixion of a substitute which are attributed to several Successors.
They differ from the account which was allegedly favoured by Ibn
al-'Abbâs. Would the Successors have propagated them if they had
known the teaching of this illustrious Companion? Similarly there
are explanations of the name Sister of Aaron which are attributed
to the Companions. They differ from the explanation which is found
in the Ḥadîth. Would the Companions have published them if they
had known the dictum of the Prophet? I cannot here attempt to
answer those questions. I raise them simply to show that there is
plenty of scope for the Christian scholar to engage critically with the
Muslim exegetical tradition.[11]

Buddhist Christianity

Peggy Morgan

I propose to discuss certain contemporary thinkers whom I think of not as working on the frontiers between the Buddhist and Christian religious traditions (the geopolitical metaphor suggests too sudden a transition) but as carving an intermediate territory of mixed status which demonstrates by its very existence that the adjoining 'nations' were not as mutually alien as had been supposed.

Some of this supposed alienness is reflected or imputed by the terminology we use. From within the Christian tradition it is easy to avoid noticing, for example, that the word 'theology' labels a distinctively Christian preoccupation. Others are not so wrapped up in *logos* (reasoned discourse) about *theos* (God).[1] This is especially true of Buddhists who set aside, as not helpful for enlightenment, belief in a personal creator God as traditionally understood by Christians.[2] But even in those traditions often assumed to be closest to Christianity, such as Judaism or Islam, there is more concern with Torah and Shari'ah – with way of life and will of God – than with articulating our understanding of the divine nature. The mere recognition that matters can be seen in a different light is surely salutary – as learning another language enriches our control of our own.

Goethe's remark about language ('he who knows one knows none') is today perhaps slightly less startling than when he first uttered it. We recapture the full shock when F. M. Müller takes that remark and applies it to the study of religions.[3] It takes a meeting with a real live bilingual (in this sense) to loosen the hold of the previously inconceivable.

Such an example is provided by Raymundo Panikkar, who was introduced by Keith Ward at the Younghusband Lecture in 1989 as 'a pointer to a human possibility'. Panikkar describes himself as a Catholic priest, initiated Buddhist and initiated Saivite (follower of Shiva) Hindu. Trilingual at least and seemingly with multiple citizenship! Listening to him speak requires some adjustment in one's understanding of the idea of identity in general, and of the relation between theological language and the life-styles of faiths.

The above analogies may be linked to two opposing styles in living and exercising the theological imagination which are at either end of the spectrum which makes up Christianity. One reflects a way of faith which inherits a revelation, asserts a truth, and does not want to live (has no wish to venture) outside the closed, protected fortress of its securities. What is outside is contaminating and hostile and if the portcullis is raised it is only to welcome others in, for there is genuine concern to share its safety with other souls who need protection, help and security.

The other way sees faith as itself a journey, without a fully known goal and during which there is no abiding city, no continuing stay and no sure protection but where the whole earth is the Lord's and fellow human beings are others on a journey which may run parallel to one's own. This model does not suggest actual physical immobility on the part of the first group of theologians and members of faith communities. Many such people have been brave missionaries and faced great personal danger in China and Africa for example. What is described is an attitude of mind, an imaginative and emotional disposition. A theologian of the second type, on the other hand, might well be quite 'stay-at-home' physically. One may have encountered the faiths of others without having lived in Japan, Thailand, Tibet or Sri Lanka. The physical journey does not guarantee that theology, or the theologian will move outwards and enter into the experience of others any more than physical isolation debars it. To many, the suggestion that fellow human beings, rather than just fellow Christians, are on a journey parallel to one's own, sounds dangerously liberal. After all, to be confident enough to set off at all one needs a sense that one's chosen way, or the instructions on how to follow that way, are distinctive and right. Yet every traveller has come across signposts pointing in opposite directions to the same place.

Nevertheless the different nature of the religious paths must be taken seriously. One of the false assumptions often made about those who teach history of religions, or are students of religions, is that they think that all religions are the same in the end really. This is frequently taken to be the meaning of the well-known story of the six blind men and the elephant which each of them identifies with the part they happen to have hold of.[4]

The story seems to fit well with the Christian emphasis on humility, and with an appreciation of the inadequate and interim nature of theological doctrine. Religion and theologizing, as human expressions, are inescapably flawed. All of our descriptions of ultimate reality are different and are full of limitations. These are all points about religious understanding which will strike the student of religion just as forcibly as any sense of 'sameness' in what he or she encounters. If it is true, as was once suggested, that the trouble with so-called comparative religion is that it makes people comparatively religious, then that might be a wholly healthy thing.

Of course, these problems are not only a challenge *between* two religions such as Christianity and Buddhism but *within* each tradition too, for all religions are plural and diverse. Kenneth Cracknell was once asked whether he ever worships with people of other faiths, and he said: 'Yes, every Sunday in my local Methodist Church.' Some of the challenges arising from Buddhist-Christian interchange, though interpreted by some as the 'Buddhizing of Christianity', are already present in the various strands within the Christian tradition, as pointed out by John Macquarrie:

> The conception of a personal God in Western religions and the conception of an impersonal ultimate in some of the Eastern religions may not be such an absolute difference between them as it seems at first sight. Personal/impersonal is one more dialectic within the divine *coincidentia oppositorum*.[5]

That Buddhist patterns of thinking and practice have been a rich resource for many Christians is undeniable. The range of these influential patterns of thinking and practice is wide and includes the following. First, there is the concept which Buddhists call 'skilful means'[6] which affirms the positive value of relating doctrines and practical teachings to cultural contexts and historical needs. Accompanying this is an attitude of tolerance towards 'views' as relative to cultural and individual human development. Then there is the sense of the inter-relatedness of the human, animal and plant worlds.[7] Buddhism also adds a fresh voice to the debate about the nature of the human person in relationship to concepts such as mind, body, heart and soul which are particularly important areas for modern bio-ethics.[8] There is here too an understanding of the mind-relatedness of the phenomenal world which links with the modern scientific world-view and therefore with modern Christianity. All the writers on Buddhism and Christianity referred to later in this paper also take up Buddhism's emphasis on practice, meditation and 'spirituality' rather than belief and intellectual assent.

Nor is this refreshment from 'outside' the first of its kind in the Christian tradition. This very question was raised in provocative terms by Tertullian's rhetorical question, 'What has Athens to do with Jerusalem?' Christianity clearly bears the marks of many such mutual influences – Jerusalem/Athens, Jerusalem/Rome, Jerusalem/-Benares[9] – with the possibility, therefore, of new cultural marriages, more fitting for another time and place.

Of course there are Christians who quite explicitly call themselves Christian Platonists, Christian humanists and even Catholic Marxists. These positions create another set of tensions with what has seemed to be the dominant (though not the only) voice in the tradition *extra ecclesiam nulla salus est*. In using such expressions no one implies a one-way influence of the adjective on the noun, any more than in 'Neoplatonic Christianity' or 'Modern Scientific Christianity'.[10] In this paper there is a deliberate choice to use the phrase Buddhist Christianity to indicate Christian faith and practice which is close to, affected by, seen to be in creative relationship with Buddhism and even changed by its contact.

But why isolate Buddhism rather than Hinduism, Confucianism or Taoism? Much depends, of course, on one's personal interest, but there are other facts and voices which witness to the significance of this particular encounter. First, Buddhism is transplanting itself in the West, among westerners, in a particularly thoroughgoing way. Twenty years ago Ninian Smart wrote that Buddhism 'has all the appearances of being the faith which will challenge Christianity most seriously in the West'.[11] Pieris comments: 'Many had hoped with Arnold Toynbee that an in-depth encounter between Buddhism and Christianity would usher in a new era in human history.'[12]

Would not a proper parallel to the situation in the first centuries of Christian history be in the encounter between East and West, as it takes place in the environment of Japan or Burma for instance? Here Buddhist language, as once in the West Greek language and thought, might be used appropriately to understand and communicate Christian truth for hearers with a distinctive 'Buddhist' background. But what is involved is more significant than the use of another language. Athens and Rome did more than provide a language for communication. They extended and formed emergent Christianity, creating a new Graeco-Romano-Christian culture. In analogous fashion the Burmese theologian Khin Maung Din sees his purpose as

> not primarily to communicate the Gospel to the Burmese Buddhists.
> But rather, the main object of this paper is to discover more about
> the Gospel itself with the aid of some Buddhist and Oriental categories.
> Genuine theology, in my opinion, should not only try to broaden the
> present boundaries of Christian Theology alone. It should also try and
> discover new dimensions for theology with the help of the spiritual
> experience and concepts of men of other faiths.[13]

This involves more than the indigenization of Christianity; it is an effort to explore God in terms such as 'the unborn, unbecome, unconditioned' or to appreciate the Theravada Buddhist position that the best way to describe ultimate reality is not to describe it at all. Din echoes di-polar and dialectical theology in advocating not an either/or mode of theological expression but a both/and, with the possibility of a 'beyond either'. In a similar way Panikkar often responds to people who present quite opposite and contradictory points of view, by saying to each, 'Yes, you are right', and then, 'You are both right'.[14]

Among other theologians who have worked in this field, J. K. Kadowaki in *Zen and the Bible* remarks more than once how similar the monastic disciplines for the Jesuit and the Zen practitioner are: 'The daily schedule in a Jesuit novitiate could easily be transferred into that of a Zen monastery.' He is one of the many Christians, in Britain as well as Japan, who continue to use Zen practice as helpful to his Christian life.[15]

William Johnston is another Jesuit deeply immersed in the Japanese Zen experience but coming to Japan from the West. He writes: 'In dialogue, just as Christians will integrate Buddhist insights into their Christian outlook, so Buddhists will integrate the truth they learn from Christianity and be committed to it.'[16] Elsewhere, he reflects that Christianity 'will find her encounter with the Orient no less enriching than her meeting with Graeco-Roman thought'.[17] One obvious meeting-point of Christians and Buddhists is in their listening to the cries of the poor. As Johnston remarks: 'No Asian theology of liberation can be construed without consulting Asian Buddhists.'[18]

This gives us a natural bridge to the thinking of Aloysius Pieris, who lives and works in Sri Lanka. Pieris is critical of any airy-fairy encounter with the 'spirituality' of the East since for him spirituality is practical involvement with the poor. He talks of the complementarity between Christian agape (speaking the language of redemptive love) and Buddhist gnosis (speaking the language of liberative knowledge), with poverty as the meeting-ground, responded to by charity in the former case and by that voluntary poverty in monasticism which Buddhism demonstrates so centrally.[19]

One of the most interesting books in the area of Buddhism and Christianity is John Cobb's *Beyond Dialogue, towards a mutual transformation of Christianity and Buddhism*.[20] Cobb notes particularly how much the Church has appropriated from neo-Platonism and from modern scientific thought. He contrasts those Christians who see the 'sharing in spirituality as dangerously close to syncretism' with writers like Knotter and Northrop who see a complementarity in the dialectic of East and West:

> The opportunities for adventure in Christian theology have never been greater. The risk is real, for we cannot predict the outcome. We cannot know in advance which of our most cherished beliefs will be dissolved. But if we do not take this risk, we will forfeit all claim to universality and exist only as a relic of times past.

Many of the points about those writers who 'pass over' into Buddhist thought and practice emerge in the writings of Don Cupitt –

indeed, too many to be summarized here. One quotation must serve, to give something of the flavour of a rich controversy:

> In the nineteenth century people defined religion in terms of belief in the supernatural. I want to see religion now as a creative activity, like art. The means by which we continually invent and try out new forms of life, new forms of consciousness, new ways of being human and infuse new values into life.[21]

Yet it seems that artists have freedoms denied to professional theologians. How many people would be particularly upset if one suggested that T. S. Eliot or R. S. Thomas are Buddhist-Christians? But to say this of a churchman in an influential position or an academic theologian rouses grave concern. There are no explicit references to Buddhism in Thomas's poetry, but for anyone immersed in Buddhist ideas there are clear echoes in much that he writes. For example in his *Via Negativa* he speaks of God as

> that great absence
> In our lives, the empty silence
> Within, the place where we go
> Seeking, not in hope to
> Arrive or find.[22]

For Eliot, 'all language is inadequate, but probably the language of poetry is the language most capable of communicating wisdom'.[23] Like Cupitt, he sees a rigorous scepticism as a 'useful equipment for religious understanding', 'the demon of doubt . . . is inseparable from the spirit of belief'.[24] Eliot's interest in, and the influence of Indian religions on him, is well documented.[25] Kearns suggests that he saw Indic and Christian ideas as complementary:

> The life of a soul does not consist in the contemplation of one consistent world but in the painful task of unifying [. . .] incompatible ones, and passing, when possible, from one or more discordant viewpoints to a higher which shall somehow include and transmute them.[26]

One last parallel, between a passage from *Murder in the Cathedral* and a poem by the contemporary Zen poet:[27]

> I have lain on the floor of the sea and breathed with the breathing of the sea-anemone, swallowed with ingurgitation of the sponge. I have lain in the soil and criticized the worm. In the air flirted with the passage of the kite. I have plunged with the kite and cowered with the wren. I have felt the horn of the beetle, the scale of the viper, the mobile hard insensitive skin of the elephant, the evasive flank of the fish.
>
> T. S. Eliot

I am the mayfly metamorphosing on the surface of the river,
and I am the bird which, when spring comes, arrives in time to eat the
  mayfly
I am a frog swimming happily in the clear water of a pond,
and I am the grass-snake who, approaching in silence, feeds itself
  on the frog . . .
My joy is like spring, so warm it makes flowers bloom in all walks
  of life
My pain is like a river of tears, so full it fills all four oceans.

Thich Nhat Hanh

Jonathan Harvey, Professor of Music at the University of Sussex, is a Christian composer who has worked a good deal with the choir and staff of Winchester Cathedral in the performance of some of his dramatic choral works. In the second annual Hussey Lecture on the relationship of the arts to Christianity (particularly music in his case), he made reference to the writings on art and religion of the English Buddhist and head of the Western Buddhist Order, the Venerable Sangharakshita.[28] Jonathan Harvey perceives himself as 'pushing my Christianity out, like a boat towards the East'. Like others working on these frontiers he recognizes the danger of the enterprise. 'Art and religion . . . are both dangerous, they push us out into the boundless . . . Religion, like art, is dangerous and iconoclastic. Art, like religion, is dangerous and iconoclastic.'

It seems to me wholly appropriate to end without a systematic conclusion. I have tried to suggest some links, between the artist as theologian and the theologian (or person of faith) as artist. In his chapter 'We are grateful to Art', Cupitt expresses the point, in a somewhat individualistic perspective: 'We keep restarting. The establishment of a settled tradition is impossible . . . everyone feels charged with the task of working out her own path through life, view of life and task in life.'[29] Sangharakshita's version has a warmer ring, despite the dominant masculine pronoun:

> The man who bears on his soul, as it were, the stamp of egolessness, whether derived from Religion through the will, or from Art by means of the imagination, will tend to act egolessly in all the relations of life. Such a one will be a good man in the noblest sense of the term, sensitive to the sufferings of others, sharing their sorrows and their joys, ready to help in time of need, not moved by 'greed or hate or fear', and ever seeking to share with his fellow men the joy of the Beauty which he has known.[30]

6 THEOLOGY AND SEXUALITY

Beyond God the Father:
an Introduction to Mary Daly's View of Christian Tradition

Ann Loades

In discussing Mary Daly I have first to encounter a 'Daly'-type view of myself. I am the product, at any rate from university level onwards, of a patriarchal culture, though I do not think that I have ever encountered a 'gangrenous patriarch'; and I am what Mary Daly would, I think, call a pseudo-feminist, promoted by patriarchs. For she writes that 'The real rebels/renegades have been driven away from positions of patriarchally defined power, replaced by reformist and roboticized tokens' (*Gyn/Ecology*, p. xv). The book here quoted was written in 1978 as a requiem for the 'earlier' women's movement, male-designed, male-orchestrated, male-legitimated, male assimilated (p. xvi). It is also her call to those whom she says have been unwittingly tokenized, to 'tear off their mindbindings and join in the Journey', a kind of alarm-clock for those former Journeyers who have merged with what she carefully indicates as 'the human (men's) community', but who can still feel nostalgia for the present/ future of their own being. The woman of whom Mary Daly might approve would be clearer than I am about what 'tokenism' represents and what can or may be achieved by it, and would no doubt respect herself differently, bond with her 'sisters' rather than with her 'sisters *and* her brothers', refuse to sell her freedom, her original birthright, for a mess of respectability.

As a pseudo-feminist in her terms, then, I make the suggestion to begin with that we should try to appreciate why the writer of the 1968 *The Church and the Second Sex* is now so profoundly at odds with those women theologians who have stayed within the Christian tradition in its Roman Catholic form – Elisabeth Schüssler Fiorenza, Rosemary Radford Ruether, Kari-Elisabeth Børresen, for instance – precisely the communion with which they have their argument, but which has nourished them as it originally nourished Mary Daly. It is important to recognize that although many Protestant women have contributed to the discussion of the relationship between Christianity and feminism (focusing not surprisingly on the use of the Bible, the issue of ministry and doctrines of God), it is the North American Roman Catholic tradition which has produced the most prolific and distinguished women theologians, including Mary Daly, the most formidable and uncompromising critic of them all. Her argument with her tradition, begun in *The Church and the Second Sex*, precipitated her out of it in the course of writing *Beyond God the Father* of 1973, now reissued with an original reintroduction, and published in the UK by The Women's Press. It is, I think, because she is so acute at hitting the nail on the head – her polemic is so lively, her ability to communicate and stimulate people to think is so powerful – that her work is widely appreciated. *Beyond God the Father* (1973), *Gyn Ecology* (1978) and *Pure Lust* (1984) will be the only books on a feminism sprung from the Christian tradition which will be read by many women. Mary Daly's work will shape the perceptions of that tradition in a way little else will do, and sharpen and deepen the divide between those who still hope to find resources from within Christianity as sufficient reason for staying within it, and those who have discovered, or simply assume, that no such resources are there to be found.

Anthropologist Gwen Kennedy Neville[1] has written about the religious socialization of women in US subcultures, at the verbal, rational, public level and at the invisible, behavioural and private level. In particular, of the kinds of religious cultures to be found in the USA, cultures torn from their European environments and reinstated there, she commented on 'Mediterranean culture' as characterized by a highly ordered and hierarchical universe, with an institution run entirely by male prelates, stressing honour of family and lineage, reverence for motherhood, idealization of women, association with buildings designed to keep arrows out and women in. And Beverly Wildung Harrison has noted that the Roman Catholic Church is one in which orders and ordination are still principally understood in terms of public sacramental mediation:

> In these churches, the patterns of sexism are legitimated at a symbolic level so potent that women struggling in them need to be forearmed with a special understanding of the emotional load their demands for change carry, where *patriarchy* and the *public* mediation of grace are deeply intertwined, there are very special problems.[2]

I have read, too, Marjorie Reiley Maguire's recent article on 'Catholic women and the theological enclave,'[3] in which she describes how renewed interest in theology after Vatican II led to women seeking entry to seminaries as laypersons, women who became candidates for teaching posts as peers of those who had equipped them to do so. They brought questions to these seed-beds, about liturgy, about the value of affective knowledge, about the recognition of ministry for women other than that of the religious education of women and children, about their exclusion from 'spiritual formation activities'. This problem has not yet been faced by the Roman Catholic Church in this country, where open access to non-denominational institutions of tertiary education with their departments of religious studies and theology has mitigated some of the problems. It is worth noticing paragraph 22 of *Ministry and Mission: Proposals for a National Policy for Lifelong Priestly Formation*[4] produced in autumn 1987 for the Bishops' Conference of England and Wales, which acknowledged the fact that a significant proportion of full-time layministers are women, reflecting the way in which the place of women in society and Church has changed, though women are still expected to play a limited role. The writer (a Roman Catholic layman and philosopher) continued:

> This is very much to be regretted and attitudes and practices need to change further so that they can contribute fully to the mission of the Church. Women must be welcomed into the work of priestly formation. They have gifts, skills and knowledge to share and their participation is essential if future priests are to develop in human maturity and avoid insensitive assumptions of male dominance.

The earlier North American versions of these points helped to precipitate the kind of situation addressed by Marjorie Reiley Maguire. The North American Roman Catholic Church has to cope not only with its laywomen, but with its formidably well educated and articulate women 'religious' all irretrievably 'lay' by virtue of their sex. Irene Woodward (a very distinguished member of the Sisters of the Holy Names of Jesus and Mary) wrote in 1986[5] of these women growing up in a Church situated in a society trying to live the American dream, a pragmatic society which told them that anything was possible; that there were always new frontiers to conquer in a society which valued free enterprise and the expression of personal opinion; and that they had a right to participate in democratic processes and determine the direction of the policies under which they lived. Membership of the Roman Catholic Church is voluntary but, once committed to it, women have a strong and active identification with it, with its marked ethnic and socio-economic character in different locations. Ten years *prior* to Vatican II, there had been a massive development in the professional education of 'religious' and as early as 1943 the first graduate programme in Roman Catholic theology for women had opened at St Mary's College, Notre Dame. By contrast, women were admitted to Harvard Divinity School only in 1955, and by 1973 only seventy-nine women had degrees, Letty Russell being one of the first three to graduate in 1958 and be ordained by the United Presbyterian Church.

By the date of Mary Daly's *Commonweal* article of 15 January 1965, 'The Forgotten Sex: a Built-in Bias', which led to the invitation to write *The Church and the Second Sex*, some 67 per cent of women religious had at least one university-level degree and 28 per cent had master's degrees. They had become one of the best-educated groups of women in the country, well equipped to assess the documents of Vatican II. There are many points which could be made about the references to women in these (Abbott Edition) documents, but we could notice especially, perhaps, the sentence added during the final drafting to paragraph 9 of the document on the laity, in the section on 'the various fields of the apostolate', pointing out the importance of women's participation in the various fields of the Church's apostolate. Readers are no doubt meant to be reassured by the footnote which draws attention to the point that this is one of the few places in all the Council documents where special attention is given to the contribution of women to the mission of the Church. The note adds that by the time the Council ended, twelve lay and ten 'religious' women were present as 'auditrices', though not, of course, that no woman was permitted to read a paper to the Council (presumably in accordance with the injunction of I Timothy 2:12) and that an attempt was made to bar women journalists from attending Council masses during its meetings.[6] And real exasperation was provoked by the closing messages of the Council, messages to men (males) regarded in terms of their diversified contributions to society, with women having a message addressed to them alone, and as is usual in Christianity, with reference to their sexual states. Women are addressed as girls, wives, mothers and widows, consecrated virgins and women living alone, though with the acknowledgement that they constitute half of the immense human family, and with the (not wholly unjustifiable) claim that the Church has 'glorified and liberated' them. Women are associated with 'the protection of the home', with cradles and deaths (cf. the nativity and crucifixion stories); mothers are exhorted to 'pass on to your sons and daughters the traditions of your fathers' (mothers presumably not having any). Women are invited to reconcile men with life, to guard purity (of course), unselfishness and piety, to aid men to retain courage in *their* great undertakings, with women's own concerns to be particularly with the peace of the world. They are clearly excluded from the address to 'workers' – 'very loved sons' (as though women did not and do not work, including producing 50 per cent of the so-called Third World's food).

The post-Vatican II renewal of religious orders was not of course without its problems. There was an 'exodus' from religious orders between 1966 and 1983, during which women's orders in the USA lost 33 per cent of their members, though still leaving 120,699 of them! But they gained other strengths by responding in 1961 to the call by a papal representative visiting the University of Notre Dame, a call to religious communities to contribute 10 per cent of their membership to work in Latin America. If feminism in the nineteenth century was forged and sharpened in the anti-slavery campaigns and the fight for the vote, the second half of the twentieth century has seen women involved in the search for justice in poor communities, honing the edge of their commitment, and this has helped, importantly, to overcome any residual antagonism between the sisters and other laywomen. Irene Woodward writes that the sisters, removed from family tensions, with opportunities for leadership and self-development, saw for themselves the abuse, helplessness and meaninglessness of many women's lives. They found that all alike wanted realization of Gospel values for themselves, inside structures which formally legitimated the religious orders, but which were now deemed to be debilitating to men and women alike. And no one could ignore the problem raised for the ecclesiastical institution by women too disaffected to transmit their faith within their families.

Readers of Mary Daly will be alert to her political criticism – the unholy trinity of rape, genocide and war run by godfather Reagan, Pentagon and company. The connections she draws between politics and patriarchy given religious legitimacy, indicate major reasons why reform, for her, could not be an option for long. And Rosemary Radford Ruether's *Women-Church* (1985) exhibits strong political criticism too, focused in her case on the conflict between 'base-Christian communities' and the Nicaraguan Roman Catholic hierarchy, and given government realization that North American Roman Catholics are now seen as a dangerous potential counter-force to American intervention in popular revolutions in Latin America. (We could also recall the North American Bishops' critique of nuclear arms and of the conduct of the economy.) Critique of foreign policy is mediated back to the Church by members of religious orders whose boundaries are transnational.

The long traditions and experience of women's religious orders may, paradoxically, provide Mary Daly herself with the option of sisterhood and the finding of 'sacred space'. Consider, in relation to her, Jacques Pohier's *God in Fragments* (1985) on the monosexual character of ecclesiastical institutions, where he writes of the kind of attitude to women and femininity engendered by spending all one's everyday life in an all-male universe, in which all important human relationships are made with men (p. 188). Although women's religious orders are legitimated by those institutions, they provided the experiences of discovering what being female and feminine might be, though this seems to have led Mary Daly to the mirroring of male-focused dualism, that is, sisterhood which wants to escape from the male world, treated as demonic, as women have been regarded by that male world as simply 'other'. Christian dualism needs to be transcended, rather than have transcendence itself understood as 'femaleness', denying the humanity of males.[7] Women need the liberating anger of her *Gyn/Ecology* (and we might add Elaine Showalter's *The Female Malady: Women, Madness and English Culture, 1930–1980*, Virago, 1987) but could still opt for a *humanly* inclusive theology and ethic – even if men have not made that option – precisely what Mary Daly herself pleaded for in the beginning.

In her *Commonweal* article at the time of Vatican II she made points that her hearers did not or simply could not hear: that props offered by social conditions in the past – false biological and philosophical theories, anti-feminist legislation – had all melted away, as had women's 'natural' timidity and ineptitude. No one was going to deny 'difference'; the problem concerned the meaning and application of the word. There was no such thing as a static, immutable conception of feminine nature which would survive scrutiny of the actual possibilities and permutations. She wanted people freed from a priori stereotypes, with polarity between groups of human characteristics fostering egoism, getting from the 'other' what 'I' lack. By the time she came to preach in Harvard on 14 November 1971 (the first time a woman had preached at a Sunday sermon in Harvard's 336-year history, to a congregation which included women training for ministry in the Divinity School), she proclaimed her irritation with the repetition of the line from Paul quoted by would-be pacifiers of women, of which, as she rightly said, *even if* in Christ there is no male and female (that used to shut them up) everywhere else there damn well is. The quotation functions as a refusal to look at specific, oppressive facts. And given that the Christ-image is male, one has still to ask what meaning-content the passage can possibly have. And if Jesus was a feminist, 'Fine wonderful. But even if he wasn't, *I am.*' Why bother to try to get back to the purity of the original revelation, as though the past has some prior claims over present experience, as if recourse to the past is necessary to validate experience now? And it is a very big assumption to make that there *are* adequate models to be extracted from the past. Women have the option of giving priority to their own experience, without looking to the past for justification. The Harvard sermon was the occasion for her 'acted parable' of 'exodus' expressing her conviction that 'women whose consciousness has been raised are spiritual exiles whose sense of transcendence is seeking alternative expressions to those available in institutional religion'. Hence her image of the women's movement as an 'exodus' community, and her invitation to the other women present to follow her out, as they did, perhaps deliberately imitating a tradition begun by Elizabeth Cady Stanton so many years before.

In another *Commonweal* article for 1971 she had in focus the familiar mechanism by which the images and values of a given society are projected into a realm of beliefs, which in turn seem to justify the social infrastructure. The belief-system becomes hardened and objectified, seeming to have an unchangeable and independent existence and validity of its own. It resists those social changes which rob it of its plausibility. But change does occur, and ideologies die, even if they die hard. So, 'Religious symbols die when the cultural system that supported them ceases to give them plausibility. This should pose no problem to authentic faith, which accepts the relativity of all symbols, and recognizes that fixation upon any of them as absolute in itself is idolatrous.' And here, too, we detect her characteristic emphasis on existential courage, displacing prudence as the virtue recommended to women, unless it is transformed into one of those 'volcanic virtues' referred to in *Pure Lust*, where we note that a 'creative Prude not only acts within a context of given circumstances. She changes circumstances and spins new ones' (p. 272).

Her articles and *Beyond God the Father* helped to put 'patriarchy' into currency,[8] connecting the political, personal, conscious and unconscious, material and spiritual together in the worship of masculine identity, patriarchy as a unifying term indicating oppression, linking consciousness of superior values, methods of control, power struggle and physical coercion. And Eugene Bianchi (in line with Pohier) in 1976 was to identify the core dogma of our patriarchal era as 'psychic celibacy', keeping women mentally and emotionally at arm's length: 'Women can be exalted as wife, virgin, mother or deprecated (and enjoyed) as temptress, playmate, whore. In whatever way this male projection works, woman is object, non-equal, manipulated, distanced.'[9]

Mary Daly's own attack on patriarchy was to be without quarter. She and Rosemary Radford Ruether were crucial in forming the women's caucus within the American Academy of Religion, at which both delivered important papers in 1971. Rosemary Radford Ruether's was to appear as 'Misogynism and Virginal Feminism in the Fathers of the Church' (available in *Religion and Sexism*, 1974). Mary Daly's much-reprinted article was called 'Theology after the demise of God the Father; a call for the castration of sexist religion', a title hardly likely to secure the ready sympathy of ecclesiastical power-brokers, unless she really thought by that time that all hope for changing social structures was to be vested in new sisterhoods. But she wrote of castrating language and images, in the sense of 'cutting away the phallus-centred value system imposed by patriarchy', asserting, too, that the value system that has been thrust upon women has amounted to 'a kind of gang-rape of minds and bodies'.

It is a form of relation to the label of 'castrating female' to retort that it is *women* who have been deprived of power, potency, creativity, ability to communicate and that sexist religion has also done damage to black males, poor males, non-competitive males, Third-World males, all of whom however could still look down on women. An alternative to castration seems to be a kind of exorcism to be performed by women, to dislodge the images which reflect and reinforce prevailing social arrangements. If women can dislodge themselves from the role of the 'other', and dislodge the problem of evil from its peculiar association with women, they can also dislodge the need for a male saviour. Inviting men to lay claim to their own complete identity has nothing to do with easy reconciliation, with cheap grace, but takes the form of a very positive refusal of co-optation.

Beyond God the Father develops this material particularly in its closing pages, in which she works on an idea taken from Virginia Woolf's *A Room of One's Own*, first written for university women in 1929. Virginia Woolf at one point asks why men are so angry with feminist women, and she came up with the answer that they were protesting against some infringement of their power to believe in themselves. She decided that women had served all these centuries as looking-glasses capable of reflecting the figure of man at twice its natural size. She asked: 'How is he to go on giving judgement, civilizing natives, making laws, writing books, dressing up and speechifying at banquets, unless he can see himself at breakfast and dinner at least twice the size he really is?' Mary Daly offers women the challenge to *become*, rather than *reflect*, moving in the current of the Verb, 'the creative drawing power of the Good who is self-communicating Be-ing, Who is the Verb for whom, in whom and with whom all true movements move'. The result of being without their mirrors will be profoundly disorientating for men, finding only within *themselves* the Eternal Woman, the Perfect Parakeet, and being forced to look at women as real things 'out there'.

Unfortunately, nothing happens as fast as one wants it to happen, and the Looking Glass Society survives, bent on killing itself off: 'It is still ruled by God the Father who, gazing at his magnified reflections, believes in his superior size. I say "believes", because the reflection now occasionally seems to be diminished and so he has to make a renewed act of faith in himself.'

Other clear attacks on Christianity's core-symbolism can be found

in her subsequent books. For instance, in *Gyn/Ecology* she writes of
the Trinity, excluding female mythic presence from the divine being,
denying female reality in the cosmos, the original love story performed by the Supreme All Male Cast, 'sublime' (and therefore disguised) erotic male homosexual *mythos*, 'the mold for all varieties of
male monogender mating'. And to 'the timid objections voiced by
Christian women, the classic answer has been: "You're included
under the Holy Spirit. He's feminine." ' As she comments: 'The
point is, of course, that male made-up femininity has nothing to do
with women. Drag queens, whether divine or human, belong to the
Men's Association' (p. 38). Not the least of the problems is that we
can hardly do justice to the feminine in ourselves, let alone in the
divine, because we can hardly know what it is to be female and
feminine in patriarchal society. And on Paul's proposal about our
adoption as sons (Galatians 4:3f.) she properly says in *Pure Lust*:
'We do not wish to be redeemed by a god, to be adopted as sons,
or to have the spirit of a god's son artificially injected into our hearts,
crying "father" '. And if the symbolism associated with 'Mary' in
Christian tradition is deemed to be 'core' symbolism, then her critique of what has been done with the symbolism also repays detailed
attention. She comes to think that there are no possible resources
in biblically-based religion to aid the journey to find out where we
should go. For tucked away in a footnote of *Beyond God the Father*
(p. 205) is her assessment of Phyllis Tribble's paper in the Journal
of the American Academy of Religion in 1973, on 'Depatriarchalizing
in Biblical Tradition', on which Mary Daly comments: 'It might be
interesting to speculate upon the probable length of a "depatriar-
chalized Bible". Perhaps there would be enough salvageable material
to comprise an interesting pamphlet.'

The first edition of *Beyond God the Father* was prepared to make
some play with 'androgyny', but even there she insisted that this
was not to do with settling for footing within patriarchal space.
Rather, it is 'something like God speaking forth God-self in the new
identity of women' (p. 41) offering a security that can absorb the
new risks of living without the securities offered by patriarchy in
return for docility. But with the 'Original Reintroduction', and after
the writing of *Gyn/Ecology*, androgyny is rejected as a confusing term
which she had used in attempting to describe integrity of be-ing.
The problem is that those who flourish in the enjoyment of both
masculine and feminine qualities may indeed by healthier, but social
structures for the time being remain the same. And the term androgyny could be said to indicate only a pseudo-wholeness combining
distorted gender-descriptions – so it is another utopian symbol leading to a dead-end. She has little sympathy, then, with those whose
'journey' was and is within 'patriarchal' culture and religion.

We may think some parts of her picture overdone. For instance, just how would one substantiate the claim that violence against women is the source and paradigm of *all* other manifestations of violence? And are women simply to be indifferent to the fact that men, too, can be afflicted with poverty of spirit, imagination, intellect, passion, and physical vigour? No one, male or female, who suffers in these ways has anything to lose by somehow, even in desperation, finding the energy for change. Some of her phrases still catch a prevailing cultural mood – 'the perpetual soap-operas of the sado-state' – but in their own way these phrases represent the linguistic impoverishment from which we may all suffer. Words may have the living, transformative power to help alter our consciousness and behaviour, but much of her own language is banal and does not serve to enthuse us to research for other possibilities. And it is especially in those North American women's communities which have stayed in connection with their tradition that one can find resources for transformation with the search already well ahead for new symbols, stories, rituals and liturgies which can be developed only with sympathy, immense patience, and over time.

Yet her work is indispensable reading none the less for those who want to begin to feel and so to think about the contribution Christian institutions and their theology have made to the distress that fuels the feminist agenda, assuming that we all stand to gain by attending to that distress. In *Pure Lust* Mary Daly turns her attention to the 'snools' who want the movement she represents to be dead. What we do with what we understand of her work in our own situation will be a struggle for us, but I think she is a leading example of one of those who can be charged in *sexist* terms with being *not feminine*, as Beverly Wildung Harrison put it. Such a woman will have said something she should not have said, aspired to do or have done something which she should not have done. In short, she has crossed that invisible but powerful boundary out of her territory. The charge of being 'not feminine', I submit, is aimed at thwarting initiative. Its message is: 'Go back.'[10] Ignore it, but go on thinking about a recent comment of Martin E. Marty's:

'Ought' and 'is' represent somewhat different worlds. 'Is' does not seem to be an area of pure disaster except to the most impatient women, and 'ought' does seem to be an area of promise for all but the most obtuse and intransigent of men.[11]

Off to See the Wizard

Richard MacKenna

It's very hard to know what to do about this minority group in our society. Luckily, they tend to keep fairly quiet about their problem, and perhaps they are grateful for the measure of acceptance that they now receive. They make up about 10 per cent of the population. No one is quite sure why they are the way they are; it is only recently that their condition has been able to be studied with a measure of objectivity. Previously it was regarded with shame and embarrassment – a terrible stigma to be concealed at all costs, and which eminent minds puzzled themselves how to cure: shock treatment, aversion therapy, punishment, condemnation. The famous criminologist Lombroso called it 'a stigma of degeneracy', and found the gaols full of it. Religion thought it evil. Is it genetic? Caused by environment? No one knows.

If 10 per cent of society do things differently from the other 90 per cent, their behaviour might well be labelled as deviant – at any rate statistically. And what are we to make of the statistics which say that such people are more likely to become alcoholics or chronic misfits? Of course the other side of their condition is that it has been known to produce wonderfully creative people like Leonardo da Vinci. But perhaps we tend to stick with the definition created in our minds by the one, rude word with which we describe such people: sinister.

Of course, the left-handed are not the only deviant group in our society, but it is interesting to speculate at what point in our history the ethical 'charge' was given to their condition – in other words, when they stopped being considered as merely different, and came to be seen as wicked. On the whole, except in primitive and ignorant communities, we have progressed to being able to think about left-handedness in terms of someone else's experience of life, rather than as something bad which is done by other people. But the left-handed still have to live in a society where it is assumed by manufacturers, designers and the bulk of society that it is normal to be right-handed, and everything must be designed and done accordingly. Small wonder that a high proportion of left-handers tend to have stammers or to have early learning problems. They are different, and everything around them tells them so.

Another deviant group, also troubled with ethical labels, is the gay community. Like the left-handed, it is only recently that the experts have come to see them less as a problem to be solved, and more as a sub-group, which expresses the healthy human emotions of love and sexuality in a different way to the main group. This is statistically interesting, but has no ethical 'charge'. Unfortunately, it isn't quite as simple as that, because the ethical clout doesn't rest with psychologists or statisticians; it is still, somewhat awkwardly, clung on to by the Church . . . and the Church . . .

Well, where *does* the Church stand about ethics? In moments of stress it tends to mutter somewhat grumpily about the Bible, and sticking to biblical morality, but somehow one gets the feeling that this has never been thought through. The Church also talks in a rather self-pitying way about being trapped in the Babylonian captivity of the suburbs; meaning, roughly, that its power base is very firmly with the 'haves', and that it hankers nostalgically after the 'have-nots'. The quandary here is that the ethical system which it pushes is very firmly that of the suburbs, and seems almost directly aimed at keeping down the have-nots. And what is this 'biblical morality'? Is it to feel admiration for the concept of invading another people's country and driving them out by war and trickery? To maintain your grip on the land by genocide and racism? Is it to accept and condone the use of slavery? To say that it is morally preferable not to marry? That it is wrong for women to open their mouths in church, to wear scarlet, or to uncover their heads? Not to eat pork sausages? To stone adulterers?

But rather than getting involved in circuitous arguments, there is another way for the have-nots to react to those who think they are in the ethical driving seat. The Jews reacted in the same way in Egypt. They were a deviant group, forced into slavery by the 'haves'. They were ordered to make bricks without using straw – an early equivalent of the church spokesmen who say that it is all right for people to be gay, as long as they don't do anything about it. The answer the Jews found wasn't to hang around and argue, but to pack up their bags and go. It is amazing how difficult it can be to carry on building ethical pyramids when you discover that all your obedient little slaves have vanished.

I watched a memorial service held by some liberated slaves. It was a procession through the streets of New York. The people were mostly dressed in white, and they were there to mourn friends, lovers, spouses, parents, children, who had died from AIDS. Many of them carried helium-filled balloons, on which they had written the name of the person they mourned. Finally, they all gathered in an open space and began to sing a hymn. As they sang, they began to let the balloons go, and as the balloons rose into the sky, the people called after them 'I love you Dad', or 'Son', or whatever the loved one's name might be. As an expression of human grief and pain, it was almost unbearable to watch.

But what sort of hymn did they sing? It had nothing to do with religion, false gods or man's exercise of power and authority over others. It was the cry of anyone confronted by the pain of life; the voice of captive humanity that longs for things to be better; Judy Garland's singing of: 'Over the Rainbow.' The pain of watching this rite of longing and letting go was such that part of me almost wanted to laugh at the childish song – anything to distance myself from this experience. But the words caught at me: pleading for a place where there is no more trouble and where the dreams we dare to dream can come true; longing to be able to fly away and to leave behind all pain and unhappiness.

Perhaps Freud would say that that is the ultimate religious expression, but what struck me most forcibly, as a professional 'religious', was the secularity of the hymn. Having freed themselves from Egypt, how can the once enslaved carry on singing the songs of Pharaoh? Freed from malevolent control, why should you willingly give yourself back into slavery?

When next *The Wizard of Oz* was shown on TV, I watched it with interest. Somehow the sweet little children's film had been transformed for me. Having heard its main song being used almost as an anthem by people who have had to reject most organized religion in order to hang on to their sense of dignity and value as human beings, suddenly the whole film seemed to talk of the mischief and danger of religion. Of course, in the end, it's just a film – but it is a film with some very helpful images on which to hang a deep sense of unease.

The heroine is Dorothy, a young girl, but of course it is also the eighteen-year-old Judy Garland, with capped teeth, breasts strapped down, and awash with pills: pills to make her eat less, pills to put her to sleep, pills to wake her up, pep pills. 'I hate the wake-up pills the worst,' Garland told a friend, 'because they make me hop around like a Mexican Jumping Bean.' Garland's entire image and behaviour had to be moulded to the approval of a man, Louis B. Mayer. The character she plays is in thrall to a world of adults who seem to have neither the time nor the will to listen to her fears or to what is going on in her life. Which brings us to another deviant group – women; not statistically deviant, but potentially deviant from a culture whose systems and concepts of authority are moulded by men. It is still male expectations which govern how women should look and how they should behave – a petty example, but if you go to an Open University summer school, it is surprising how many women will tell you that their decision to 'better' themselves has led to conflict in the marriage and, quite often, divorce; their husbands couldn't cope when willing Cinderellas suddenly wanted to emerge from the kitchen and go to the ball. The Church, kept alive by faithful women who form the vast majority of churchgoers in every denomination, is governed and dedicated to the glory of man, or, at least, a male god.

So faithful women come to church and faithfully recite how 'for us *men* . . .', and are filled with male images of warfare, authority, power. We forget that God, according to Genesis, created humanity in his/her own image, 'male and female he created them'. The Old Testament, written in a deeply patriarchal culture, is still full of images of God as female: nursing mother, midwife, pelican, she-bear, mother-eagle, mother hen, female home-maker. The very word for Spirit is female, and so is Wisdom. Imagine how short the New Testament would be if Mary had said No instead of Yes. In the three central acts of the gospels, Christ's role is passive; he is born, he is crucified, he is raised.

Dorothy, snatched from home by a tornado and dumped in a strange land, stands for all women's aspirations to be taken seriously in their own right, not as adjuncts to men. Alone in a strange country, she wants to find her way to where she belongs.

But Dorothy isn't alone for long. On her way, she meets a scare-crow, a tin-man, and a lion. They too have problems. The scarecrow has no brain; in other words, like many of us, he finds it hard to understand or make sense of the world in which he finds himself. What is right thinking? And how do you work out what is really true, what really matters? The tin-man has no heart, again a common problem. Our society has to work out what caring means in practical terms, and whether we want to care at all. In our own lives there is a desperate need to feel loved and wanted, which all the pay rises and new cars in the world cannot fill. Or there is the risk of a generation of tin-men who are proud not have hearts, and, having kidded themselves, will try to kid us too that human values aren't important, what matters is success, achievement, rank, power, money, belonging, status.

The last to join the pilgrimage is a lion. His problem is that although he looks and sounds like a lion, and tries to behave as is expected of him, inside he is afraid. And how many of us feel stuck in some kind of role or image, at work, at home, with friends, with strangers, which it can become an almost intolerable burden to maintain? Or the pressure of cultural roles and stereotypes; police-men mustn't cry or show emotion, even when they are digging up a child's body; men must be strong and provide for their families, but what happens when they lose their jobs and their wives become the wage-earners? They get embarrassed when I cry in church, so now I tell the vicar that I've found peace after my husband's death, and I sit alone and smile at people, but I take my pain back home with me . . .

So now there are four of them, in search of a heart, a brain, a home and courage – quite a religious quest. They are told that the only person who can help them is the mighty Wizard of Oz, but when eventually they reach him, he doesn't seem very interested in their problems – or rather, he says that he will be interested, provided they join his cause and do what he wants them to do; he is too busy worrying about wicked witches to have time for them. No, they must do as he wants, and if they are successful in that, then he may help them. Dorothy and friends must kill the wicked witch.

The wizard lives in a stupendous temple, full of lights and smoke and terrifying noises. He is surrounded by childlike people who seem quite happy under his benevolent despotism. The witch lives in a gloomy castle, surrounded by slaves. Magic, it seems, can produce childlike euphoria or embittered slavery, but isn't very good at dealing with human problems. Nor is the wizard. He refuses to help the successful Dorothy and party, and tries to frighten them out of his temple. It is Toto the little dog who suddenly pulls aside a curtain to reveal a little old man, desperately pulling levers, pushing buttons and shouting into microphones – the wizard is a fake.

But strangely enough, it is only when the wizard is forced to explain that he is no magician, but is just another lost human being who felt constrained by people's expectations to become a mighty wizard, that things start to go right. He tells them his story, and listens to their stories, and it is in the listening and the telling that the answers seem to lie. The wizard is just as much a victim as a villain. He sees that it was in the journeying together that healing lay, as the pilgrims learned to trust one another, to bear one another's burdens, to accept one another's weaknesses, to care for each other. Supernatural figures may have provided the initial impetus for the journey, but in the end they were irrelevant; all they had to offer was fear and domination, manipulation and exploitation, and in the end, one was a charlatan, and one dissolved away with a little cold water. What was real, what mattered, was the journey.

There is an almost intolerable demand made on many clergy to be the wizard. Some people use religion to stay as happy little Munchkins, sheltered from nasty witches by kind wizards. Or else the clergy must be seen to be bigger and better than anyone else. A sub-Christian moralism that sees the world as fallen and dangerous and demands perfection in its followers, demands even more perfection in its leaders. Or perhaps the clergy put pressure on themselves. It can be very galling to work for an organization which is regarded with total lack of interest by the vast majority of the population. So when the people come to the wizard for help, it can be a wonderful opportunity to get your own back. Recently, a group of young clergy was discussing funerals. I'd better not tell you which diocese – although, on the other hand, perhaps I should, so that you could make sure never under any circumstances to allow a young wizard from there anywhere near any funeral you may be involved with. Anyway, one bright spark said that he found funerals a wonderful time to 'be hard on them'. For once these annoying people were in his power, and so he took his chance to lay down the rules of his organization. The dead person wasn't a member, so the wizard can take no responsibility for their current safety. Unless the mourners join the wizard's gang, it is likely that they will face the same punishment as their loved one. This is called 'putting the fear of God into them' or, possibly, 'kicking them while they're down'.

The frightening thing about this story is that the other young clergy didn't shout down this pocket-Hitler, but decided that frightening the bereaved was an absolutely wizard idea. All of this, hopefully, is for the best of motives, but such vicious behaviour directed against those least able to defend themselves is powered and motivated by the pique of a wizard whom nobody wants any longer. It isn't Christianity, but spite.

And if that is the sort of god they represent, perhaps it is just as well that no one except Munchkins and slaves wants him any longer. If there were a General Election next week, and the Prime Minister were returned to power, suppose for a moment that instead of saying, 'I have been elected to serve the whole country, not just the people who voted for me and I accept that those who voted for other parties did so after careful thought, even though I happen to disagree with them', suppose the Prime Minister said, 'This election was the last chance for everyone. Those who voted for me are going to have an absolutely fabulous time. Those who voted against me, or who couldn't be bothered to vote at all, will either be sent to prison for the rest of their lives, or else will be executed.' So the day after the election results, mass executions begin. What might we say about such a person? And yet some of us seem able to carry on worshipping just such a god. If we haven't joined their party by the time we die, they're really going to take it out on us. The wizard isn't just wicked – he's a spoiled brat.

But then there are those who fight against being turned into wizards and witches; who refuse to divide life into sacred and secular, Us and Them. And perhaps they take encouragement from the

Gospel stories which show us that the main criterion for being a disciple was to keep getting things wrong. Not a day goes by without the disciples misunderstanding Jesus, lacking faith, wanting status instead of service. In the end they betray him and run away. After the resurrection Peter wanders back to being a fisherman again, and when confronted by the risen Christ is unable to say anything except that he quite likes him. Would any of them have got through a Church selection conference? But they were human – they weren't hiding behind curtains pretending to be powerful and perfect. It was the squeaky-clean people, those who led good devout upright blameless lives, who plotted and committed murder.

If all this sounds far-fetched, I think it is actually about a conflict that is threatening the heart of our religion at the moment. It is a conflict about whether, like the Boers, Christians withdraw into their kraals where they can feel the safety and assurance of being with the like-minded, and to where people may come to them when in need, provided they are willing to treat them like the wizard; or whether Christians can bear to live with the uncertainty and diffi- culty of shedding the robes of power and trying to live out their human journeys among other humans, following the path of love set by their powerless master. 'If only there were evil people some- where', says Solzhenitsyn, 'insidiously committing evil deeds, and it were necessary only to separate them from the rest of us and destroy them. But the line dividing good and evil runs through the heart of every human being.' Those who go off to see the wizard will see very clear dividing lines; those who have grown out of the need for wizards will see all the ambiguity and complexity of our human venture, and the desperate need not to throw up more distinctions and divisions between people, but to break down the barriers as Christ did.

At the end of the movie, Dorothy has to say goodbye to her companions; she is to return home and face the problems that await her there. But she is no longer a passive victim; she has learned to accept that she is worthy of love. All of the pilgrims are stronger; they haven't just come to terms with themselves, but they have also learned to like and value themselves for what they are. And their care extends to others – they have even learned to feel sorry for the wizard.

People tweak the Church's curtain to expose the all-too-frail wiz- ards hiding behind it, and shout: 'It's a fraud.' But perhaps the Church can itself step out from behind the magic curtain and go out of the temple and join the people in the streets. Outside the temple we can see what God has made, and perhaps we can dare to look both at the world and at ourselves and see that it is good. Religious concern isn't about something over the rainbow; it is about the here and now. And it is in the here and now that we have to ask whether the religion we stand for works like a wizard or an Egyptian, keeping people enslaved by the force of tradition and prejudice, or whether it is a force that can break down barriers and set the broken victims free. Because our path is through the desert to the land of God's promise beyond – not a yellow brick road.

7 Theology and Science

The Interaction of Science and Theology

John Polkinghorne

The subject of this paper is one of particular significance for me, since I am now a priest and I was for twenty-five years a theoretical physicist. I have to face the problem of how these twin worlds of my personal experience relate to each other. Various unsatisfactory answers have been propounded:

Theology swallows science. The authority of God is invoked to override purely human inquiry. We see such an attitude being taken today, in perplexing power, through the creationist movement so active in the United States. I cannot subscribe to an obscurantist rejection of the impressive story that science has to tell about the universe and its history. Nor can I believe that those who with rational integrity seek to unravel the pattern and structure of the physical world are being woefully misled. My belief in that world as God's creation is an endorsement of the validity of scientific investigation into its character.

Science swallows theology. The claims of scientism, that science alone provides true knowledge and that it answers all questions that it is sensible to ask, seem to me to be manifestly false. There are questions – such as whether there is a purpose at work in the world's process, and whether there is a fulfilment and a destiny beyond death – which are meaningful to ask but which go beyond the power of science to answer. It is necessary for us, all the same, to do all that we can to seek for answers. There are forms of knowledge – for example, that love is better than hate and that truth is better than a lie – to which we have access as surely as we do to the evidence of our senses. Science by its very self-limiting nature is unable to address these issues. If we relied upon its insights alone, our lives would be stunted and sub-human. In particular, we have to take account of the claim, widespread in time and space, of human experience of an Other, standing over against us in mercy and judgement. The 'history of holiness', witnessed to in every generation by men and women of transparent integrity and clear vision and, for me as a Christian, focused in the person of Jesus Christ, is something which I just have to take with the utmost seriousness in forming my view of the way that things are. It is the indispensable role of theology to investigate these matters.

Science and theology co-exist in insulated separation. This is, perhaps, the most widespread of the mistaken views held about their mutual relationship. It has a certain specious plausibility. Science is concerned with matter, with asking the mechanistic question 'How?'; theology is concerned with spirit, with asking the teleological question 'Why?' Each, therefore, has its own domain, its own language (indeed, its own language game, in the Wittgensteinian sense). So the story goes, and it leads to a *modus vivendi* in which science is allocated its role in a public domain of fact, while theology is relegated to a private domain of opinion. ('True for me' is the best that it can aspire to.) Lesslie Newbigin had eloquently warned us of the dangers of such a compromise.[1] The true God is not a private existentially meaningful symbol; he is the Lord of all that is – the God of science as well as the God of the soul. Such a compartmentalized view of the relation between science and theology would be false to history. The two disciplines have always interacted. One has only to think of the changes in the tone of theological discourse brought about by Darwinism and by the discoveries of physical cosmology to get the point. Necessarily science and theology impinge upon each other because, inescapably, they meet in us. We are both evolved physical systems with a continuous history stretching back over thousands of millions of years, and also, if Christianity is true, men and women for whom Christ died. Science and theology just cannot be treated in isolation from each other.

What then is the true nature of their relationship? I think that the answer is to be found in that area of intellectual activity traditionally called natural theology. I see natural theology as the completion of the task, instinctive to the scientist, of seeking the deepest possible explanation of what is going on, the most comprehensive available account of the one world of our experience. In that search for an understanding through and through, the insights of science are to be taken with the utmost seriousness. In its own terms, it is very successful. Scientific questions demand scientific answers, and they seem to get them. Yet that success is purchased by the modesty of the inquiry. Science limits itself to a certain general, impersonal, testable sort of knowledge. Within the realm of that kind of experience, I am sure that it needs no augmentation from theology. The one god who is well and truly dead is the God of the Gaps, appealed to as the 'explanation' of the currently scientifically inexplicable, and so always liable to evaporate with the advance of scientific knowledge. We have learnt not to make rash claims, such as 'Scien-

tists will never understand how life arose from inanimate matter –
only the direct intervention of God could achieve that'. At present
we do not actually have a good account of that remarkable development of terrestrial life, but there is no reason to think that the
scientifically posable question of how it came about will not, one
day, receive a scientifically statable answer. In that sense, science *is*
complete, but in another it is woefully incomplete.

First, it describes a beautiful, clear world, rather like a lunar landscape. It can speak of metastable replicating systems, but there are
no people in the world that science portrays. To talk of them we
must move from the general, impersonal, testable inquiry of science
to the realm of particular, personal, trusting encounter. No account
of the way things are which can describe a Rembrandt self-portrait
only as a collection of specks of paint of known chemical composition, is in the least adequate to the richness of reality.

Second – and this is the point I most want to emphasize – there are
questions which arise from science and which insistently demand an
answer, but which by their very character transcend that of which
science itself is competent to speak. There is a widespread feeling
among practising scientists, particularly those of us who have
worked in fundamental physics, that there is more to the physical
world than has met the scientific eye. As a result of that feeling, we
are living at a time when there is a revival of natural theology
taking place, largely at the hands of the scientists rather than the
theologians.[2] Thus, someone like Paul Davies, who is rather hostile
to conventional religion, can nevertheless write: 'It may seem bizarre
to say so, but I believe that science offers a surer path to God than
religion.'[3] In fact, I think that remark is rather bizarre, a fact that
Davies himself might be able to recognize if he showed signs of a
greater acquaintance with what religion has to say. There is a long-
standing tradition of natural theology which would find no surprise
at science's offering a path to God. In Christianity, this view has
been maintained particularly in the tradition of theological thought
stemming from St Thomas Aquinas. A modern neo-thomist, Bernard
Lonergan, has written extensively of God as the great and all-suf-
ficient explanation. He says: 'God is the unrestricted act of understanding, the eternal rapture glimpsed in every Archimedean cry of
Eureka.'[4]

This new natural theology is not only a revived natural theology
but it is also *revised* in two important aspects. First, it is more modest
in its aim than the old-style natural theology of Anselm, Aquinas
and Paley. The latter spoke of the 'proofs' of God's existence. We
recognize today that we are operating in an area where a mathematical type of demonstration is not available either to the theist or to
the atheist. Instead we must speak of 'insight', of a way of looking

at the totality of things which has coherence and intelligibility. It is not the claim of the new natural theology that atheism is stupidity, but that theism offers a more satisfying explanation of what is going on.

Second, and most importantly, the appeal of the new natural theology is not to particular occurrences ('Only God could have made the complex system of the eye') but to the law and circumstance which underlie all physical occurrences. This law and circumstance is science's given, the starting point it assumes as the basis necessary for all its explanation. It is, therefore, something which science itself is powerless to explain, though it has not seemed something without need of explanation. This further understanding is a task that naturally falls to theology in its role of providing the deepest possible explanation. In this way theology is not attempting to rival science in the latter's own domain. It leaves the explanation of how occurrences happen for science to deal with, but it seeks to set that explanation within a more profound and comprehensive understanding. The appeal is not to the God of the Gaps (only discerned in the murkier parts of physical process and so apt to prove a vanishing shadow as the light of knowledge increases) but to the true creator (who is the ground of *all* physical process).

The two pillars of this new natural theology are the appeals to intelligibility and to the cosmological anthropic principle. The physical world is marvellously rationally transparent to our inquiry and mathematics is 'unreasonably effective' (in Wigner's phrase) in providing the key to its structure. Some of its most beautiful patterns, dreamed up by the mathematicians in the isolation of their studies, are found actually to occur in the physical world around us. Whence comes this deep-seated congruence between the experienced rationality of our minds and the observed rationality of the universe? It is surely a significant fact demanding an explanation. Einstein once said that the only incomprehensible thing about the universe is that it is comprehensible. Cosmology and elementary particle physics deal with regimes so remote from everyday experience, and need for their formulation mathematics so abstract in its character, that a mere appeal to the evolutionary need to survive will not serve to explain how this comes about. A coherent explanation of the consonance of the reason within and the reason without would be that both have their origin in the Rationality of the creator. The appeal to intelligibility is a variation on the cosmological theme of natural theology (that great question, 'Why is there something rather than nothing?').

Second, we have come to realize in recent years that we do not seem to live in 'any old world'. The insights of the cosmological anthropic principle point to a delicate balance in the law and circumstance of the universe – one might almost say a 'fine tuning' – necessary in order that its evolving process might produce such complex and interesting systems as ourselves.[5]

For example, the whole history of the universe, on the largest scale, has been a great tug-of-war between two opposing principles. One is the fiery explosion of the big bang, throwing matter apart. The other is the contractive force of gravity, pulling matter together. These two effects are in almost exact balance in our universe. In fact, at the earliest time in its history that we can even pretend to be able to talk about (the Planck time, when the cosmos was 10^{43} seconds old) they appear to have been equal to one part in 10^{60} – an accuracy equivalent to hitting a target an inch wide on the other side of the universe! Astonishing you say, but if it had not been so you would not be here to be amazed by it. If expansion had predominated a little more, the world would have flown apart too fast. In the resulting dilute universe, stars and galaxies would have been unable to form, and their existence is essential for the coming-to-be of life. On the other hand, if gravity had predominated a little more, the world would have collapsed in upon itself before we had time to appear on its scene. It takes some fifteen thousand million years to make men and women. It may be that this delicate balance of expansion and contraction resulted from a process in the early universe called inflation – a sort of boiling of space – as Alan Guth has ingeniously suggested. Even if that is so, inflation requires for its possibility a certain form for the laws of physics. It cannot happen in 'any old world'. So it seems that this universe is special in its characteristics in ways that relate directly to its having been able eventually to evolve forms of life. Many more examples could be invoked to support that claim.

It is against the instinct of a scientist just to say, 'We're here because we're here'. The remarkable fruitful coincidences of the cosmological anthropic principle seem to call for some explanation. Some have suggested that there is a great portfolio of different universes, each with its own law and circumstances. If that were so, it would not be surprising if one of them were more or less 'right' to evolve life, and that of course is the one that we live in since we could appear in no other. This somewhat prodigal suggestion is not physics (which knows only this universe) but metaphysics. A metaphysical suggestion of equal coherence and greater economy would be that there is only one universe, which is the way it is because it is not 'any old world' but the creation of a creator who wills it to be capable of fruitful process. This appeal to the cosmological anthropic principle is a wholly new variation on the design theme of natural theology, based on a designed potentiality built into the very fabric of cosmic law and circumstance.

What sort of a universe is it that is thus perceived as God's creation? It is characterized by three features:

1 *The interplay of chance and necessity.* This is seen not only in evolutionary biology (random genetic mutations sifted and preserved in a regular environment), but also, for instance, in the coming-to-be of galaxies by gravitational condensation. This role of chance implies that the end is not foreseeable in the beginning. Some have thought that this challenges theology's claim that there is a purpose at work in the world. The great French biochemist, Jacques Monod, wrote with Gallic passion and intensity: 'Pure chance, absolutely free but blind, is at the very root of the stupendous edifice of evolution.'[6] The word where Monod puts the knife in is, of course, 'blind'. Yet one need not see things that way. The theist can interpret the dialectic of chance and necessity as reflecting the gifts of freedom and reliability to the creation by a God who is at once both loving and faithful. The random 'shuffling' operations of chance are then seen as the way in which the universe explores its God-given (anthropic) potentiality, incorporated in the lawfulness of necessity. If the resulting picture is of a precarious process, that is because love always accepts the precariousness inherent in the independence of the beloved. As W. H. Vanstone wrote: 'If the creation is the work of love then its shape cannot be predetermined by the Creator, nor its triumph foreknown; it is the realization of vision, but of vision which is discovered by its own realization.'[7]

Vanstone makes no reference to the insights of modern science, but his picture of 'the realization of vision, but of vision which is discovered by its own realization' is strikingly consonant with our understanding of physical process as the interplay of chance and necessity.

2 *No mere mechanism.* The apparently clockwork universe of Newton has disappeared in modern science, not only because of the cloudy fitfulness of quantum theory at the constituent roots of the universe, but also because even classical dynamical systems are now known, in general, to be so exquisitely sensitive to circumstance as to be intrinsically unpredictable.[8] That observation is epistemological in character (it concerns what we can know about such delicate systems) but I believe that it also points to an ontological openness present in physical process. Science is beginning to discern what we, as humans, experiencing choice and responsibility, have always known, that the future is not just a spelling out of what was already present in the past, but it is something really new. We live in a world not only of being, but also of genuine becoming.

3 *Ultimate futility.* Science can not only peer in to the cosmic past, it can also seek to discern the eventual cosmic fate. In the end, the universe will either fly apart for ever and decay, or it will fall in

upon itself and collapse. We are not sure which, because the balance between expansive and contractive forces is too fine for us to be sure which will prove to be in the ascendancy. Either way the future is bleak, in terms of a final fulfilment solely within the physical process of this world. However, I do not think that this need present a difficulty for the theologian. He has always known that the only possible source of lasting hope is God himself, whether we are thinking of ourselves or of the cosmos. Our physical bodies will decay on a timescale of tens of years, the universe on a timescale of thousands of millions of years. If there is a true hope for either (as I believe there is), it lies in the redeeming faithfulness of the eternal creator alone.

I have sought to survey the interaction of science and theology. I claim that they do impinge upon each other in ways that are fruitful. The resulting interplay is not without its perplexities but I think that it is mutually enhancing. I have written elsewhere:

> Einstein once said that 'Religion without science is blind. Science with religion is lame.' His instinct that they need each other was right, though I would not describe their separate shortcomings in quite the terms he chose. Rather I would say, 'Religion without science is confined; it fails to be completely open to reality. Science without religion is incomplete; it fails to attain the deepest possible understanding.' The remarkable insights that science affords us into the intelligible workings of the world cry out for an explanation more profound than that which it can itself provide. Religion, if it is to take seriously its claim that the world is the creation of God must be humble enough to learn from science what that world is actually like.[9]

The instinct of the physical scientist is to seek the most all-embracing explanation available to him. Hence the search for GUTs (grand unified theories) in elementary particle physics. The thirst for that unified understanding will not be quenched by science alone. Ultimately it will prove to be the search for God, and so natural theology will have an indispensable role in its achievement. In that way I find a fruitful reconciliation of my experience as a theoretical physicist and my experience as a priest.

Chance in God's World

David J. Bartholomew

seventeenth/

The great set pieces in the conflict between science and religion are well known but tend to be seen nowadays as things of the past. Galileo's contretemps with the Church in the sixteenth century, the findings of geology about the age of the earth and – most spectacular of all – the Darwinian revolution in biology have all been largely assimilated into Christian thinking and now fail to arouse much passion. It is true that echoes of old battles continue to be heard and the appearance of 'creation science' across the Atlantic reminds us that the skirmishing is not over. Nevertheless, even where differences remain, tolerance and peaceful co-existence have largely replaced the old hostilities. But if we assent to this account we are in danger of being lulled into a false sense of security because there is now a fundamental threat to belief which comes from the way that scientists see the world. It springs from the fact that chance seems to play a fundamental role in the scheme of things. If this is true, it undermines not so much belief in the divine origin of the world but in the idea that its creator can have any control or influence over it.

see previous article, p. 136

The challenge of chance

The challenge is not entirely new. It goes back at least as far as Epicurus, but in more recent times the American philosopher Charles Peirce has posed it in modern dress. Ian Hacking sees Peirce's importance in the fact that he was the first person to articulate the idea that we live in a universe of chance.[1] He concluded that it is the laws of probability which account for our false conviction that nature is governed by regular laws. In physics Heisenberg's uncertainty principle marked a point when the universe could no longer be seen as the vast well-oiled machine of Newtonian mechanics. Instead the quantum theory revealed an irreducible uncertainty at the heart of matter. For most practical purposes this did not challenge the appearance of lawfulness in the world since Newton's laws remained a perfectly adequate approximation at the level of everyday experience. But what it did do was to ground those laws in a sub-stratum of randomness rather than in what had been commonly seen as the will of God. However, there also appeared to be unpredictable happenings at the sub-atomic level which could have effects on the course of events in the macro-world. This fact undermined the machine-like character of the universe.

It was with Darwin's theory of evolution by natural selection that the trouble really started. For it now appeared that the line of development of living things was not according to some divine blueprint but was the outcome of the rough-and-tumble of the struggle to survive. This thus disposed of the need for any purposeful direction from the supreme being and it was this, rather than the challenge to the literal truth of the Genesis account of creation, which posed the real threat to belief. However, the axe which Darwin had laid to the root of the tree penetrated further under the impetus of the discoveries of molecular biology. Darwin knew that variation occurred in nature and that this provided the raw material on which natural selection worked but he did not know what caused the variation. We now know that it is the result of accidental copying errors in the replication of the DNA in the reproductive process. Such errors are not random in the sense of having no cause but we *What is cause?* are justified in speaking of them as chance, or accidental, events *Or effect?* since their effects bear no relation to the viability of the resulting organism.

The new outlook on evolution which this discovery provides is at the heart of the 'New Biology'. It is set out with admirable clarity by the late Jacques Monod, the French Nobel laureate, in his book *Chance and Necessity*.[2] To his way of thinking, modern biology had dealt a death blow to any notion of a purposeful God. The words in which he expressed the essence of his conclusion admit of no compromise and, though often quoted, bear repetition:

> We say that these events are accidental, due to chance. And since they constitute the *only* possible source of modification in the genetic text, itself the *sole* repository of the organism's hereditary structures, it necessarily follows that chance *alone* is at the source of every innovation, of all creation in the biosphere. Pure chance, absolutely free but blind, at the very root of the stupendous edifice of evolution: this central concept of modern biology is no longer one among other possible or even conceivable hypotheses. It is today the *sole* conceivable hypothesis, the only one compatible with observed and tested fact. And nothing warrants the supposition (or the hope) that conceptions about this should, or ever could, be revised.

Few of us are scientists with the specialist knowledge fully to *No, it's philosophy they lack* appreciate the revolution in the scientific view of the world which these discoveries have precipitated. But all of us have experienced the seemingly random and inconsequential happenings which so often seem to determine the course of our own lives. The accidental meeting which eventually leads to marriage or a new career is common enough. Looking back we see how easily things might have turned out differently. W. H. Vanstone from whom I shall quote again, catches the feeling exactly as he reflects on the church and the circumstances surrounding who was in and who was out:

> For I was acutely aware, in the first place, that life in the Church was different only in detail from life outside it: and, in the second place, that the presence of some people within the Church, and the absence of others, owed much to factors of chance and circumstance. This second point weighed particularly heavily. In many cases I knew the occasion of a person's first association with the Church: and I knew how often chance rather than choice had determined this occasion. It was repugnant to belief in a God of love and justice that chance passengers in the Ark should be so richly rewarded, and those, who, equally by chance, were absent so heavily penalized. If the new Church were God's instrument for selecting, identifying or preserving those who should be saved, then it was a crude and random instrument. To assert that God so intended or so used the Church would be to degrade and brutalize the concept of God.[3]

If we accept this as an accurate picture of the way things happen then some of the ideas which many see as central to Christian belief are challenged. In particular, the notion of a providential God creating all things and directing their course does not sit easily with the haphazardness which is so much a part of life. One may well feel that the only rational course in the choice of God or chance is to choose chance.

We should beware of falling into the error of thinking of chance as some kind of metaphysical entity which causes things. That is why we have avoided writing it with a capital letter. To speak of chance as an alternative to God is merely to deny that God exists and to assert that things 'just happen'. Whether or not this can be described as an explanation is a moot point. Nevertheless, if the way that things happen shows no rhyme or reason the outlook for the believer is bleak. The scientific picture is compelling in its coherence and correspondence with reality. The account rings true and, for many of us, bears out our own experience of the way the world is. What then are believers to do?

A common reaction

The natural reaction of believers to the foregoing scenario is to deny its premiss. That is to claim that what looks like chance to us is none other than the working out of God's purpose. It is our ignorance rather than the inherent randomness of nature which is the source of the uncertainty which pervades the world around us. This line of argument is put very clearly in the literature of *The Summit Lighthouse*, a rather curious sect which believes that its present prophet, Elizabeth Prophet, transmits teachings of the 'Ascended Masters'. It says

> The writings of the great masters published by The Summit Lighthouse point to the fact that nothing happens by chance but everything happens according to natural and spiritual laws which may often appear as chance. The universe was set into motion by Infinite Law and Infinite Wisdom. Even its finite characteristics show the scientific accuracy behind the manifestation.

This is a common view which is by no means confined to the outer fringes of the believing community. Among scientists it has been advocated by the late Donald Mackay in several of his books, especially in his Riddell Memorial Lectures published as *Science, Chance and Providence*.[4] According to him the cause of every single event can be traced back to the will of God. Sometimes we can trace the casual chain for some distance, and sometimes not, but in either case everything is ultimately under the sovereign will of God. This *No such thing* is a regular part of popular piety nicely illustrated by an item in the *Billy Graham Mission England Newsletter* (East Anglian Region South No. 5). Under the heading 'This is the age of the miracle', it told how Mrs Fiona Castle had been on her way to speak at a meeting in Newmarket. She missed her connection in Cambridge and a special train was provided to get her to Newmarket where she duly arrived in time to speak at the meeting. To those familiar with the ways of British Rail this does indeed have the mark of a miracle but the writer was quite serious in seeing the hand of God intervening to get Mrs Castle to Newmarket in time. We were not told whether the delay on the way to Cambridge was outside God's control or whether the delay was arranged to provide the occasion for the miracle. In spite of the inconsistencies into which this kind of argument so easily leads, it provides a perfectly defensible way of accommodating science and religion when stripped of its more credulous aspects. Furthermore, it appears to have a solid biblical foundation – in the Old Testament at least. The key text is Proverbs 16:33: 'The lots may be cast into the lap but the issue depends wholly on the Lord.' With few exceptions God is pictured in the Old Testament as the one who holds the whole world in his hand, as one who can stop the sun in its tracks, change the direction of the wind and control the outcome of battles. For the nervous believer it offers security since it is a view which cannot be falsified no matter what science may turn up. It is always possible to assert that everything that happens conforms to the divine blueprint laid down in heaven. Even Monod was prepared to allow as much in a broadcast conversation with Sir Peter Medawar following the publication of *Chance and Necessity*.

Why then do I claim that it is an inadequate defence? There are several arguments against it which to my mind are compelling. First, what cannot be disproved does not, thereby, become credible. To argue that what looks like a purely natural process calling for no external agent is actually the work of just such an agent sounds like special pleading in which only someone with a vested interest would indulge.

Secondly, it is not so well-founded in the Bible as its protagonists seem to suppose, especially if one looks at the New Testament. I reviewed the matter in some detail in *God of Chance*,[5] but the gist of the case rests on two lines of argument. One is that there are instances where Jesus expressly denied that God is directly involved in the way that his questioners supposed. The cases of the man born blind (John 9:3) and the tower which fell in Siloam (Luke 13:4) are two examples. More important is the fact that no sense can be made of the healing and caring ministry of Jesus if sickness and need were directly willed by God. What justification could there be for the Son undoing the work of the Father?

Moving in a more philosophical direction a third objection is that a theology which sees God's sovereign will as ruling all things leaves very little room for human freedom – something with which Calvinists have long had to wrestle. It is then difficult to escape the conclusion that the human drama is no more than a puppet show and that our sense of self-determination, however restricted, is but a cruel illusion. It is hard to reconcile this with a gospel to which we may freely respond – or not.

The claim that God is directly responsible for everything would be easier to sustain if all the happenings in the world were beneficial but this is clearly not the case. It then has to be explained *how* it is that God, whose nature is love, can cause the undeserved suffering which so many of his children endure. All theologies have to contend with the fact of evil but in none is it posed so acutely as in this one.

However, to my mind, the decisive argument against this understanding of nature is that if it were true it would rule out an alternative explanation which is both more credible and more consistent with the Christian understanding of God. Anything which diminishes our view of God, as I believe this does, must be highly suspect theologically.

God's world of chance

The alternative view, which is developed more fully in *God of Chance*, turns the matter on its head. Setting God in opposition to chance is fallacious and unnecessary. My contention is simply that chance is part of God's plan; that there are advantages to a creator in building into the world a measure of uncertainty. At first this may seem absurd or self-contradictory, but like many simple but unfamiliar ideas it has to be lived with and thought about for its appeal to take hold. The idea is not a new one. According to Hooykaas, Sebastian Basso in the seventeenth century saw that there could be happenings in physical systems which were not individually directed to some intended end.[6] Prior to that the French philosopher, scientist and priest Pierre Gassendi, had revived Epicureanism, combining it with belief in God, particular providence and the existence of an immortal soul. He may, perhaps, be regarded as the father of the view proposed here but in a modern scientific context it is in the writings of Arthur Peacocke that it was first given serious attention.[7] He envisages the random processes of nature as God's way of sorting through the options available and thus exploring the potential of the creation. In *God of Chance* I developed a similar idea but with somewhat different emphases. However, the idea was already abroad and had been mooted by a modern hymn-writer in the verse:

> When you started off the universe, Lord most high,
> Did you know just what would happen as years went by?
> Did you in your infinite mind everything foresee?
> Or does being God mean you make a place for uncertainty?
>
> John Gregory, Hymn 107, *New Church Praise*

Bishop John Taylor had said much the same thing in conversation with Gerald Priestland: 'I think that God is engaged in a much longer and more dangerous adventure, in which there is a great deal of accident around: that's the sort of world that God has made and allowed and has submitted Himself to.'[8]

To sum up, we are saying that chance is not wholly an illusion but was designed into the system by God for good reason.

This may be an interesting way of looking at things but is there any good reason for believing that it is a true account? I believe that there is.

In the first place, it has the merit of doing full justice to the scientific view of how things actually are. The scientific view changes, of course, and it would be foolhardy to nail our colours to any particular scientific mast but it seems hardly conceivable that a new scientific revolution would oust chance.

Secondly, it actually seems a better way of doing things. It is presumptuous to put one's self in the place of God but even an inadequate attempt to take a God's-eye view can give us a fresh perspective. To take a relatively simple example, imagine that as creator you have decided that there should be two sexes in the animal kingdom in roughly equal numbers. One option would be deliberately to plan the sex of each individual to be born; another would be to leave it to chance as if by the tossing of a fair coin. The end effect would be the same with roughly equal numbers of each sex but the latter method would be a much simpler and more elegant method bringing with it several other advantages. The variety of family composition, the uncertainty and surprise surrounding each birth add something to the richness of life, in human populations at least. It is the element of uncertainty which creates the surprise which adds so much spice to life. In her autobiography, Janet Baker remarks:

> So-called 'technical perfection' seems out of place to me. The human experience and the world of nature contain an element of risk, of error, of unpredictability. The possibility of something new, or of change, is closely bound together with the idea of life. Take away that possibility and you have something different, which shouldn't be confused with the living reality.[9]

In theology too, the notion of God is enlarged rather than diminished by getting away from the precisely determined world of an automaton-like God. W. H. Vanstone captures the essence of the argument when he says:

> The God Who will not abandon and to Whom nothing save Himself is expendable is often misinterpreted in popular devotion as the God of fore-ordained and programmed purposes. It is assumed that for that to which He gives purpose He already has purpose, and that of that which He uses He has predetermined the use. To make this assumption is to destroy the basis for any real analogy between divine and human creativity, and to exclude from the activity of God all the precariousness and all the poignancy of love.[10]

Thirdly, the new view does not rule out providence, as superficial examination might suggest. The lawfulness of the world arises partly from the average effects of large numbers of random happenings – the gas laws, for example. There can be a providence in the aggregate effect of events just as in the isolated happening. Even if we denied God's direct involvement in all the detailed happenings of the world this would not rule out purpose in their aggregate effects. Many examples showing how determinate ends can be achieved by processes whose component parts are random are given in *God of Chance*. G. Theissen puts it thus:

In all probability, evolution has no pre-existing goal. At least, such a goal cannot be formulated within an evolutionary framework of thought. However, the properties of the system of all reality may have been created in such a way that tendencies in particular directions are constantly strengthened. Here we need not assume any guiding hand. Chance can be at work. Whatever direction a flyer may take by chance at the North Pole, he will always eventually arrive at the same point, the South Pole, regardless of his intention, simply because of the properties of a sphere. So we cannot rule out the possibility that the world-process has an intrinsic goal, which follows from properties of the system which are still hidden from us. Trial and error can also bring us nearer to it.[11]

As we noted earlier, there is also much in the New Testament to justify the line we are taking. Jesus was not a fatalist and he clearly regarded much that happens in the world just as we do, that is as unfortunate accidents which, even if they could not be avoided, could be the occasions for him to demonstrate where God's true intentions lay.

Perhaps the most powerful argument of all is that our view permits a degree of genuine human freedom. It leaves room in the scheme of things for an openness to the future on which our decisions have a real influence. It thus adds to human dignity and worth and thereby to the greatness of God.

Lastly it alleviates, even if it does not entirely eliminate, the problem of evil. When it is no longer necessary to attribute every evil happening to the inscrutable will of God it is easier to understand why there should be suffering in the creation of an all-powerful and loving God. There is no need for the guilt which some feel through the belief that their suffering is a punishment for sin. There is assurance for the victims of earthquake, famine and congenital illness that they are not more deserving of punishment than others. It still has to be explained why there should be accident and disaster at all but that, I suggest, is a less intractable problem than that of reconciling the power and goodness of a God who is responsible for all suffering. Again W. H. Vanstone sums it up succinctly:

> We do not believe, of the children who died at Aberfan, that God willed their death as a means to some greater good. If we so believed, we should find that alleged 'good' tainted, compromised and unacceptable: like Ivan Karamazov, we would have no part in it and would 'hand in our ticket'. We believe that, at the moment when the mountain of Aberfan slipped, 'something went wrong': the step of creative risk was the step of disaster: the creative process passed out of control.[12]

Problems remain

It would be idle to pretend that the conflict with which we began has been fully resolved. Theologies are not fashioned as easily as that and much hard thinking still needs to be done. What I do feel confident about is that we have hit upon a significant clue to the unravelling of one of the most perplexing features of our world. Rather surprisingly, it appears that the threat to orthodox Christian belief is less severe than at first seemed probable, especially when the accretions of time engendered by a mechanical view of the universe and undue emphasis on the Old Testament to the detriment of the New are stripped away. Nevertheless, difficulties remain and let me leave you with two of them.

The first takes us back to the question of God's providence. We have argued that our viewpoint does not rule out providence but the providence envisaged was of the general kind which has traditionally been seen in the lawfulness of the physical universe. Most Christians want to go much further than this and see God's hand at work in a more specific and direct manner. The uneasiness which they feel about God's world of chance is well put by H. Montefiore:

> Perhaps in other aspects of the universe as well, it is the element of chance which makes new developments possible. 'Time governs all . . .' Is this a godless vision? I do not believe so. This is certainly not a *godless* vision, but it is one that is hard to reconcile with the God who is the Father of our Lord Jesus Christ. This kind of God winds the clock up and lets it run down, confident that through trial and error and blind chance what he wants will in the end turn up. He is the God of the deists, remote, unmoved, unloving. Chance and necessity may produce creativity, but they cannot produce purpose.[13]

I have argued that the last assertion is not entirely true, that chance *in the aggregate* can express purpose but that does not deflect the full force of the Bishop's objection. To meet it fully one must enlarge the field of discussion to include that part of the realm of being which, so far, has been entirely excluded from our discussion, namely, that of mind. It is in the province of that mysterious entity which we call mind, in which our own free acts originate, that God's action must primarily be located. And it is precisely in the flexibility with which the physical world is endowed by the chance within it that the scope for exercising our will and his resides. Bishop John Taylor came close to the truth, I think, when he said in the passage immediately following the earlier quotation:

> I think He intervenes through that part of the universe that is capable of being open to Him, namely ourselves . . . But I don't believe in a God

who can suddenly raise up a storm or make the sun stand still or take away something that is there threatening.[14]

The second area which needs deeper exploration is the incarnation. This seems to have required a very specific act on the part of God which could admit of little error in miscalculation. The whole sequence of events from conception to resurrection hang together as a piece. According to the ideas developed here each must have been subject to all the hazards and uncertainties which the rest of us face. This implies that things could have easily turned out otherwise and the whole plan of redemption might have foundered. How, if at all, can we defend the particularity of the incarnation in the face of the risks which it must have run? G. Theissen goes too far when he says:

> If faith in historical 'mutations' of our existence is related to the history of Israel leading up to Jesus of Nazareth, it is related to 'chance' events. By that I mean that there is no reason why a decisive turning-point in the history of evolution should have taken place in Israel, of all peoples – and not in another. There is no need for this turning point to have taken place in a small strip of land between the sea and the wilderness in the eastern Mediterranean – away from the cultural centres of the old world. There is no reason why these events should have happened when they did – between the great migrations of peoples in the Mediterranean about 1200 B C and the establishment of the Roman empire under the first emperors. However, all that is no argument against the belief that if we approach and adapt ourselves to the central reality only through unplannable mutations, any alternative to biblical faith is no less fortuitous than this.[15]

I do not believe that the incarnation derives its significance and meaning from the attitude which we take to a 'random' happening in Palestine which might just as well have occurred elsewhere at some other time. This hardly does justice to an act on a par with creation itself. We shall have to do better in seeking an explanation which transcends, without contravening, the scientific account of the world. But it would be a dull subject indeed which left no challenges for the student.

8 THEOLOGY AND SOCIETY

William Temple and British Society Today

Alan M. Suggate

One of my earliest recollections as a child is of my parents being aghast when William Temple's sudden death was announced in October 1944, just a few months before the end of the Second World War. Their reaction was widespread. Clearly he had been seen as a tower of strength in a country shaken to the foundations by war. His leadership of the Church of England was established long before 1939. It grew during his years as Bishop of Manchester from 1921, and Archbishop of York from 1929. Winston Churchill had no option but to call him to Canterbury in 1942, grumbling the while that he was a half-crown article in a sixpenny bazaar.

What were the ingredients of this strength? First and foremost there was his spirituality, which was moulded by sacramental worship and his study of St John's Gospel.[1] He impressed with a serenity and joy which enabled groups he chaired to work through their controversies constructively. This was particularly valuable in his work for the ecumenical movement.[2]

Secondly, he had a fine intellect. He was a Christian philosopher whose style of thinking was shaped by the British Hegelians, and especially Edward Caird, the Master of his Oxford College. Temple adopted their view that philosophy was a constructive enterprise, 'a determined attempt to think clearly and comprehensively about the problems of life and existence'.[3] In his three main philosophical works, *Mens Creatrix* (1917), *Christus Veritas* (1924), and the Gifford Lectures, *Nature, Man and God* (1932–34), he was engaged in the search for a coherent account of the universe, and he believed that it was in the incarnation of Jesus Christ which provided the decisive clue to that coherence.

Thirdly, he was convinced that the Christian faith embraces the whole of life, so that no part of it is wholly autonomous. *Christianity and Social Order* is his best-known defence of this view, and it suggests ways in which the Christian faith can be a resource for dealing with social questions, in that it provides principles which can serve as criteria for judging the status quo and hint at ways of making the social order more Christian.[4] Let us look at the development of Temple's social ethic, which was integral to his philosophy.

By both temperament and upbringing Temple was an optimist. Hegelian philosophers believed in the rationality of the universe; and the dominance by Great Britain of great tracts of the globe gave every ground for optimism, if you were British. In his early manhood Temple was a liberal moral idealist. He looked quite uncritically on the latest social movements, especially the Labour Movement and the Workers' Educational Association. The Labour Movement exemplified the ideal of brotherhood over against selfish individualism. The WEA (Temple became President in 1908) was praised in the language of faith, hope and love for being a movement which sought the spiritual and not merely the material advancement of the working class.

The First World War did for a while dent Temple's optimism about human progress. He asked some searching questions in 1914 about the applicability of the concept of self-sacrifice to the conduct of nations. He found himself compelled to reject pacifism. An individual might choose it, but a government could not commit a whole nation to it against its will. In any case, a refusal to fight would do nothing to stop the triumph of evil forces. We were caught in what he called 'the entanglement of sin' and had to make compromises and do the best we could in the circumstances.[5]

Yet by the end of the war he shared in the general optimism that a radically new social order could be created in Britain. It was as if ideals could be realized by a sheer act of will. He set in motion preparatory work for a large scale Conference on Christian Politics, Economics and Citizenship (COPEC), which took place in Birmingham in 1924. The specially headed notepaper for the Conference claimed that the Christian faith gave the vision and the power essential for solving social problems.[6] Temple modified his idealism to the extent that he now spoke of social principles. The phrase was designed to mark the fact that ideals had to be implemented with close attention to social circumstances. He described his method as idealist in that it went beyond mere tinkering with the status quo and suggested positive social relationships, but realist in that it was always concerned with the application of principles to what is, rather than with dreams of what might be.[7]

Temple's principles at this time were four: the freedom and dignity of the individual, based on the doctrine that each person is made in the image of God; fellowship, or the social nature of human beings, which he grounded in the Pauline concept of the Church as the Body of Christ; service, drawn from the picture of the servant Messiah and also from the idea of the parts of the Body of Christ each contributing to the life of the whole; and sacrifice, which marked the fact that service could be very costly.

These principles were used at the Birmingham Conference to make judgements on contemporary society and to suggest directions for the future without getting as far as programmes of action, which were the province of government and citizens. Thus, workers were to have an increasingly effective voice in the management of industry; there was to be a living wage; unemployment was to be eliminated if possible; wealth was to be more justly distributed.

Temple continued to use the first three of these social principles (which I consider sound) for the rest of his life. (He eventually dropped the fourth on the grounds that sacrifice could only be practised freely by individuals.) We see their operation in *Christianity and Social Order*. In the 1930s Temple had initiated an investigation of long-term unemployment which approached the matter from the standpoint of the unemployed as persons. In *Christianity and Social Order* he wrote that the unemployed feel that they have fallen out of the common life. Worse than physical need is the fact that they are not wanted. The only answer to this moral isolation is for them to do something needed by the community: 'For it is part of the principle of personality that we should live for one another.'[8]

The main problem with COPEC was that its strong moral critique was not adequately supported by analysis of the social situation. This weakness was exposed by the General Strike and the miners' strike of 1926, the economic crises from 1929, and the rise of Hitler in the 1930s. Temple perceived the need to get to grips with the hard realities of the world by more detailed analysis. The study of long-term unemployment was carried out by experts in social investigation. In his analysis of international politics he came to recognize much more thoroughly the problem of power, and especially the self-interested exercise of power.

As a consequence Temple came to question the Christian philosophy he had elaborated up to 1934. He could see that Anglican theology had thrown great emphasis on the incarnation, interpreting it in a way which permitted the building of a Christocentric philosophy. What was needed was a shift to a greater emphasis on redemption.

> A theology of Redemption . . . tends to sound a prophetic note; it is more ready to admit that much in this evil world is irrational and strictly unintelligible, and it looks to the coming of the Kingdom as a necessary preliminary to the full comprehension of much that now is . . . We have been learning again how impotent man is to save himself, how deep and pervasive is that corruption which theologians call Original Sin. Man needs above all to be saved from himself. This must be the work of Divine Grace.[9]

Christians had to start out in their thinking from the tension between the doctrine of the love of God and the actual facts of daily experience.[10]

In attempting to reach a deeper theological position, Temple was heavily influenced by the discussions he had with continental theologians, especially in preparation for the ecumenical conference at Oxford in 1937 on Church, Community and State, and also by the American theologian Reinhold Niebuhr. He drew on Niebuhr's ideas about the relationship of love and justice, which stressed the acute difficulty nations have in practising love. Love indeed applied both to individuals and to groups, but in the case of groups the principal task was to harness self-interest to the cause of justice, and here little more might be achieved than balances of power which were very rough justice.[11]

Temple was thus trying to set his social principles within a stronger theological framework. At the centre was a vision of the Kingdom of God, whose presence already in history stood in tension with its final coming. Christian existence is lived out in this tension. It is a vision which squares with the Gospels and with the writings of St Paul. A similar framework is not only still used within the Anglican tradition – for instance by the eminent social theologian Professor Ronald H. Preston – but finds a basic confirmation within contemporary Roman Catholic and Lutheran thought.[12] Liberation Theology is rather different in focus, but has many points of contact. It is too much to say that there is an ecumenical consensus, but at least such a framework has a serious claim to consideration, and contrary models carry the onus of showing their superiority.

In the last decade in this country a contrary model has been promoted which has led to disagreements between Church and State in the area of social ethics. I wish to make some critical remarks on this recent development, using an article which Temple wrote a few months before his death, called 'What Christians Stand for in the Secular World'. Professor Donald MacKinnon once told me that this was the piece above all others in Christian social ethics by which Temple wished to be remembered. It can be found in *Religious Experience*.[13] It gathers up many of the ideas I have briefly referred to, and offers a number of thoughts which serve as a warning against current attitudes. I offer three lines of criticism.

'The Christian religion is primarily a religion of redemption, a gospel. It is good news, not a philosophy or good advice.' Those words are not actually from Temple, but from V. A. Demant, an eminent Anglo-Catholic theologian who complained that the British exhibited a 'rancid moralism cut off from its religious roots'.[14] He meant by this that the British are prone, while claiming to be Christian, to interpret the Christian faith essentially as a set of moral rules, thus forgetting the sense of the basic dynamic of God's dealings with human beings as revealed in Scripture and summarized in doctrine. Temple was not very original in his social ethics, but he was good at picking up other people's good ideas, weaving them into his own thought and presenting them lucidly. In his article he wrote:

> The first task is to disabuse the minds of people of the notion, which
> is widespread, and infects to a large extent current Christian
> preaching, that Christianity is in essence a system of morals, so that
> they have lost all understanding of the truth, so prominent in the
> New Testament, that to be a Christian is to share in a new movement
> of life, and to co-operate with new regenerating forces that have
> entered into history.[15]

This construing of the Christian faith as essentially morality appears in various forms. One form is the kind of liberal moralism found among the pioneers of the Labour Party, and perhaps Temple saw in Demant's comments an implicit criticism of his own early social thought. Another is a hard bourgeois Protestant version. In a recent thesis on the churches in Bermondsey from 1880 to 1939, Dr Alan Bartlett noted that the Protestant churches preached a creed of self-improvement, and appealed therefore to people who had got on in life or who hoped to get on. Those who declined to attend church neatly fed this moralism back by declaring that they were not good enough to go to church.[16] There was therefore collusion in the idea that Christianity is primarily a system of morals. Today we appear to be confronted with a variant of this bourgeois Protestant version, which lays great stress on moral rules and looks to the Church to propagate them and so assist in the process of social control.

Temple develops his point in a section called 'Man as rooted in nature', which attacks the reduction of Christianity to morality in two directions. First it involves neglect of the doctrine of creation.

> A fundamental duty which man owes to God is reverence for the world
> as God has made it. Failure to understand and acknowledge this is a
> principal cause of the present ineffectiveness of the Christian witness
> in relation to the temporal order. It is one of the chief points at which a
> fundamental change of outlook is demanded from Christians. Our false
> outlook is most of all apparent in the exploitation of the physical
> world. As animals we are part of nature, dependent on it and
> interdependent with it. We must reverence its economy and co-
> operate with its processes. If we have dominion over it, that is as
> predominant partners, not as superior beings who are entitled merely
> to extract from it what gratifies our desires.[17]

Subsequent theological reflection has confirmed Temple's insight.[18] However, the setting up of freedom as an absolute moral good and the insistence on the freedom of the market run counter to our respect for the natural world. It is claimed that such freedom is entirely compatible with the Christian faith.[19] But the reigning philosophy has little to do with the stewardship of nature given to the human race by God, and has more affinity with the Enlightenment view that man is the completely free manipulator of a mechanistic natural world.

The second direction in which Temple turns is towards society, and especially those forms of association which spring up naturally from our social life. He writes (again drawing on Demant):

> The present plight of our society arises in large part from the breakdown of these natural forms of association, and of the cultural pattern formed to a great extent under Christian influences. New dogmas and assumptions about the nature of reality have taken the place of the old. New rituals of various kinds are giving shape to men's emotional life. The consequence is that while their aims still remain to a large extent Christian, their souls are moulded by alien influences. The real crisis of our time is not primarily a moral, but a cultural crisis. In so far as this is true, the remedy is not to be found in what the Church is at present principally doing – insisting on ideals – or in efforts to intensify the will to pursue them. The cure has to be sought in the quite different direction of seeking to re-establish a unity between men's ultimate beliefs and habits and their conscious aims.[20]

A Church which preaches moral ideals or rules, therefore, and fails to examine the basic assumptions of society is a defective Church.

The latest dogmas and assumptions which need examination include the idolizing of the market-place, as if Adam Smith's doctrine of the invisible hand were true; and the dogma that since there is nothing wrong with wealth, we have nothing to do but accumulate it in abundance and distribute it individually with some generosity. There is an especial danger for the Church at the present time if it focuses on morality. For many of those who propagate the new dogmas maintain that the competitive market provides the most moral order available to human beings as we know them. The free market presupposes values centring on individual responsibility, and fosters them. The moral responsibility of individuals must not be attenuated. Moral growth and personal fulfilment require the widest freedom for individuals to make their choices and accept responsibility for their own decisions.[21] Clearly there is some point of contact with the Christian faith in the insistence on individual responsibility; but it must be said that it is an abstraction of moral elements from the Christian faith, and it is patently a selection which is used as a weapon by the successful and the powerful against certain groups which are presumed to be guilty of fecklessness and irresponsibility, until they succeed in proving otherwise. I have in mind in particular the unemployed, who are treated so often as if their unemployment is the result of their own idleness or incompetence; or the homeless, who are so often treated as if they had become homeless through their own ineptitude or intent.

Underlying this attitude, again characteristic of the Enlightenment, is the belief that human beings can make simple choices between good and evil, right and wrong. This easily generates a hard self-righteousness which contrasts markedly with the way Jesus himself consorted with the outcasts of society and gave them the assurance that in him God was graciously taking the initiative to include them within his kingdom.

The reference to inclusion brings us to my second point, which can be summarized in the aphorism 'I belong, therefore I am'. Temple was concerned with the way in which so much democratic thought considered only the relation of the individual with the State. What was missing was the sense that personality is inherently social.

> Only in social groupings can it mature, or indeed fully exist. These groupings must be small enough to enable the individual to feel (not only to think) that he can influence the quality and activity of the group, so that he is responsible for it, and also that it needs his contribution, so that he is responsible to it. He must feel that he belongs to it, and that it belongs to him . . . If we are to save freedom, we must proceed . . . from democracy of the individual to democracy of the person, and recollect that personality achieves itself in the lesser groupings within the State – in the family, the school, the guild, the trade union, the village, the city, the county. These are no enemies of the State, and that State will in fact be stable which deliberately fosters these lesser objects of loyalty as contributors to its own wealth of tradition and inheritance.[22]

Once again Temple's thought has been confirmed by subsequent theological reflection, and also by the development of the social sciences. The fashionable thinking of the right is highly individualistic. It operates in polar terms of individual freedom and State socialism, and has little sense of community. So great is its hostility to any notion of socialism, that it is prepared to break up lesser groupings which might pose a threat to its hegemony. Nowhere is this clearer than in the policy behind the Housing Action Trust. In Sunderland the housing stock is generally well maintained, and there is a genuine community sense within many areas of the town. But the Housing Action Trust is taking over an area which is by no means the worst, and handing it over to private developers. It is no accident that the area is a Labour stronghold, which at present returns the Leader of the Council and the Head of the Housing

Department. Under the dogma that there is no such thing as society, the right gets no further than the idea of the active citizen, which is a concept more attuned to propagating the interests of certain groups in society in accordance with the reigning values than to the genuine creation and sustaining of community. The citizen's typical action is the defence of property in the Neighbourhood Watch scheme. Clearly new thoughts are required here, and one of the great merits of *Faith in the City*, the Archbishop's Report on Urban Priority Areas, is its focus on the development of genuine community.[23] I am myself happy to be involved in a Faith in the City project in inner Sunderland, which is employing a community worker whose object is to help the local inhabitants of a very depressed area to find a renewed sense of dignity and community.

Thirdly, I pick up the central concept of the Kingdom of God and focus on its particular dynamic of hope. Temple writes that it is the task of Christians 'to restore hope to the world through a true understanding of the relation of the Kingdom of God to history, as a transcendent reality that is continually seeking, and partially achieving, embodiment in the activities and conflicts of the temporal order'.[24]

By contrast, the current ideology of the right is often presented unashamedly as a politics of imperfection, which is underwritten by appeal to the Christian doctrine of original sin. There is great stress upon the insolubility of many of our political problems. People must scale down their expectations of politics. There is an emphasis on human ignorance and irrationality, upon the need for a firm framework of coercion to hold society together.[25]

Clearly there is a point here against a romantic utopianism of the left. But it is certainly not a straight choice between that utopianism and this kind of realism. Temple offers us clues. He writes:

> There is need of a much clearer recognition of the part played in human behaviour by sub-conscious egoisms, interests, deceptions and determinisms imposed by man's place in nature and history, by his cultural patterns and by his sinfulness. It has to be recognized that society is made up of competing centres of power, and that the separate existence of contending vitalities, and not only human sinfulness, makes the elimination of power impossible. What has to be aimed at is such a distribution and balance of power that a measure of justice may be achieved even among those who are actuated in the main by egoistic and sinful impulses.[26]

Those are important points to be taken. But Temple's theology did not revolve round a doctrine of sin, and he would certainly have resisted the current politics of imperfection. For it is likely to be extremely conservative in a rigorous defence of the status quo and will tend to play into the hands of those who already have power.

Logically they come under the greatest suspicion; in practice those who have most to lose are likely out of fear to identify more and more enemies within and hold them at bay through a dogged defence of law, order and property. The divisiveness engendered by a hard moralism and individualism can easily develop into what I would call a bunker mentality, under the power of the symbol of original sin and the politics of imperfection.

Temple by contrast speaks of the restoration of hope through the inbreaking of the Kingdom of God. The decisive act was the life, death and resurrection of Christ. From that point on in human history the Kingdom repeatedly breaks in, judging the status quo, including all our finest achievements, and beckoning us on, suggesting and opening up new ways of living the Kingdom. This pattern seems to me to reflect the dynamics of the Gospel. The Old Testament tells us of God's rescue of a rabble from Egypt, and how he made them into the covenant community of Israel. Within the community there is a particular concern for those who are marginalized, the poor, the widow and the orphan. If the relations within that community are right there will be no poor. The Old Testament also gives us glimpses of the extension of that community to incorporate all nations, to the point where in Psalm 87 (the basis for the hymn 'Glorious things of Thee are spoken') there is a picture of the nations dancing and singing that in Jerusalem they all find their home.

When God acts in Jesus Christ, he comes to call people home into a newly constituted community of Israel. He goes particularly to the outcast. He does not lecture them on morality, but offers them God's forgiveness, restores and heals them. He treats them graciously as those who are loved by God, and they respond gladly. His criticism is reserved for the exclusive leaders, those who say, 'I thank Thee, Lord, that I am not as other men are'; those who would put a fence around their faith to keep it pure; thus excluding lesser breeds within Israel, and the Gentiles too, unless they join on Jewish terms. Jesus makes himself vulnerable for the sake of including the outcast. The hostility of the leaders towards him is so great that he pays the price of crucifixion. Yet God raises him up. He does not appeal again to the Jews, to secure some Palestinian base for faith. He goes before his disciples into Galilee, and sends them out into all the world, with the sole assurance, 'Do not be afraid; I am with you.' They are to break down all divisions; for all are to be brought home. It is this hopeful vision which has to be maintained against the current pessimism about society, and though the vision cannot be neatly translated into a political programme, it should at least set accents to guide its basic direction.[27]

The Christian Critique of Thatcherism

Kenneth Leech

Readers of G. K. Chesterton will recall the 'Song against Grocers' from *The Flying Inn*. It begins:

> God made the wicked grocer
> For a mystery and a sign
> That men might shun the awful shops
> And go to inns to dine . . .

The song continues:

> The righteous minds of innkeepers
> Induce them now and then
> To crack a bottle with a friend
> Or treat unmonied men.
> But who hath seen the grocer
> Treat housemaids to his teas,
> Or crack a bottle of fish sauce,
> Or stand a man a cheese?

This song, in which the grocer stands as a symbol of competition and grasping individualism, and the innkeeper a symbol of co-operation, sharing and solidarity, may be somewhat romantic in its view of inns, but it acquired a new relevance in the decade of the grocer's daughter, a decade through which Britain has recently passed.

My aim in this paper is not to analyse the political ideology of Thatcherism – which has been done many times by such diverse writers as Stuart Hall, Andrew Gamble, Peter Jenkins, Robert Skidelsky and others[1] – but rather to focus on its specific claim to be a Christian ideology; and to examine this claim in the light of the Christian tradition. I want to attempt to assess the nature of the conflict between the Churches and the Thatcher government; to describe briefly what I take Thatcherite ideology and practice to have been; to identify those elements in Thatcherism which derived from, or were alleged to derive from, Christianity; and to suggest that what we experienced was something very far removed from Christian orthodoxy. In other words, to anticipate the conclusion, I shall argue that we were confronted by an ideology which paid lip-service to a

Christian and moral vocabulary while denying its substance at every important point. But I shall also suggest that these distortions do have their roots in a specific type of Christianity, and that the Church has only itself to blame for this particular mutant of its faith. While this essay was written during the Thatcher period, most of it is still applicable to the present government's approach to Christianity.

The conflict between the Churches and Thatcherism

Here the first point that must be made is that for most members of the Churches there was no conflict. The recent study by Kenneth Medhurst and George Moyser shows that most ordinary members of the Church of England are still attached to the Conservative Party.[2] Churches tend to reflect the dominant values of their society, and I saw no evidence of any widespread revolt against Thatcherite values in the Churches as a whole, or in the Church of England in particular. There 'the Tory Party at prayer' is still a valid description of the laity, if slightly less so of the clergy.

Nevertheless, conflict there was and is, in the sense, first, that most mainstream Christian Churches, through their leaders and synods and boards, have found themselves in opposition to government policy on issues ranging from nuclear weapons and South Africa to child benefit, the community charge or poll tax, the National Health Service, the British Nationality Act, and urban policies, and, secondly, there is undoubtedly a process of 'radicalization' going on among Christians of all traditions, as there is in the USA, and this process has been aided, and in some cases initiated, by the experience of the Thatcher and Reagan regimes. We can be grateful to them for that.

Now this is very interesting because the Thatcher government, more than any other British government since the war – and possibly this century – claimed to be a government rooted in Christian principles. Journalists have often spoken of this: Clifford Longley of *The Times* said in 1978 that Thatcherism was 'consciously and explicitly theological in its foundations,'[3] while *New Society* called the Thatcher regime 'the most determinedly Christian government since the war.'[4] The Christian links, and especially the links with the Church of England, of course, go back to the party's origins. It was originally, as Mrs Thatcher has stressed, a Church party. It is fascinating to read the official Conservative Party policy document for 1949, *The Right Road for Britain*:

> Conservatism proclaims the inability of purely materialist philosophies to read the riddle of life, and achieve the necessary subordination of scientific and economic progress to the needs of the human spirit. Man

is a spiritual creature adventuring on an immortal destiny, and science, politics and economics are good or bad so far as they help or hinder the individual soul on its eternal destiny.[5]

In her insistence on maintaining a link with Christianity, Mrs Thatcher was well within the Tory tradition. But this was not the case with her economic policies and her political philosophy (which ironically owed something to the eighteenth-century Anglican clergymen Malthus and Paley). And it was in her break with traditional Tory paternalism which dominated the party from Disraeli to Macmillan, the High Church party of hierarchy and old wealth, that some of the roots of the conflicts with the Church of England were to be found. For the hierarchy of the Church has not suddenly shifted to the left, still less adopted a Marxist perspective. There are many discernible influences on recent Church social utterances, but Marx is certainly not one of them. Rather has the Church remained faithful to the paternalistic social liberalism of an earlier conservative age. *The Independent* perceptively described the Church of England as a 'citadel of exiled liberalism.'[6] It is one of the few large British institutions which did not succumb to Thatcherism. However, one by-product of Margaret Thatcher's revolution has been to force Christians in all the Churches to rethink the theological roots of their social concern; and this has led to a revival of the socialist Christian tradition. So now we have the paradoxical situation of a government which more and more emphasizes religion and morality, confronted by churches which, at all significant points, reject its perspective and its practice. Again, the parallels in the USA are very close, though Reagan and now Bush have massive fundamentalist churches on their side. My own guess is that Mrs Thatcher and some of her cabinet were taken aback by the strength and persistence of the opposition from the Church of England. Strong and persistent has that opposition been: the attack on the Nationality Act and on the abolition of the Greater London Council, led by the former Bishop of London; *The Church and the Bomb*; report after report on the issues of poverty, unemployment and social welfare; the Falkland Islands; *Faith in the City*; the role of the Churches in the miners' strike; former Archbishop of Canterbury Runcie's comments on the Pharisee society; and so on. And I think it is for this reason that we saw attempts by Margaret Thatcher and Douglas Hurd in 1988, in their addresses to the Church of Scotland and the Church of England, to regain lost ground. But the attempts were not successful. On the contrary, they probably served only to emphasize how wide was the gulf between Thatcherism and the Churches, at least at the official level.

Thatcherism

I am assuming that Thatcherism existed, which would be denied by many conservatives, as well as by Tony Benn (for whom capitalism is capitalism is capitalism) and by David Selbourne (who speaks rather of working-class Toryism). But the fact that Margaret Thatcher, alone of all twentieth-century Prime Ministers, gave her name to an 'ism' does suggest that there is some basis for it. I want to use 'Thatcherism' to mean a body of thought and practice which combines economic liberalism and authoritarian conservatism in a somewhat unstable fusion. The two tendencies have been in conflict since the early days of Thatcher's rise to power. It was the neo-liberals, the economic disciples of von Hayek, Friedman and the Institute of Economic Affairs, who promoted her to power; but it was in 1978 that the social authoritarians produced *Conservative Essays*. The history of the Thatcherite ideology and practice is in large part a history of tension and struggle between these two tendencies.

The Thatcherite commitment to the dominance of the market derived from the thinking of the Institute of Economic Affairs and its Journal. As the lady said: 'All policies are based on ideas. Our policies are firmly founded on those ideas which have been developed with such imagination in the Journal.'[7] For the social-authoritarian wing of the movement, we need to go to the gurus of Peterhouse – Maurice Cowling, Peregrine Worsthorne, George Gale and Roger Scruton and the *Salisbury Review* group – with their stress on social discipline rather than on individual freedom. 'The most important need today', wrote Peregrine Worsthorne, 'is for the state to regain control over the people,'[8] while Scruton has argued that most sections of local government should be eliminated.[9] The years since the 1981 uprisings, the miners' strike and the abolition of the Greater London Council and the metropolitan councils saw the strengthening of this aspect of Thatcherism. 'Never let anyone say I am laisser-faire. We are a strong government.'[10] So from a minimalist doctrine of State intervention in public welfare we moved very quickly to a centralized and authoritarian State in terms of political and social control.

Thatcherism and Christianity

I want now to look at some of the links which Thatcherism had with Christian ideas and values. There will be some who argue that Thatcherism (and indeed capitalism as a whole) is fundamentally anti-Christian, an utterly ungodly system of Mammon-worship, and at one level I would agree. Yet it is foolish for Christians to deny that, both in ideology and in practice, the Thatcher regime drew on strands within Western and particularly post-Reformation Christianity. Ironically, it was precisely at those points where it was most faithful to the theology of the Reformation that it came into conflict with a Christian community which had moved beyond that framework. The crucial period in which the Christian social consciousness was re-formed or renewed, both among Roman Catholics and evangelicals (the Church of England catching up later) was the 1960s, the era of Martin Luther King, of the peace movement, of the Second Vatican Council, of John Robinson and the rediscovery of Bonhoeffer, and so much else. But this period, the most creative social and spiritual decade of post-war Christianity, was for Margaret Thatcher, Norman Tebbit and Rhodes Boyson a period of 'fashionable theories and permissive claptrap'. 'We are reaping what was sown in the 60s.'[11] The rejection of the values and insights of the 1960s was crucial to Thatcherism as it is to the New Right in the USA.

However, there is a sense – though perhaps not the sense that Margaret Thatcher intended – in which she was right. For Thatcherism, with all its harshness and materialism, was a predictable reaction to the often naive optimism, utopian socialism and apolitical spirituality of the 1960s. In a sense Thatcher and Tebbit were mirror opposites of the flower children of 1967.

But that is another and longer story. The historical point about the Church – Tory conflict is that its seeds were sown in the radicalizing trends of that decade (though the dispute between Thatcher and Runcie went back to their undergraduate days at Oxford). At the same time, while the Thatcherites found themselves in conflict with mainstream Christianity, they most certainly drew on elements within Christian theology and Christian tradition, specifically on that of the sixteenth-century Reformation.

First, they were individualists. Margaret Thatcher believes that there is no such thing as society: 'Really, you know, there is no such thing as society . . . If the families and the Church and the great voluntary organizations were really doing their job, there would be no need of governments to intervene.'[12] Mrs Thatcher has said that she always regarded individualism as a Christian mission, and has even claimed that the New Testament is 'preoccupied with the individual' and that all biblical principles refer back to the individual.[13]

The contrast between this and traditional Catholic Christianity could not be more dramatic. As a former Archbishop of Canterbury, Michael Ramsey, pointed out in 1936, there is no place for individualism in Christianity: it is implacably hostile to it. The New Testament says virtually nothing about personal spirituality or personal salvation; all its emphasis is on the Body of Christ, the Kingdom of God, the New Humanity in Christ. One of the key biblical studies of the 1960s was John Robinson's *The Body*, which stressed how central is the theme of solidarity (a word unknown to Thatcherite vocabulary) to the New Testament. The post-war period has seen a major critique of and rejection of individualism by thousands of Christians, especially by evangelicals who have seen it to be unChristian, unbiblical and untrue.

So Thatcherism came preaching an individualist gospel at a time when Christians, evangelical and Catholic, had rediscovered the importance of society, social justice and human interdependence.

Secondly, Thatcherites had a low and pessimistic view of human nature, especially of human beings in groups. The view of human society as non-perfectible was shared by critics of Thatcherism, 'wets' such as Sir Ian Gilmour: 'Human nature is not perfectible, and . . . government has no business to seek to alter it.'[14] Mrs Thatcher often linked original sin and imperfection with the impossibility of utopias and of any significant social transformation; people are basically sinful and must be firmly disciplined, taught to obey and kept under control. This view is stated most clearly in Nigel Lawson's tract *The New Conservatives* (1980). Human imperfection, he claims, is the basis of conservatism.

The Christian Church, however, while it accepts the doctrine of original sin, does not offer this as the basis of policy, and it rejects a politics rooted in a belief in irredeemable human degeneracy. It rejects a static view of 'human nature' as unchangeable. Both human beings and human society are constantly open to the possibility of transformation and fulfilment, and this calls for both spiritual and political struggle. To say that they are not easily perfectible is not to say that they are not perfectible at all. And again it was precisely in the period that Margaret Thatcher was calling for obedience, treating the nation as immature, rebellious children, that Churches were coming to stress the importance of questioning, of criticism, of doubt and of other adult virtues.

Thirdly, in spite of their belief in human depravity, Thatcherites also had a central belief in freedom, but it was freedom of choice for individuals. And this was linked in Margaret Thatcher's thought with the rejection of the notion of equality: 'Free choice is ultimately what life is about. From saying we are all equal it is only a small step to saying that we cannot make any choice for ourselves.' She even claimed 'that the right to choose is the essence of Christianity'.[15] However, freedom is the freedom to maintain existing inequalities or to restore lost ones. Now, of course, the Christian Church also believes in freedom. The biblical word is redemption, best translated 'liberation', and it is essentially about the setting free of a people from oppressive forces. In the New Testament it is used both of the human community and of the creation itself. It is a theology very far removed from the Conservative privatized view of enterprise by which the upwardly mobile leave the rest behind. The Churches at the grass roots had a better and clearer view of what free choice meant in terms of human bondage than Mrs Thatcher did. They saw that freedom for some can mean misery for others, and they therefore went back to the biblical teaching that what happens to the poor is the criterion of how authentic is our freedom.

Fourthly, Thatcherites held an Erastian view of the Church as an agent of social control and as moral cement for the established order – the view summed up by Brian Walden in 1985: 'If the working classes in our cities . . . are not restrained by Christian morality then they are not restrained at all.'[16] There is no reason to doubt that this is still mainstream Tory thinking. The Church is primarily a force for stability and social control. It should provide the moral and spiritual resources for national unity. That it failed to do so was at the heart of the row over the Falkland Islands service. Denis Thatcher was quoted as saying: 'I've just been with the Boss [he did not mean God] and she's hopping mad.' It came out very clearly also in Douglas Hurd's address to the General Synod of the Church of England on 10 February 1988, the day after that body denounced the community charge. Hurd, in a patronizing and simplistic address, advised the body of clergy to stick to morality and not to 'occupy itself' with lesser matters. Church and State, he suggested, should work together 'to rebuild moral standards and values which should form the sure foundations of a cohesive and united nation'.[17]

It is in fact the refusal of the Church to be no more than the religious arm of the civil power which periodically sends the *Daily Express* and the *Daily Mail* into apoplexy. These papers are not afraid to face the issue of what happens when morality and politics conflict. So Tony Dawe wrote in the *Express* after the Falklands service that 'instead of a triumphal service thanking God for our victory the congregation was treated to a sermon on the morals of war'.[18] Morals! What a thing for the Church to talk about on such an occasion!

There is a second, and secondary, role for the Church in Thatcherite philosophy: to care for the casualties of our society, even the casualties of government policy. To care for the poor was conceded as part of the Church's job. (The government's job, it may be suggested, was to ensure that there is a constant supply of them to care for.) But it is emphatically not the Church's job to ask questions about the causes of poverty. There was no notion of the Church as a critical community with different and perhaps conflicting values to those of the State.

Finally, Thatcherites held a 'two kingdoms' theology of the type which was held by the German Churches at the time of the rise of

Nazism and which made the Nazi conquest of the Church so easy. In this theology, Church and State, God and Caesar, have clearly defined and differentiated roles: moral and political respectively. God must not trespass on the territory of Caesar, and vice versa. 'Render to Caesar' (the first part of the sentence at any rate) was one of Mrs Thatcher's favourite texts. As she said in 1978 in an address in St Lawrence Jewry in London:

> For the truth of the matter is this: the Bible as well as the tradition of the church tell us very little directly about political systems or social programmes. The nearest we get is Christ telling his disciples to render unto Caesar that which is Caesar's and unto God that which is God's.[19]

Even clearer was Norman Tebbit in his reply to some London Church leaders who had expressed their views on the future of the Greater London Council:

> I am sure you will continue to follow the injunction to render unto Caesar that which is Caesar's but resist the temptation to initiate a comparative search of the testaments to justify our positions. Whilst this government, concerned as ever to operate within the widest consensus, asked for comments on its White Paper, I see no reason why the Churches should enter a specifically political arena.[20]

Jesus 'got it about right', Mrs Thatcher told us in 1984, when he said, 'Render unto Caesar'.[21]

Mrs Thatcher repeated her sentiments when she addressed the Church of Scotland on 21 May 1988. Her address ended with the recital of the words from the hymn 'I vow to thee, my country'. It was a revealing choice of hymn. For not only is the hymn deeply heretical in its other-worldliness and its sharp distinction between this world and 'another country', but it is also uncritical in its devotion to the fatherland. Indeed the fatherland is all but deified. In Thatcherite theology Caesar clearly wins the victory.

I have so far looked at Thatcherite thinking as it relates to Christian theology. But it should be stressed that Christians judge governments not by what they say alone, but by what they do: by their fruits we shall know them. And in fact the principal reason for the conflict between the Church and the Thatcher government did not lie at the theoretical level: it lay in the fact that the Churches, especially in the inner cities and in the run-down economies of the north-west and north-east, had seen the devastation and the cruelty as well as the demoralizing effects of Thatcherism in practice. They had seen that the government's assurances that all was well did not correspond to their own experience on the ground: and they therefore raised the issues of truth and illusion. And this is still so. When Church leaders from Liverpool, Manchester and the East End of London talked to the government, it is as if they were talking to

people on Mars, so great was the comprehension gap. And so for
many of these Christians the government became, in the literal
sense, incredible: they did not speak the truth which these Christians perceived. Rather they bore false witness. But more than that:
for in biblical terms, the truth is not spoken, it is done. It is those
who do justice who know the Lord. And so these Christians went
back to the scriptures and found such words as 'Woe to those who
decree iniquitous decrees . . . those who grind the faces of the poor'.
They read again about the fate of the alien, the orphan and the
widow; the condemnation of riches and of the service of Mammon.
And they realized that Caesar, far from sharing a divided realm with
God, is often an enemy at whose overthrow the saints rejoice. They
read Revelation 19, the lament over Babylon, the prosperous city
which trafficked in human souls, and found in it renewed relevance.

At this point it is important to remind ourselves of a vital fact: not
all Christians, and not all the Churches, are white. Indeed, in the
inner urban areas of many cities the majority of practising Christians
are black. They too have seen the effects of Thatcherism in practice,
not only in terms of unemployment and despair but in the operation
of the immigration rules by which the party of the family persistently
kept and keeps Asian families divided, in the insecurity and inferior
status created by the Nationality Act, and in the explicit and crude
racist nationalism of some Tory MPs, many councillors and most of
the right-wing press. Here a crucial reference-point was Mrs Thatcher's 'swamping' interview on Granada TV on 30 January 1978. It
was the reference to the British (that is, the white British) fear of
being 'swamped' by an alien influx which is remembered, and which
tipped the polls within days in favour of the Conservatives. But in
that interview Mrs Thatcher was also asked whether she wanted to
bring the support which had gone to the National Front back to the
Conservative Party. She replied: 'Oh, very much back, certainly.'
And this is what happened. In 1979 the National Front vote collapsed due to the public identification of the Conservative Party
with a 'tough' line on immigration. There were massive swings to
the Conservatives in all the areas of NF support, from Islington
Central through the East End to Dagenham. The marginalization
and fragmentation of the NF was primarily due to the fact that the
Conservative Party had made them obsolete.

Here we need surely to recall that devout Christian who can claim
to be the father of Thatcherism. For the Gospel according to St
Margaret was originally written in the Book of Enoch. As Peregrine
Worsthorne wrote:

> It was Enoch Powell who first sowed the seeds whose harvest Margaret
> Thatcher reaped last Thursday. What is now called Thatcherism was

originally known as Powellism: bitter-tasting market economies sweetened and rendered palatable to the popular taste by great creamy dollops of nationalistic custard. In his case immigration control was the custard and it was a bit too rich for any but the strongest digestions. She was lucky to have the Falklands campaign handed to her on a plate which did the same job more effectively, turning fewer stomachs . . . But the original formula was Enoch's.[22]

I believe it is a very serious mistake to treat Powell as a rejected and tragic wilderness figure of no further political significance. The Conservative Party has officially rejected him – though whether it would have done so had Thatcher been the leader instead of Heath is open to question – but it has taken many of his key ideas on board, not least on matters of race and nation. It has done so at a time when Christians are more and more conscious of their international solidarity with their black brothers and sisters and of the destructive power of institutional racism.

The Churches, then, have witnessed the effects of the Thatcher regime on the most vulnerable sections of the community. They have remembered Tawney's words that the test of any philosophy or system of government is how it responds to those who fall by the wayside. They have seen the devastation of the inner cities, and the incomprehension and perplexity of those ministers who have descended, heavily guarded, usually after some disturbance. They have watched the decline in health care, documented in report after report, and the refusal of the government to accept the evidence. They have watched the marked shift from agitprop to satisprop,[23] from struggle to complacency, and the institutionalization of selfishness. (On the same day as Thatcher's address to the Church of Scotland a Harris Poll showed that 61 per cent of people believed we were a more selfish society.) They have seen the growing materialism. They have seen the young housewives from the north forced into prostitution in London ('Thatcher's girls' they were called in King's Cross), the bitter flip-side of the consumer culture. But, in a sense, in the crude materialism of Thatcherite values we have all become prostitutes. Even the Good Samaritan is remembered only for his money. 'In the Thatcherist view there is nothing else beyond the satisfaction of desires . . . In the Thatcherist society we each become a Faust whose endless and innumerable desires can all be satisfied provided only that he gives up his identity, his soul.'[24]

At heart the Christian critique of Thatcherism, and of régimes which reflect the same features, is a spiritual critique: Thatcherism represents a form of Mammon-worship, rooted in the moral sin of avarice, which is an assault on human dignity and which erodes the human spirit. Because of this Christians are bound to work for its end, for, as St Thomas Aquinas taught, an unjust government has forfeited the right of obedience and the Christian task is to seek to end it. So we can pray, in words first used in South Africa on 16 June 1986, but applicable here also:

We now pray that God will replace the present unjust structures of oppression with ones that are just, and remove from power those who persist in defying his laws, installing in their place leaders who will govern with justice and mercy . . .
The present régime, together with its structures of domination, stands in contradiction to the Christian gospel, to which the churches of this land seek to remain faithful . . .
We pray that God in his grace may remove from his people the tyrannical structures of oppression, and the present rulers in our country who persistently refuse to hear the cry for justice.
We pledge ourselves to work for that day,

Notes

Introduction

1 H. E. Fosdick, 'Shall the Fundamentalists Win?' in *The Christian World Pulpit*, 4 January 1923, p. 3.
2 'The Doctrinal Commission: Full Summary of Epoch-making Report', *Church Times*, 14 January 1938, p. 47. For the full report see *Doctrine in the Church of England*: the Report of the Commission on Christian Doctrine appointed by the Archbishops of Canterbury and York in 1922, SPCK, 1938, esp. pp. 81–7.
3 J. A. T. Robinson, *Can We Trust the New Testament?*, Mowbrays, 1977, pp. 13–29.
4 P. Tillich, *Sytematic Theology*, Vol I, Part 1, SCM Press, 1978, p. 3.
5 Fosdick, op. cit., pp. 4–5.

Wiles: The Authority of Scripture in a Contemporary Theology

Author's note. A more specialized treatment of the issues discussed in this essay will be found in my 'Scriptural Authority and Theological Construction: The Limitations of Narrative Interpretation', in G. Green (ed.), *Scriptural Authority and Narrative Interpretation*, Fortress Press, 1987, pp. 42–58.
1 See J. Barr, *The Bible in the Modern World*, SCM Press, 1973, p. 27.
2 Augustine, *On Christian Doctrine III*, 1, 2.
3 L. Hodgson, *For Faith and Freedom*, Vol. 2, Basil Blackwell, 1956, p. 12.
4 J. Fenton, 'Controversy in the New Testament' in *Studia Patristica* (ed. E. A. Livingstone), Vol. 3, 1978, pp. 97–100.
5 S. Sykes, *The Identity of Christianity*, SPCK, 1984, pp. 251–6.

Roe: Authority and Freedom – Yesterday and Today

1 W. G. Roe, *Lamennais and England*, OUP, 1966, p. 137.
2 H. J. Laski, *Authority in the Modern State*, New Haven UP, 1927, p. 189.
3 For a detailed account of the first part of Lamennais' life see A. R. Vidler, *Prophecy and Papacy*, SCM press, 1954. His religious development may be studied in Louis Le Guillou, *L'évolution de la pensée religieuse de Félicité Lamennais*, Armand Colin, 1966. A recent popular account is Tanguy Kenec'dhu, *Lamennais, un prêtre en recherche*, Tequi, 1982 (in the series 'L'auteur et son message'). Most revealing of all is his *Correspondence générale*, ed. Louis Le Guillou, 10 vols (1971–81).
4 *Correspondance*, Armand Colin, p. 283.
5 Ibid., p. 305.
6 *Essai sur l'indifférence en matière de religion*, vol. 2, 1817–23, p. 1.

7   Ibid, pp. 279–80.
8   Vidler, op. cit., p. 114.
9   Cited by Vidler, op. cit., p. 159.
10 *L'Avenir*, 22 December 1830.
11 Louis Le Guillou, *Les Discussions critiques, journal de la crise mennaisienne*, Armand Colin 1967, p. 37.
12 Paul Vuillaud, *Les* Paroles d'un croyant *de Lamennais* Société Française d'éditions littéraires et techniques, 1928 (in the series 'Les Grands événements littéraires').
13 *Les Paroles d'un croyant de Lamennais*, ed. Yves Le Hir, Armand Colin, 1949, p. 127.
14 Ibid., p. 156.
15 Ibid., p. 258.
16 Ibid., p. 198.
17 *Lamennais*, Une voix de prison, ed. Yves Le Hir Presses Universitaires de France, 1954, p. 28.
18 A. Ruge, *Zwei Jahre in Paris*, vol. 1, Leipzig, 1846 pp. 146–51.

Blythe: All Mine and Seen So Easily: the Inclusive Vision of Thomas Traherne

1   Lewis Thompson, *Mirror to the Light*, Coventure, 1984, pp. 30.

Bayfield: Still Chosen?

1   Ellen M. Umansky, 'Election' in *The Encyclopædia of Religion*, Macmillan, 1987, p. 78.
2   Lou H. Silberman, 'Chosen People' in *Encyclopædia Judaica*, Vol. 5, Keter Publishing, Jerusalem, 1972 p. 499.
3   Tanna d'Vey Eliyahu (Seder Eliyahu Rabba), beginning of Chapter 10.
4   Henri Atlan, 'Chosen People' in *Contemporary Jewish Religious Thought* (eds A. A. Cohen and P. Mendes-Flohr) Free Press, 1987, pp. 57–8.
5   *The Condition of Jewish Belief*, Macmillan, 1966, p. 7.
6   Arnold Toynbee, *A Study of History*, Vol. IV, 1961, OUP p. 262.
7   *The Condition of Jewish Belief*, p. 218.
8   Ibid., p. 219.
9   Ibid., p. 121.
10 Ibid., p. 13.
11 Ibid., p. 111.
12 Ibid., p. 112.
13 T. B. Shabbat 88a.
14 Mekilta, JPS edition, Vol. 2, p. 234.
15 *The Condition of Jewish Belief*, p. 40.
16 Ibid., pp. 40–41.
17 George Steiner, 'A Kind of Survivor' in *Language and Silence*, quoted in *George Steiner – a Reader*, Penguin 1984.
18 *The Condition of Jewish Belief*, p. 26.
19 Ibid., p. 72.
20 Ibid., p. 127.
21 Ibid., p. 87.
22 Ibid., p. 88.

23 Ibid., p. 54.
24 Ibid., p. 175.
25 Ibid., p. 270.

Robinson: Christian and Muslim Perspectives on Jesus in the Qur'ân

1 For detailed information on the development of anti-Muslim polemic the following works should be consulted: G. C. Anawati, 'Polémique, apologie et dialogue islamo-chrétiens. Positions classiques médiévales et positions contemporaines', *Euntes docete*, Rome, Urbaniana, 22, 1969, pp. 375–472; A.-Th. Khoury, *Les Théologiens Byzantins et l'Islam* Nauwelaerts, Louvain and Paris, 2e tirage, 1969; and N. Daniel, *Islam and the West: the Making of an Image*, Edinburgh University Press, 1964.

2 In its full-blown form this approach seems to be a twentieth-century phenomenon. Two classic statements are: C.-J. Ledit, *Mahomet, Israel et le Christ*, La Colombe, Paris, 1956, pp. 144–58, and R. C. Zaehner, *At Sundry Times: an Essay in Comparative Religion*, Faber & Faber, London, 1958, pp. 195–217. Ledit differs from Zaehner in that he admits that at one level the Qur'ân does deny the crucifixion.

3 The most comprehensive and up-to-date treatment of the penetration of Christianity into Arabia is J. S. Trimingham, *Christianity among the Arabs in Pre-Islamic Times*, London and New York, Longman, 1979. The similarities between the Qur'anic Jesus material and the apocryphal Gospels is documented in D. Sidersky, *Les origines des légendes musulmanes dans le coran et dans les vies des prophètes*, Geuthner, Paris, 1933. On the Qur'ân's possible debt to Monophysism, see further H. Grégoire, 'Mahomet et le monophysisme', *Mélanges Charles Diehl*, Paris, 1930, pp. 107–19, and J. Bowman 'The Debt of Islam to Monophysite Syrian Christianity', *Nederlands Theologisch Tijdschrift* 19, 1964–65, pp. 177–201. On Jewish Christianity, see M. P. Roncaglia 'Eléments Ebionites et Elkésaïtes dans le Coran', *Proche-Orient Chrétien* 21, 1971, pp. 101–25.

4 H. Michaud, *Jésus selon le coran*, Neuchatel, 1960; H. Raïsänen, *Das Koranische Jesusbild*, Helsinki, 1971; and C. Schedl, *Muḥammad und Jesus*, Vienna, Herder 1978. For a detailed discussion of the Qur'anic material exclusively along these lines see Neal Robinson, 'Jesus and Mary in the Qur'ân: Some Neglected Affinities', *Religion* 20, 1990, pp. 211–25.

5 There are brief extracts from some of the classical commentaries in H. Gätje, *The Qur'ân and its Exegesis: Selected Texts with Classical and Modern Interpretations*, tr. and ed. A. Welch, London and Henley, Routledge and Kegan Paul Rippin, OUP, 1976. On the history of exegesis see A. Rippin (ed.), *Approaches to the History of the Interpretation of the Qur'ân*, Oxford, 1988.

6 'Imâd al-Dîn Abû al-Fidâ' Isma'îl Ibn Kathîr, *Tafsîr al-Qur'ân al-'Azîm*, 7 Vol., Beirut: dâr al-andalus 1385 A H, Vol. 1. This is the work referred to as TIK.

7 Abû Ja'far Muhammad b. Jarîr al Tabarî, *Jâmi' al-Bayân fî Tafsîr Qur'ân*, 30 parts in 12 Vols, Bûlâq 1324 A H. The first volume of an abridged English translation is published by Oxford University Press.

8 Fakhr al-Dîn al-Râzî, *al-Tafsîr al-Kabîr*, 8 Vols, Beirut, dâr al-fikr 1398 A H/1978 C E. See further Neal Robinson, 'Creating Birds from Clay: a

Miracle of Jesus in the Qur'ân and in Classical Muslim Exegesis', *Muslim World* 79, 1989, pp. 1–13.

9 A good example is G. Parrinder, *Jesus in the Quran*, London, 1965. On the whole it is a balanced and scholarly work but its eclecticism makes it very difficult for the non-specialist to evaluate. The polemical element is minimal, although on p. 78 the author mentions the possibility that Mary has been confused with Miriam without referring to the provenance of this theory.

10 See e.g. K. Cragg, *Jesus and the Muslim*, London, George Allen & Unwin, 1985.

11 I have attempted to do this at length in my book, *Christ in Islam and Christianity*, Macmillan, 1991.

Morgan: Buddhist Christianity

1 This is well explored in W. Cantwell Smith, *Towards a World Theology*, Macmillan, 1981.

2 Process theologians do, of course, articulate a theology which might seem naturally closer to Buddhism. See the summary in Chapter 4 of P. O. Ingram and F. J. Streng, *Buddhist-Christian Dialogue*, University of Hawaii Press, 1986.

3 For a discussion of this in the context of the history of religions see E. Sharpe, *Comparative Religion*, Duckworth, 1975, Chapter 2.

4 The original Buddhist text of this story can be found in L. Stryk (ed.), *World of the Buddha*, Anchor Books, 1969, pp. 216–17.

5 J. Macquarrie, *In Search of Deity*, SCM Press, 1984, p. 244. Also interesting are T. J. J. Altizer, 'Dialectic vs Di-Polar Theology' in *Process Studies*, Vol. 1, No. 1, 1971, pp. 29–37; P. Berger, *The Other Side of God*, Anchor Books, 1981; and K. Ward, *Images of Eternity*, DLT, 1987.

6 See M. Pye, *Skilful Means*, Duckworth, 1978.

7 For extensive recovery of Christian views see the work of A. Linzey and T. Regan, *Animals and Christianity*, SPCK, 1989.

8 See D. Parfitt, *Reasons and Persons*, Oxford, 1984.

9 'Between Jerusalem and Benares', title of the last chapter in P. Berger, *The Heretical Imperative*, Anchor Books, 1980.

10 See J. Cobb 'Can a Christian be a Buddhist too?' *Japanese Religions*, Vol. 16, Part 3, 1978, pp. 1–20.

11 N. Smart, *The Religious Experience of Mankind*, Fontana, 1971 , p. 692.

12 A. Pieris, 'Buddhism as a Challenge to Christianity' in *Christianity among World Religions* (eds H. Kung and J. Moltmann), T. & T. Clark, 1986, p. 60.

13 K. M. Din in *Christianity and the Religions of the East* (ed. R. W. Rousseau), Ridge Row Press, 1982, pp. 77ff.

14 Panikkar reflected on this at the Younghusband Lecture, 1989.

15 J. K. Kadowaki, *Zen and the Bible*, Routledge Kegan Paul, 1977, pp. 5–9, viii.

16 W. Johnston, *The Mirror Mind*, Collins, 1981, pp. 5–22.

17 W. Johnston, *The Still Point*, Fordham University Press, 1970, p. 187.

18 Ibid., p. 73.

19 A. Pieris, *An Asian Theory of Liberation*, SPCK, 1989.

20 J. Cobb, *Beyond Dialogue*, Fortress Press, 1982.

21 D. Cupitt, *Taking Leave of God*, SCM Press, 1980. See particularly the review article by W. Schwarz in the *Guardian* 21 September 1987 after the publication of *The Long Legged Fly*, SCM Press, 1987.

22 R. S. Thomas, 'Via Negativa from H'm, *Later Poems*, Macmillan, 1983, p. 23.

23 T. S. Eliot, *On Poetry and Poets*, Farrar Straus, 1957, p. 264.

24 T. S. Eliot, *Selected Essays*, Harcourt, 1950, pp. 363, 399.

25 C. N. Kearns, *T. S Eliot and the Indic Traditions*, Cambridge University Press, 1987; A. N. Dwivedi, *T. S. Eliot's Major Poems: An Indian Interpretation*, Salzburg Studies in English Literature, 1982; D. Ghosh, *Indian Thought in T. S. Eliot*, Calcutta, 1978; A. K. Jha, *Oriental Influences on T. S. Eliot*, Allahabad, 1988. S.-Y. Killingley, *Time, Action, Incarnation: Shades of the Bhagavad-Gita in the Poetry of T. S. Eliot*, University of Newcastle, 1989.

26 Unacknowledged quotation from Eliot in Kearns, op. cit., p. 132.

27 The first from T. S. Eliot, *Murder in the Cathedral*, Faber and Faber, 1935, p. 67, the second from Thich Nhat Hanh, *Please call me by my true names*, Buddhist Peace Fellowship.

28 Sangharakshita, *The Religion of Art*, Windhorse Publications, 1988.

29 D. Cupitt, *Radicals and the Future of the Church*, Chapter 2, SCM, 1989

30 Sangharakshita, op. cit., p. 114.

Loades: Beyond God the Father: an Introduction to Mary Daly's View of Christian Tradition

1 Gwen Kennedy Neville, 'Religious Socialization of Women within US subcultures', pp. 77–91 in *Sexist Religion and Women in the Church: No More Silence* (ed. Alice L. Hageman), Association Press, 1974, pp. 84–5.

2 Beverly Wildung Harrison, 'Sexism and the Contemporary Church: When Evasion becomes Complicity' in Hageman, op. cit, pp. 195–216.

3 Marjorie Reiley Maguire, 'Catholic Women and the Theological Enclave', *Christian Century*, 3–10 February 1982, pp. 109–11.

4 Published as *Briefing 87* by the Bishops' Conference of Great Britain.

5 Irene Woodward, *The Catholic Sisters of the United States: Signs of Contradiction or Signs of the Times?* Pro Mundi Vita: Dossiers 4/1986; cf. Mary E. Hines, 'Women Religious in Transition', *New Theology Review*, 1; 1 February 1988, pp. 93–106.

6 Anne E. Carr, *Transforming Grace: Christian Tradition and Womens' Experience*, Harper and Row, 1988, p. 30.

7 Cf. Rosemary Radcliffe Ruether, *Sexism and God-talk*, SCM Press, 1981, p. 284: and see Lynda Birke, 'Clearing the mind: Speculations on Conceptual Dichotomies' in *Against Biological Determinism*, (ed. Steven Rose), Allison and Busby, 1986, pp. 60–78.

8 John Rowan, *The Horned God*, Routledge, Kegan Paul, 1987.

9 Quoted in Rowan, op. cit., pp. 42–3.

10 As in Hageman, op. cit., p. 197. See also Beverly Wildung Harrison's appreciative essay on Mary Daly in 'The Power of Anger in the Work of Love: Christian Ethics for Women and Other Strangers' in *Making the Connections: Essays in Feminist Social Ethics* (eds Beverly Wildung Harrison and Carol S. Robb), Boston, Beacon Press, 1985, pp. 3–21.

11 Martin E. Marty, *Christian Century*, 3–10 February 1982, p. 107.

Polkinghorne: The Interaction of Science and Theology

1 L. Newbigin, *Foolishness to the Greeks*, SPCK, 1986.
2 P. Davies, *God and the New Physics*, Dent, 1983; H. Montefiore, *The Probability of God*, SCM Press, 1985; A. R. Peacocke, *Creation and the World of Science*, Oxford University Press, 1979; *God and the New Biology*, Dent, 1986; J. C. Polkinghorne, *One World*, SPCK, 1986; *Science and Creation*, SPCK, 1988.
3 Davies, op. cit., p. ix.
4 B. Lonergan, *Insight*, Longman, 1957, p. 684.
5 J. Barrow and F. Tipler, *The Anthropic Cosmological Principle*, Oxford University Press, 1986; see also Montefiore, op. cit.
6 J. Monod, *Chance and Necessity*, Collins, 1972, p. 10.
7 W. H. Vanstone, *Love's Endeavour, Love's Expense*, Darton, Longman and Todd, 1977, p. 63.
8 P. Davies, *The Cosmic Blueprint*, Heinemann, 1987; I. Prigogine and I. Stengers, *Order out of Chaos*, Heinemann, 1984; J. Gleick, *Chaos*, Heinemann, 1988; see also Polkinghorne (1988), op. cit., Chapter 3.
9 Polkinghorne (1988), op. cit.

Bartholomew: Chance in God's World

1 I. Hacking, *Representing and Intervening*, Cambridge University Press, 1983, p. 141.
2 J. Monod, *Chance and Necessity*, Collins, 1972, p. 110.
3 W. H. Vanstone, *Love's Endeavour, Love's Expense*, Darton, Longman and Todd, 1977, p. 26.
4 D. M. Mackay, *Science, Chance and Providence*, Oxford University Press, 1978.
5 D. J. Bartholomew, *God of Chance*, SCM Press, 1984.
6 R. Hooykaas, *Religion and the Rise of Modern Science*, Scottish Academic Press, 1972.
7 See especially A. R. Peacocke, *Creation and the World of Science*, Clarendon Press, 1979.
8 G. Priestland, *The Case Against God*, Collins, 1984, p. 130.
9 J. Baker, *Full Circle*, Penguin, 1984, p. 66.
10 Vanstone, op. cit., p. 65.
11 G. Theissen, *Biblical Faith: an Evolutionary Approach*, SCM Press, 1984, p. 167.
12 Vanstone, op. cit., p. 65.
13 H. Montefiore, *The Probability of God*, SCM Press, 1985, p. 98.
14 Priestland, op. cit., p. 130.
15 Theissen, op. cit., p. 150.

Suggate: William Temple and British Society Today

1 See W. Temple, *Readings in St John's Gospel*, Macmillan, 1939–40.
2 A good example is to be found in F. A. Iremonger, *William Temple, Archbishop of Canterbury*, Oxford University Press, 1948, pp. 417–18.
3 W. Temple, *Mens Creatrix*, Macmillan, 1917, p. 7.
4 *Christianity and Social Order* was originally published by Penguin in 1942. A new edition was produced by Shepheard-Walwyn and SPCK

in 1976, with a foreword by the Rt Hon. Edward Heath and a valuable introduction by Professor Ronald H. Preston.

5   W. Temple, *Christianity and War*, Oxford University Press, 1914, pp. 10–13.

6   *Conference on Christian Politics, Economics and Citizenship Commission Reports*, and *Proceedings of COPEC*, Longmans Green, 1924; E. R. Norman, *Church and Society in England, 1770–1970*, Clarendon Press, 1976, Chapter 7, esp. p. 284.

7   *The Pilgrim*, January 1923, pp. 218–25.

8   W. Temple, *Christianity and Social Order*, p. 12 (1942 edition).

9   'Chairman's Introduction', in W. Temple, *Doctrine in the Church of England*, SPCK, 1938, pp. 16–17.

10   In 'Theology Today', *Theology*, November 1939 and reprinted in W. Temple, *Thoughts in War-time*, Macmillan, 1940, pp. 94–107.

11   See the articles of Temple and Niebuhr in *Christian Faith and the Common Life*, Vol. IV of the Oxford Conference on Church, Community and State, Allen and Unwin, 1937.

12   For Preston's own assessment of Temple see note 4 above and also *The Future of Christian Ethics*, SCM Press, 1987, pp. 99–112. Among Roman Catholics Charles Curran probably stands nearest to Temple. See e.g. his *New Perspectives in Moral Theology* or *Directions in Catholic Social Ethics*, University of Notre Dame Press, 1976 and 1985 respectively. An example of Lutheran thought is W. Huber and H.-E. Tödt, *Menschenrechte*, Stuttgart, Kreuz Verlag, 1977.

13   W. Temple, *Religious Experience and other Essays and Addresses*, collected and ed. with an introduction by A. E. Baker, James Clarke, 1958, pp. 243–55.

14   V. A. Demant, *The Religious Prospect*, Muller, 1939, pp. 232, 11.

15   *Religious Experience*, p. 254.

16   A. Bartlett, *The Churches in Bermondsey, 1880–1939*, unpublished PhD thesis, Birmingham University, pp. 375ff.

17   *Religious Experience*, p. 251.

18   See, for example, A. R. Peacocke, *Creation and the World of Science*, Clarendon Press, 1979, esp. Chapter VII.

19   See, for example, Lord Harris, 'The Morality of the Market' in *The New Right and Christian Values*, Occasional Paper No. 5, Department of Christian Ethics and Practical Theology, Edinburgh.

20   *Religious Experience*, pp. 251–2.

21   Harris, op. cit.

22   *Religious Experience*, pp. 246–7.

23   *Faith in the City*, The Report of the Archbishop of Canterbury's Commission on Urban Priority Areas, Church House Publishing, 1985, pp. 57ff.

24   *Religious Experience*, p. 254.

25   See R. H. Preston, 'The New Right: a Theological Assessment' in *The New Right and Christian Values*, op. cit.

26   *Religious Experience*, p. 252.

27   For a fuller treatment of Temple see my *William Temple and Christian Social Ethics Today*, T. and T. Clark, Edinburgh, 1987. For a more extensive critique of the New Right see my article, 'The New Right', *Crucible*, October-December 1988, pp. 148–59.

Leech: The Christian Critique of Thatcherism

1   Stuart Hall and Martin Jacques, *The Politics of Thatcherism*, Lawrence and Wishart, 1984; Stuart Hall, *The Hard Road to Renewal*, Verso, 1988; Andrew Gamble, *The Free Economy and the Strong State*, Macmillan, 1988; Peter Jenkins, *Mrs Thatcher's Revolution*, Cape, 1987; Robert Skidelsky (ed.), *Thatcherism*, Chatto and Windus, 1988.

2   K. Medhurst and G. Moyser, *Church and Politics in a Secular Age*, Oxford, Clarendon Press, 1988, p. 33.

3   *The Times*, 17 April 1978.

4   *New Society*, 24 October 1986.

5   *The Right Road for Britain*, Conservative and Unionist Central Office, 1949, p. 65.

6   *The Independent*, 27 October 1987.

7   M. Thatcher, cited in G. Hodgson, 'Now is the time for all right-thinking men . . .', *Sunday Times* Magazine, 4 March 1984, p. 49.

8   P. Worsthorne in *Conservative Essays* (ed. M. Cowling), Cassell, 1978, p. 149.

9   R. Scruton, 'Abolish council elections too', *The Times*, 18 October 1983.

10   M. Thatcher interviewed by P. Jenkins, *The Independent*, 14 September 1987.

11   M. Thatcher, 27 March 1982. See D. Edgar, 'The free and the good' in *The Ideology of the New Right* (ed. Ruth Levitas), Polity Press, 1985; and P. Gordon and F. Klug, *New Right, New Racism*, Searchlight Publications, 1986, p. 52.

12   Mrs Thatcher's statement was made in an interview with *Woman's Own* in November 1987. Cf. Epicurus: 'There is no such thing as human society' (cited in A. D. Lindsay, 'Individualism', *Encyclopaedia of the Social Sciences*, 1932 ed., p. 675).

13   Address at St Lawrence Jewry, 4 March 1981.

14   Ian Gilmour, *Inside Right*, Hutchinson, 1977, p. 158.

15   *The Times*, 10 May 1978; *Financial Times*, 31 March 1979; Jimmy Young show, BBC Radio, 5 June 1987; *The Independent*, 6 June 1987.

16   *The Standard*, 4 June 1985.

17   Douglas Hurd, Address to the General Synod, 10 February 1988, reported in the press the following day. See also Douglas Hurd, 'God versus Cæsar?', *Church Times*, 9 September 1988.

18   Tony Dawe, *Daily Express*, 17 August 1982.

19   Address at St Lawrence Jewry, 30 March 1978. Text from Conservative Central Office News Service.

20   Norman Tebbit, correspondence with the Rev. Peter Sutcliffe, cited in *Guardian*, 8 September 1984.

21   *Guardian*, 16 October 1984.

22   P. Worsthorne, *Sunday Telegraph*, 12 June 1983. Anthony Barnett has called Thatcherism 'Powellism in government' (in *World View 1985*, Pluto Press, 1984, p. 117).

23   H. Young, *Guardian*, 14 July 1988.

24   Nicholas Boyle, 'Thatcher's dead souls', *New Statesman and Society*, 14 October 1985, pp. 29–30.

Contributors and Editors

David J. Bartholomew was born in 1931. After undergraduate and postgraduate study at University College, London, specializing in statistics, he worked for two years in the operation research branch of the National Coal Board. In 1957 he began his academic career at the University of Keele and then moved to the University College of Wales, Aberystwyth, as lecturer, then senior lecturer in statistics. This was followed by appointment to a Chair in statistics at the University of Kent in 1967. Six years later he moved to the London School of Economics where he is now Pro-Director and Professor of Statistics. These have been interspersed with visiting appointments at Harvard University, the University of California at Berkeley, the Technion Haifa, the University of Melbourne and the University of Indiana. He is a Fellow of the British Academy, a Member of the International Statistical Institute, a Fellow of the Institute of Mathematical Statistics and has served as Honorary Secretary and, currently, Treasurer of the Royal Statistical Society. He has acted as a consultant on a wide range of statistical matters to many governmental and other organizations and has taken a particular interest in medical manpower planning questions. Within the Methodist Church, in which he has been a local preacher since 1956, he has carried out studies on the supply of ministers and local preachers. He has authored, co-authored or edited eleven books and about seventy-five research papers, mainly in technical journals. The books include *Stochastic Models for Social Processes* (3rd ed., 1982), *Statistical Techniques for Manpower Planning* (with A. F. Forbes, 1979) and *Latent Variable Models and Factor Analysis* (1987). His *God of Chance* represents an attempt to grapple with the theological implications of the critical role which chance appears to play in the natural world. This theme has been pursued in lectures and articles and a further book on uncertainty and belief is in preparation.

Anthony Bayfield was born in 1946. He read law at Magdalene College, Cambridge, and studied for the rabbinate at Leo Baeck College, London. He received semichah in 1972 and was appointed rabbi of the North West Surrey Synagogue. During his time in Surrey he published a number of works in the field of Jewish education, including *Churban, the Murder of the Jews of Europe* and 'Religious Education – Towards a New Approach' in D. Marmur (ed.), *A Genuine Search*. He lectures in education at the Leo Baeck College. He was Chair, Assembly of Rabbis, Reform Synagogues of Great Britain, 1981–88, and later Chair of the Council of Reform and Liberal Rabbis. In 1983 he was appointed Director of the Sternberg Centre for Judaism, a major Jewish educational and cultural centre in north-west

London. During the 1980s he developed a deep interest in the theology of Jewish–Christian relations and published 'Repentance and Forgiveness', *European Judaism*, 1988, 1/2 and 'Judaism and Religious Pluralism', *European Judaism*, 1989, 1. He is Editor of the quarterly journal *Manna*; a member of the Executive of the Council of Christians and Jews and a regular reviewer for the *Church Times*.

Ronald Blythe was born in Suffolk in 1922 and has had a life-long working association with the rural Church. He is a poet, short-story writer, essayist, historian and literary critic. He is a Fellow of the Royal Society of Literature and has received the Heinemann Award, the Society of Authors' Travel Scholarship and other literary prizes. His books include: *The Age of Illusion* (1963), *Akenfield* (1969), *William Hazlitt: Selected Writings* (1970), *The View in Winter* (1979), *From the Headlands* (1982), *The Visitors* (1985), *Divine Landscapes* (1986) and *Each Returning Day: the Pleasure of Diaries* (1989). He has written a number of films and has at various times reviewed for most British and American literary journals, including *The Tablet*.

David Conner was born in 1947. He read Theology at Exeter College, Oxford, and trained for the priesthood at St Stephen's House, Oxford. Ordained in 1971, he became Assistant Chaplain and then Chaplain of St Edward's School, Oxford. Later he was appointed also as Team Vicar of the Parish of Wolvercote with Summertown in which he was given special responsibility for educational matters. In 1980 he became Senior Chaplain to Winchester College and for some of his time in the Winchester Diocese was Examining Chaplain to the Bishop of Winchester. In 1987 he became Vicar of St Mary the Great, the Cambridge University Church.

Morna D. Hooker was born in 1931. She read theology at the University of Bristol, and then spent two further years in Bristol researching into the use of the Servant Songs in the New Testament. After a spell in religious publishing (editing Sunday School lessons) she did further research work at the University of Manchester and the University of Durham, where she was a Research Fellow 1959–61. She moved to King's College, London, in 1961 as a temporary stop-gap lecturer in New Testament, and stayed there for nine years. In 1970 she was appointed to the first University lectureship in Theology in Oxford, and was elected to a Fellowship at Linacre College. In 1972 she took on the additional task of Lecturer in Theology at Keble College. Elected to the Lady Margaret's Professorship (Cambridge's oldest Chair) from 1976, she became a Foundation Fellow of Robinson College (Cambridge's newest college). She has been a Visiting Fellow at Clare Hall, Cambridge, and a Visiting Professor at McGill University and Duke University, and has lectured widely in the UK and in America, and in Australia and Africa also. She is a Fellow of King's College, London, and an honorary Fellow of Linacre College, Oxford. In 1988–89 she was President of the Studiorum Novi Testamenti Societas, the international society of New Testament scholars. Her publications include *Jesus and the Servant* (1959), *The Son of Man in Mark* (1967), *Pauline Pieces* (1979), *Studying the New Testa-*

ment (1979), *The Message of Mark* (1983), *Continuity and Discontinuity* (1986) and she has two books in the press, *From Adam to Christ* and *Commentary on Mark*. She has also jointly edited two other books, *What about the New Testament?* (1975) and *Paul and Paulinism* (1982). Since 1985 she has been joint editor of the *Journal of Theological Studies*; she has also contributed articles to many scholarly journals. She is a Methodist local preacher, and is married to a Methodist minister (the Rev. Dr. W. David Stacey, former Principal of Wesley College, Bristol) and has served on various connexional committees, including the Faith and Order Committee of the Methodist Church.

Leslie Houlden was born in 1929. He read Modern History and Theology at The Queen's College, Oxford, and trained for the priesthood at Cuddesdon Theological College, Oxford. Ordained in 1955 he went to be curate of St Mary, Hunslet, Leeds, in the Diocese of Ripon, and in 1958 he joined the staff of Chichester Theological College, first as Tutor and then as Chaplain. From 1960 to 1970 he was Chaplain and Fellow of Trinity College, Oxford, and in 1970 he was appointed Principal of Cuddesdon Theological College. When Ripon Hall and Cuddesdon merged in 1975 he became the first Principal of the newly formed Ripon College, Cuddesdon. In 1977 he became Lecturer in New Testament at King's College, London, and from 1985 was Senior Lecturer. In 1987 he was honoured with a personal Chair in Theology. He has been a member of the Church of England Liturgical and Doctrine Commissions, and from 1980 has been a member of General Synod. His publications include *Paul's Letters from Prison* (1970), *The Johannine Epistles* (1973), *The Pastoral Epistles* (1976), *Ethics and the New Testament* (1973), *Patterns of Faith* (1977), *Explorations in Theology 3* (1978), *What Did the First Christians Believe?* (1982), *Connections* (1986) and *Backward into Light* (1987). He was a contributor to *The Myth of God Incarnate* (1977), *Incarnation and Myth: the Debate Continued* (1979), *Alternative Approaches to New Testament Study* (1985) and *The Reality of God* (1986). He is co-editor of the *Dictionary of Biblical Interpretation* (1990). In 1983 he became joint editor of the journal *Theology*.

Kenneth Leech is a Community theologian based at St Botolph's, Aldgate. He was recently Director of the Runnymede Trust, an educational and research unit concerned with racial justice, located in the Brick Lane area of East London. A graduate of King's College, London, and Trinity College, Oxford, he is an Anglican priest and has worked in the East End of London for over twenty years. He became involved with the beginnings of heroin addiction among young people in 1964, and founded the Soho Drugs Group, a pioneer group in the field of community drug care, in 1967. As Assistant Priest at St Anne's Church in Soho (1967–71), he was heavily involved with the problem of homelessness in the 1960s, and founded Centrepoint, the first all-night centre for homeless young people in Britain, in 1969. After three years as Chaplain of St Augustine's College, Canterbury, he was Rector of Bethnal Green 1974–80, and Field Officer of the Church of England's Board for Social Responsibility 1980–87. As Rector of Bethnal Green he helped to organize the resistance to the National Front which had established its main base in the parish. In the latter post he was responsible for setting up two major conferences on the Church of England and racism which led to much greater commitment of the churches in the field of race relations. He was one of the founders of the Jubilee Group, a network of mainly Anglican socialists, in 1974. He became Director of the Runnymede Trust in 1987. He is author of *Pastoral Care and the Drug Scene* (1980), *Keep the Faith Baby* (1972), *Youthquake: the Growth of a Counter Culture through Two Decades* (1973), *Soul Friend* (1977), *True Prayer* (1980), *Brick Lane 1978: the Events and Their Significance* (1980), *The Social God* (1981), *True God* (1985), *What Everyone Should Know about Drugs* (1985), *Spirituality and Pastoral Care* (1986), *Struggle in Babylon: Racism in the Cities and Churches of Britain* (1988) and other works.

Barnabas Lindars was born in 1923. He read Oriental Languages and Theology at St John's College, Cambridge, his studies being interrupted by service in military intelligence during the Second World War. After training for the priesthood at Westcott House, Cambridge, he was ordained in 1948 to be curate of St Luke's, Pallion, Sunderland. In 1952 he joined the Society of St Francis, and served on the staff of St Francis House in Cambridge from 1953 to 1978. He was appointed Assistant Lecturer in the Faculty of Divinity in the University of Cambridge in 1961 and Lecturer in 1966. He became Fellow and Dean of Chapel of Jesus College, Cambridge, in 1976. Two years later he was appointed Rylands Professor of Biblical Criticism and Exegesis in the University of Manchester until his retirement in 1990, when he returned to community life at the Hilfield Friary in Dorset. He was awarded the DD degree of Cambridge in 1973, and was President of the Society for Old Testament Study in 1986. He has been a Canon Theologian of Leicester Cathedral since 1977. He has served on the Doctrine Commission of the Church of England and the Faith and Order Group of General Synod, and was a member of General Synod from 1980 to 1990. His best known book is *The Gospel of John* in the New Century Bible (1972). Other publications include *New Testament Apologetic* (1961), *Behind the Fourth Gospel* (1971), *Jesus Son of Man* (1983), *The Study and Use of the Bible* (joint author, 1988). He was editor of and contributor to *Church Without Walls* (1968), *Words and Meanings* (1968), *Christ and Spirit in the New Testament* (1973), *Law and Religion* (1988). A small volume on *The Theology of Hebrews* and a study guide to *The Gospel of John* are in the press.

Ann Loades was born in 1938. She read Theology in Durham University and in McMaster University, Ontario. After working at St Mary's College, Durham, she moved into full-time lecturing in the Theology Department there in 1975. She is currently Senior Lecturer and Chair of the Department, and has begun to chair St Chad's College Council. Some of her research has been in discussions of theodicy, but accepting an invitation from the Scott Holland Trust to give lectures on 'theology and the significance of gender' has turned her attention to the study of feminist theory/theology. She has lectured widely in Europe as well as in the USA, and has had two stints as a visiting professor in American colleges. She has edited W. A.

Whitehouse, *The Authority of Grace* (1981) and co-edited two books related to the work of Austin Farrer – with J. C. Eaton *For God and Clarity* (1983) and with Michael McLain, a book about hermeneutics (1991). Her two monographs are *Kant and Job's comforters* (1985) and her Scott Holland Lectures, *Searching for Lost Coins* (1987). Her next collection is a reader in *Feminist Theology* and she is co-editing with Loyal Rue a book of contemporary readings in philosophy of religion. She has edited a special number of the *Journal of the History of European Ideas* on Kierkegaard (1990). She has also taken part in a number of television and radio programmes, and helps the Civil Service select its young administrators.

Richard MacKenna was born in London in 1949, and educated at Westminster School and Pembroke College, Cambridge, where he was an English Exhibitioner and President of Footlights. After a short time as an actor, he became one of the first men ever to be employed on a national agony column, answering personal correspondence to Clare Rayner and Angela Williams at *Woman's Own*. He trained for the ministry at Ripon College, Cuddesdon, and then worked at St Dionis', Fulham, where he was also acting chaplain at Charing Cross Hospital, and St James' Paddington. In 1985 he was appointed Director of Studies in the Mission and Ministry of the Church at Westcott House, Cambridge, and later became Convenor of the Director of Pastoral Studies of the Cambridge Federation of Theological Colleges. He is currently Vicar of All Saints, Kingston-upon-Thames. He is the author of *God for Nothing* (1984) and *Is there Anyone There?* (1987).

Peggy Morgan was born in 1940. She read Theology at the University of Nottingham and went on to take a postgraduate Certificate in Education. After a post as Head of RE in a Hampshire grammar school, she moved to Lancaster to lecture in the Department of Theology and Religous Studies at the newly founded St Martin's College. Marriage and children brought a career break but with it the opportunity to do postgraduate work at the Lancaster Religious Studies Department. She moved to Oxford in 1976 where she was self-employed for many years, tutoring for the Open University, Oxford Theology Faculty and Westminster College, where she is now a senior lecturer. Her publications include *Six Religions in the Twentieth Century* (with W. Owen Cole), *Buddhist Stories, Buddhist Iconography*, an illustrated dictionary on *Buddhism*, and *Being a Buddhist*. She also has chapters in *Religion and Education* (ed. A. Wood) and in *Religious Education in Junior Schools* (eds. R. Jackson and D. Starkings). She has written encyclopædia articles for OUP and contributed to *Theology, Religion Today, The Journal of Belief and Values, BJRE* and *Children's Literature in Education*. She is a member of the SHAP Working Party for World Religions in Education, lectures regularly at their conferences, and is reviews editor for their journal *World Religions in Education*, to which she has also contributed many articles. She is actively involved in the British Association for the Study of Religions and in inter-faith dialogue at many levels.

John Polkinghorne was born in 1930. He read mathematics at Trinity College, Cambridge, where he became a Fellow in 1954. He worked for many years in theoretical chemistry particle physics, teaching at Edinburgh University and then Cambridge University, where he was Professor of Mathematical Physics, 1968–79. He was elected a Fellow of the Royal Society in 1974. After two years training at Westcott House, Cambridge, he was ordained in 1981 and served curacies in Cambridge and Bristol. He was Vicar of Blean, Kent, 1984–86, but then returned to Cambridge as Fellow and Dean of Trinity Hall. In 1989 he was elected President of Queens' College, Cambridge. His writings include *The Particle Play* (1979), *The Way the World Is* (1983), *The Quantum World* (1984), *One World* (1986), *Science and Creation* (1988), *Science and Providence* (1989), *The Rochester Roundabout*. He is a member of the Church of England Doctrine Commission.

Neal Robinson was born in 1948. He read Theology at Worcester College, Oxford. After spending two years studying Medicine at London University and a further two years teaching Religious Studies and Biology in comprehensive schools in Coventry, he trained for the priesthood at The Queen's College, Birmingham. In 1977 he was awarded a PhD from Birmingham University for a thesis on the New Testament. He was ordained in 1976 to be curate of St Saviour's, Folkestone, in the Diocese of Canterbury. In 1979 he moved to Bradford as Anglican Chaplain to Bradford University and Bradford College. In 1984 he was awarded the Stephen Bayne Scholarship of the St Augustine Foundation which enabled him to spend six weeks in Tunisia and a year at the Sorbonne studying Arabic and Islamics. On returning to Bradford he was made Honorary Senior Research Fellow in Interdisciplinary Human Studies at the University. In 1987 he moved to Cheltenham as Lecturer in Religious Studies at the College of St Paul and St Mary, becoming Senior Lecturer a year later. He is now Lecturer in Theology at the University of Leeds. He has published a number of articles on Islam and was a contributor to *Essex Essays in Theology and Ethics* (1986). In 1988 he was Visiting Lecturer at the Centre for the Study of Theology in Essex University, and an expanded version of his lectures on *Christ in Islam and Christianity* has now been published by Macmillan.

Gordon Roe was born in 1932. He read Modern Languages at Jesus College, Oxford, and after doing National Service in Germany he returned to Oxford for theological training and to start work on a Doctorate about Lamennais. This was published in a revised form in 1966 as *Lamennais and England*. After ordination in 1958 he was curate at St Peter's, Bournemouth, and from 1961 priest in charge of St Michael's, Abingdon. He moved to Durham in 1969 as Vice-Principal of St Chad's College and taught both Theology and French in the University. In 1974 he moved over the river to be Vicar of St Oswald's, Rural Dean of Durham, Chaplain of Collingwood College and Chairman of the University Chaplains. In 1980 he became Bishop of Huntington in the diocese of Ely, where he is particularly involved in education, social matters, communications and training for the Church's ministry.

Graham Stanton was born in New Zealand in 1940. He read History and Theology at the University of Otago, Dunedin, and trained for the ministry of the Presbyterian Church of New Zealand. In 1969 he was awarded the PhD degree in New Testament Studies from the University of Cambridge; he also studied at the Universities of Zürich and Tübingen. In 1970 he was appointed to a lectureship at King's College, London; since 1977 he has held the Chair of New Testament Studies at King's College. From 1976–82 he served as secretary of the International Society of New Testament Scholars. Since 1982 he has been Editor of the journal *New Testament Studies* and of the associated monograph series. He has been a member of the Doctrine and Worship Committee of the United Reformed Church. His publications include *Jesus of Nazareth in New Testament Preaching* (1974), *The Gospels and Jesus* (1989), *A Gospel for New People: Studies in Matthew* (1990). He is currently working on aspects of the parting of the ways between early Christianity and Judaism.

Alan M. Suggate was born in 1936. He was educated at King Edward VII school, Sheffield, and read Classics at Peterhouse, Cambridge, followed by a part of the Theological Tripos. He taught Classics and Religious Education at Kingston Grammar School and Queen Elizabeth Grammar School, Wakefield, for a total of seven years before moving to Durham to take up the post of Lecturer in Religious Studies at Bede College. Here he completed an external London BD in 1971. During the 1970s, partly through contacts with Industrial Mission and the pressures for the reorganization of higher education he became very interested in issues of Church and society, and embarked on doctoral work on William Temple's Christian social ethics, which he completed in 1981. He became Senior and then Principal Lecturer, but in 1979 his career in teaching-training was cut short by the closure of the College of St Hild and St Bede, as Bede College had then become, as a College of Education. He was able to take up a post as Lecturer in Theology in the University of Durham, where he developed courses in Christian social teaching. Since 1984 he has built up strong links with Germany and initiated a series of consultations with colleagues in Tübingen and Durham. He serves in the West European Network on the Churches, Work and Unemployment. He is also visiting Japan in order to explore the challenges of Far Eastern theology to Western theology. He has been involved with numerous projects in the north-east of England, including the Arts and Recreation Chaplaincy, the North of England Institute for Christian Education, consultancy work for Traidcraft plc, and a Faith in the City venture based in Sunderland and linked with the Oxford Diocese. He has published several articles and essays, and a book *William Temple and Christian Social Ethics Today* (1987).

Maurice Wiles was born in 1923. He read Moral Sciences and Theology at Christ's College, Cambridge, and trained for the priesthood at Ridley Hall, Cambridge. Ordained in 1950, he was curate at St George's, Stockport, in the diocese of Chester, and in 1952 he joined the staff of Ridley Hall. From 1955 to 1959 he was lecturer in New Testament Studies in University

College, Ibadan, in Nigeria, and from 1959 to 1967 was University Lecturer in Divinity at Cambridge and Dean of Clare College. In 1967 he moved to the University of London, King's College, as Professor of Christian Doctrine, and since 1970 has been Regius Professor of Divinity at Oxford and Canon of Christ Church. His publications include *The Spiritual Gospel* (1960), *The Christian Fathers* (1966), *The Divine Apostle* (1967), *The Making of Christian Doctrine* (1967), *The Remaking of Christian Doctrine* (1974), *What is Theology?* (1976), *Faith and the Mystery of God* (1982), *God's Action in the World* (1986).

Andrew Linzey was born in Oxford in 1952. He is Director of Studies of the Centre for the Study of Theology in the University of Essex. He has written or edited eleven books including *Research on Embryos: Politics, Theology and Law*, edited with P.A.B Clarke (1988); *Theology, the University and the Modern World*, co-authored with P.A.B. Clarke (1989); *Christianity and the Rights of Animals* (1989); and *Animals and Christianity: A Book of Readings* (1988) and *The Song of Creation* (1989) – both edited with Tom Regan. He is co-editor with Paul A. B. Clarke of a *Dictionary of Theology and Society* which will be published by Routledge in 1993.

Peter Wexler was until recently Reader in the Department of Language and Linguistics at the University of Essex. His publications touch on Racine, taxonomy, railways, the morphology of French, explanation, the history of vehicle-brakes, applications of graph theory, lexicography, and rat-liver lysosomes – but never on theology, unless you include some camouflaged parts of a just-completed *Teacher's PerpLexicon*. He is a Fellow of the Centre for the Study of Theology in the University of Essex.

Andrew Linzey and Peter Wexler have edited a previous collection entitled *Heaven and Earth: Essex Essays in Theology and Ethics* published by Churchman Publishing in 1986.